Writing the New Ethnography

Ethnographic Alternatives Book Series

SERIES EDITORS
Carolyn Ellis   Arthur P. Bochner

ABOUT THE SERIES

Ethnographic Alternatives publishes experimental forms of qualitative writing that blur the boundaries between social sciences and humanities. Some volumes in the series stand as exemplars of new ethnographic writing that experiment with novel forms of expressing lived experience, including literary, poetic, auto-biographical, multivoiced, conversational, critical, visual, performative, and co-constructed representations. Other volumes explore methodologies of research and writing in these new genres, providing bold and candid discussions of fieldwork and writing processes, and offering stunning examples of the work they encourage.

Ethnographic Alternatives are topically diverse, and promote narration of local stories; literary modes of descriptive scene setting, dialogue, and unfolding action; and inclusion of the author's subjective reactions, involvement in the research process, and strategies for practicing reflexive fieldwork. They are ideal for classroom use in the social sciences and humanities, and will inspire students, instructors, and researchers alike to new, creative forms of scholarship and expression.

PLEASE SEND CORRESPONDENCE OR PROPOSALS TO
Carolyn Ellis and Arthur P. Bochner
College of Arts and Sciences; Department of Communication
University of South Florida
4202 East Fowler Avenue, CIS 1040
Tampa, FL 33620-7800

WRITING
the new
ETHNOGRAPHY

H. L. (BUD) GOODALL, JR.

ALTAMIRA
PRESS

A Division of
ROWMAN & LITTLEFIELD PUBLISHERS, INC.
Lanham • New York • Toronto • Oxford

ALTAMIRA PRESS
A Division of ROWMAN & LITTLEFIELD PUBLISHERS, INC.

Published in the United States of America
by Rowman & Littlefield Publishers, Inc.
4501 Forbes Boulevard, Suite 200, Lanham, Maryland 20706

http://www.altamirapress.com

12 Hid's Copse Road
Cumnor Hill, Oxford OX2 9JJ, England

British Library Cataloguing in Publication Information Available

Library of Congress Cataloging-in-Publication Data

Goodall, H. Lloyd.
   Writing the new ethnography / H.L. Goodall, Jr.
      p.   cm.
   Includes bibliographical references and index.
   ISBN 0-7425-0338-0 (cloth : alk. paper) — ISBN 0-7425-0339-9
(paper : alk. paper)   ISBN: 978-0-7425-0339-7
      1. Ethnology—Authorship. 2. Ethnology—Field work. 3. Communication in
ethnology. 4. Academic writing. I. Title.
   GN307.7.G66 2000
   305.8'007'32—dc21   99-049581

Printed in the United States of America

Contents

The Idea

Four tasks are involved in learning how to become an ethnographer:

You have to learn how to do fieldwork.

You have to learn how to write.

You have to learn who you are as a fieldworker, as a writer, and as a self.

And you have to learn how—and where—those activities are meaningfully connected.

In sum, these four tasks are what this book is about.

FIELDWORK IS A DIFFICULT SUBJECT to learn about because it is a difficult subject to teach. It is difficult to teach because no matter what you say about it, it is what is left unsaid that will be likely to prove the character and creativity of the fieldworker.

Nevertheless, a lot of useful things can be said about fieldwork.

Wade Davis, while still a graduate student at Harvard, once asked Charles Schultes, the legendary ethnobotanist, "What is the best preparation for fieldwork?" Schultes, a pale white man who had disappeared alone for eight years into the Brazilian Amazon to study hallucinogenic plants, and—in addition to writing the definitive history and personal experience of these plants—had located a new source of rubber, replied: "Don't worry about getting a good pair of boots."

WRITING ETHNOGRAPHY IS DIFFICULT TO LEARN because no matter how many exemplars you locate, no matter how many hours you devote to editing and rewriting, and no matter how much you love language, are skilled with metaphor, and are aware of representational limitations, what may be truest about writing is this: The tensions that guide the ethnographic writer's hand lie between the felt improbability of what you have lived and the known impossibility of expressing it, which is to say between desire and its unresolvable, often ineffable, end.

LEARNING WHO YOU ARE as a fieldworker, as a writer, and as a self is difficult because what you learn evolves out of lifelong habits of self-reflection and conversations with others about everything—about lived experiences, what you've read, whom you've loved, what you think about this, that, and the other. This means that whatever you learn about the self—about the self as writer, about the self as a field-worker, about the self as a self—it is always going to be derived from the quality of those conversations and habits of self-reflection, but it is also going to be incomplete.

This would be all right, except that as a scholar, whatever you say about what you've learned is expected to be complete. Herein lies an important tension. To speak and write from this tension—a tension between incomplete personal evolution and the desire for complete scholarly arrival—is part of the new ethnographic text. Writing that tension honors the incompleteness, the desire, the learning. It shows the self, and the self's construction of knowledge, as a jointly produced work in progress.

LEARNING TO UNDERSTAND the meaningful connections between fieldwork and writing is difficult because "pattern recognition"— the basis, as Gregory Bateson put it, of all human communication— requires the application of disciplined imagination to personal experience. The goal of fieldwork is to recognize patterns. The goal of writing ethnography is to express them.

These goals are difficult to accomplish because the need for disciplined application seems most urgent when personal experience seems either not to have added up to very much, or to have added up to something beyond the anticipated sum, or even contrary to it.

Therein lie the pull, and the call, of this mystery.

When you feel pulled in, called to the mystery of it, you have arrived. You must now begin to write.

Preface

This book is about writing the "new" ethnography. By new ethnographies, I mean creative narratives shaped out of a writer's personal experiences within a culture and addressed to academic and public audiences. This book aims to provide students with a foundational understanding of the creative writing processes associated with crafting new ethnographies.

In some disciplines these new ethnographies are labeled as autobiographies, or autoethnographies, but the advice given in this book is not limited to these two genres. Topics in this book—writing as a form of inquiry in academic cultures; the construction of a personal voice; development of self-reflexivity in relation to an issue or research problem; writing and analyzing fieldnotes; the ethics of field research and writing practices; and a narrative focus on examined accounts of experiences in one's own life—are all rhetorical strategies that may be used in other, more traditional forms of qualitative research writing and report making. Because most graduate students and academic professionals are neither trained as creative writers nor schooled in the development and deployment of these particular techniques, this book may serve as a short course in writing as a method of qualitative inquiry.

I have been teaching ethnography for nearly fifteen years, but have been studying writing for a lot longer time. Because I live and work as an academic ethnographer, I am keenly aware of the unique tensions and institutional pressures on writers, especially on young writers who seek alternative or experimental forms of expression. Throughout this volume I have written some of these experiences and lessons into the text to give a better, or at least more contextual, account of the personal, social, professional, and institutional stakes in becoming an academic ethnographer. Particularly one who wants to explore and engage in new ethnographic work.

❏   ❏

I don't think anyone grows up wanting to become "an ethnographer." At least I've never heard a child, or an adolescent, say so.

Some of my trusted colleagues say ethnography is a calling. Maybe it is. I think you don't choose to do it so much as it chooses *you.*

Nobody is exactly sure how that happens. For some people it is through the influence of a teacher. For others it happens when they enroll in a qualitative methods class and are suddenly "turned on" by it. And for others, ethnographic methods just seem to do a better job at getting at what is important about social research.

I've also heard some bad reasons for becoming an ethnographer. People think writing about culture is easier than doing quantitative research. Or people who think doing so gives them license to avoid including scholarly sources in their work, which basically means they don't have to visit the library as often. Or those who believe that claiming to be "an ethnographer" sounds exotic, or sexy. Or people who don't know what else to say they want to do in school because they don't ever intend to do very much.

One thing I do know for certain: Nobody with a bad reason ever became a good ethnographer. Ethnography is not the result of a noetic experience in your backyard, nor is it a magic gift that some people have and others don't. It is the result of a lot of reading, a disciplined imagination, hard work in the field and in front of a computer, and solid research skills, all of which are crafted into compelling stories, narratives, or accounts.

New ethnography is hard work. Even for students who apply themselves, who work very hard, who read very deeply, who think creatively, and who have the requisite desire for an ethnographic life, there are no guarantees. Unlike other methods of inquiry and writing, simply acquiring the knowledge and understanding the processes involved doesn't make you into an ethnographer.

To become an ethnographer who writes new ethnographies requires habits of being in the world, of being able to talk and listen to people, and of being able to write—habits that are beyond method. These ethnographic practices involve a craft that anyone can learn, but there is also *art* to it, a confluence made out of a person and the process, one that separates those who know about and can theorize new ethnography from those who know about, theorize about, and *do* it.

It is a difference that emerges on the written page.

Which is to say: New ethnographers are not researchers who learn to "write it up," but *writers* who learn how to use their research and how they write to "get it down."

This book is about writing to "getting it down." To *really* get it down.

THE PROCESSES THAT PRODUCE new ethnographies—living, studying, reflecting, and storying—are intimately and experientially connected through the writing process.

I want to share with you why I think this writing process should be imagined, that is, theorized, as an enlarged *conversation*. To do that, I want to reframe the writing process as a choice between a *monologue* and a *dialogue*.

For most of the twentieth century, traditional forms of ethnographic writing were constructed out of a metaphor of argumentative *speechmaking* to a relatively passive audience. As a speechmaker in book form, the ethnographic writer argued for a representation of reality that could be critically approached and validated (or dismissed) by examining how the writer's claims were technically and rationally supported by the detailed evidence given. The preferred format for these arguments was the traditional scholarly essay.

This model for ethnographic writing-as-speechmaking, and for modern argument in scholarly texts in general, is predicated on the presumption of a reality external to the perceiver, whose particulars may be known through the application of scientific reasoning. It is a reality whose truths may be revealed and made known through detailed, objective observation and detached, dispassionate analysis. It is a reality that the properly trained and institutionally credentialed ethnographer is trusted to accurately describe. It is a place where truth about an other's culture is supposedly located.

The format for writing up the results of fieldwork are, like all scientifically informed reports, *formulaic*. First and foremost, the preferred form for a scholarly study is the scholarly essay or edited book chapter. The brevity imposed by these preferred formats is intended to ensure clarity and narrowness of purpose, as well as uniformity, in the reading experience. The goal of the reading experience is not pleasure, or literary richness, or close identification between the reader and the writer, but rather scientific elegance, where elegance means—as it does in mathematics—the most generalizable result gotten with the least amount of writing. The classic expression of scientific elegance is Einstein's formula $E = MC^2$.

Brevity of form carries with it a preference for following a prescribed written method. For this reason, the traditional scholarly essay begins with an introduction that locates a research question, or questions, within an established scholarly literature and field of study, proceeds through a collection and analysis of data that represent the fieldwork and reasoning processes, and concludes with a set of "findings" that add to the professional literature, as well as a set of heuristics—recommendations for future research—for other ethnographers to consider. The rules for writing within these margins are rigidly enforced. The traditional scholarly essay is not the place to "try out" experimental forms of writing. Instead, the point of the essay is to add another finding to the accumulative storehouse of knowledge. It was this view of ethnography, and of ethnographic writing, that helped establish and maintain its status as a social science through the modern era.

However, this view of ethnographic writing—what it was supposed to look and read like, and what it was intended to do—was, along with all forms of dominant, scientific narratives, challenged during the rise of the postmodern era. One result of this challenge has been a "crisis of representation" (Denzin, 1996; Van Maanen, 1995). Why? Because representation is literally about *re-presenting* a reality, which assumes a *correspondence between language used to create the representation and the reality that gets represented.* Because language is symbolic and reality is not, these two domains are obviously *not* alike, so the ethnographer's task was to get as close to the truth of a given reality as possible through the application of scientific reasoning. Scientific reasoning—induction and deduction—teaches us what is rational. When looked at one way, what is called rational is, at least in part, about how to account for the gap between language and reality by agreeing that what is logical is what may be linked through representational premises to entailed conclusions.

One of the gifts of the postmodern challenge has been the cool but sometimes chaotic dismantling of this model of representational truth telling. Postmodernists assert that the logical assumptions and scientific methods guide—some say, privilege—a particular reasoning elite's consensual view of reality: the grand narrative (Lyotard, 1984) of Western, mostly white, mostly male, science. The problem with this construction of rationality is that there are "realities" more so than there is a "reality." What counts as the truth depends on where you are standing when you observe or participate in it, what you believe about it in the first place, and what you want to do with it—or who is paying you to do something with it—once you name it. With representation thus challenged, the *legitimacy* of scientifically informed ethnographic reports was also fouled. "Who has the right to speak for a culture?" is very much a question about *who is entitled* to represent it.

Furthermore, regardless of who represents it, or what gets represented, cultures are *not* "out there" for inspection and amenable solely to received scientific truths. Rather, cultures are apprehended, theorized, studied, explained, storied, and otherwise rendered *symbolic* through language. They are *constructed*. We locate (from the languages we collect through fieldwork) and invent (out of our professional training and individual sensitivities) a language of contextual meanings for describing, analyzing, and storying a culture as we go along. We write our ethnographic stories for a purpose, which, when understood within an academic environment, is usually associated with the ethnographer's academic promotion and institutional tenure. As one postmodern author put it, with all these attacks on it, with all these possibilities for invention and expression, "reality isn't what it used to be" (Keval, 1995).

Neither, as a result, is *ethnography*.

Hence, the *crisis*. The crisis of *representation*.

NOBODY AGREES ON HOW TO RESOLVE this crisis. Probably nobody ever will.

In times of academic revolutions, when old explanatory models don't work as well anymore and new questions challenge existing paradigms, new models and answers emerge. In the final quarter of the twentieth century, as postmodern critiques were being circulated and debated, new experiments with the forms and methods of ethnographic writing occurred (see Van Maanen, 1988; Rose, 1990; Denzin, 1996). Perhaps this arose from the fact that each ethnographer who absorbed and agreed with the postmodern critiques needed to resolve the crisis of representation in her or his own way. Or perhaps some ethnographers outgrew the need to have their writing adhere to a master narrative or to an overarching model of inquiry and expression to guide practice. Or perhaps some ethnographers simply tired of talking, of arguing, *about* the crisis of representation, and instead wanted to perform the writing experiments that were being talked about and theorized. Perhaps it was all of these reasons. But clearly what has happened is that new ethnographies were born.

I am not going to take up a lot of space in this book with theoretical arguments about, or models of, new ethnographic writing. What I *am* going to do is assert that new ethnographic writing is constructed out of a writer's ability to hold an interesting *conversation* with readers. Viewed this way, the pertinent issues, goals, and rhetorical and narrative methods for writing new ethnographies shift from those associated with modern *speechmaking* to issues, goals, and methods aligned more formally with *interpersonal communication.* Where writing derived from speechmaking gains its authority from the principles and practices of argumentation and debate, writing based on interpersonal relationships gains authenticity from the quality of personal experiences, the richness and depth of individual voices, and a balance between engagements with others and self-reflexive considerations of those engagements. Where writing based on speechmaking prizes "winning over" an audience by defeating opponents and minimizing the importance of alternative ways of knowing, writing based on interpersonal effectiveness prizes the working out of dialectical tensions, dialogic vulnerability, and a profound openness to differences. Viewed this way, new ethnography is about how writers experiment with forms of *communication* to create meaningful relationships with readers.

We—writers and readers—can still argue. We can still debate. But, as Wayne Brockriede (1972), a rhetorical theorist, pointed out years ago, the *attitude* the writer has toward his or her reader is one of *love* rather than domination and control. It is more *dialogic,* less singularly red-faced; more *dialectical,* less confrontational. The aim is to develop *in our relationship* an appreciation for differences that lead to improved understandings of ourselves in contexts of others. To write—and to read—the new ethnographies is akin to providing a space for language to help shape a professional meeting into an intellectually and emotionally rewarding friendship.

Think of the new ethnography as writing that *rhetorically enables intimacy in the study of culture.* The new ethnographers want readers to take what we say *personally.* We want our words to make *differences* in their lives.

❑   ❑

I have divided *Writing the New Ethnography* into six chapters.

Chapter 1, "On Becoming an Ethnographer in the Academy," is a personal tale that locates the practices of fieldwork and writing within academic contexts and interpretive communities. It is also about how I learned to define an *audience* for my writing, why my writing took shape as storytelling, and why and how I learned that my relationship with that audience is better understood as an enlarged conversation than as a speech. It concludes with a series of "Writing Experiments" designed to help you connect your autobiographical life to your selection of academic discipline and to your writing purpose and choices of genres.

Chapter 2, "Finding the Story in Ethnographic Words," is about the idea that all new ethnographies are really *two stories* that shape and inform each other—one personal and one professional. I begin the chapter with a personal account of how I took "the interpretive turn" as an ethnographer, and how, within that turning, I learned to locate my fieldwork and theoretical issues within an existing professional literature. It tells the story of what many academics call the "gap" in a professional literature, and explains why ethnographers must be mindful of the ongoing professional conversation in their disciplines. The chapter then details a version of new ethnography's emerging storyline. By "storyline," I mean the historical, methodological, and theoretical arguments, debates, and dialogues that have shaped the rhetorical and narrative commonplaces in the ethnographic literature. I then explain how writing and merging these two stories—the personal engagement of a disciplinary conversation—creates choices among styles of presentation. The chapter concludes with a series of "Writing Experiments" designed to induce readers to find storylines they want to pursue, investigate the rhetorical and narrative choices and techniques available to them, and become involved in drafting traditional and alternative forms of literature reviews in their chosen subject areas.

Chapter 3, "Representing Ethnographic Experiences: From Fieldwork to Fieldnotes to Stories," is a "how to do it" chapter that has been subdivided into five subsections amenable to an individual instructor's teaching preferences and available time. The subsections are:

"What Is a Fieldnote?"—Provides a detailed examination and comparison of personal diaries, professional journals, and notebooks, as well as information on how to adapt material from these sources into an ethnographic account.

"Verbal Exchanges"—Provides a descriptive analysis of various types of "conversations"—from phatic communion through dialogue—with examples drawn from ethnographic fieldnotes and texts. It also provides a guide to questions that may be raised about the various types of verbal exchanges.

"Practices"—Provides detailed accounts of how to "observe" others' practices and make cultural sense out of them. Also provides help on the coordination and management of ethnographic and personal information.

"From Coding, Analysis, and Making Connections to Writing Stories"—Provides an extended analysis of how I wrote "On Becoming an Organizational Detective" (1989a) from fieldnotes, including various problematics associated with that undertaking and narrative writing style. "Writing Experiments"—Concludes the chapter with exercises designed to encourage readers to apply what they have learned about writing fieldnotes.

In Chapter 4, "Voice, Reflexivity, and Character: The Construction of Identities in Texts," I describe how writing choices create the author's narrative *persona,* or soul, for the story or account. Using the interpretive categories of "positionings" (for example, fixed, or "standpoint"; subjective; textual) and "processual developments" to inform the available writing choices, the chapter demystifies the construct of "voice." I then offer readers a way of understanding self-reflexivity as a strategic and ethical part of any new ethnography that can be accomplished by applying a series of known questions to passages that make evaluative statements about the meaning of others and contexts in cultures. To encourage readers to apply the information in each section, "Writing Experiments" are provided within the chapter, as well as at the end.

In Chapter 5, "The Ethics of Writing Ethnography," I investigate a little-appreciated aspect of constructing ethnographic accounts and tales. Specifically, the chapter goes beyond the ethics of fieldwork to consider the ethics of editing and translating fieldnotes into ethnographic accounts or stories. This chapter also includes a discussion of how texts are gendered, as well as practical advice about the do's and don'ts of ethnographic editing. The chapter concludes with a series of "Writing Experiments" that asks questions about the ethics of text constructions, genres of reporting/evoking cultures, and editing processes.

Finally, Chapter 6, "The Future of New Ethnographic Writing," is organized around a series of heuristic questions about reading and writing the new ethnographies. To respond to the questions, I provide excerpts from what I consider to be exemplary work. I conclude the chapter by reconsidering the evaluative standards used to assess the scholarly merits of new ethnographies.

HLG
Greensboro, North Carolina
June 1999

Dedication

This book is proudly dedicated to
new ethnographers
who want to write from their hearts about the truth
of their own and others' experiences,
but who lack someone standing behind them,
or with them,
urging them on.

With this book I will try to be that person for you,
that colleague and mentor and maybe even friend,
who urges you on.

Acknowledgments

This book came about because Art Bochner and Carolyn Ellis supported the initial idea I pitched to them. Since then, the book has evolved as a result of their guiding influences and the input of many valued and cherished people, as well as what happens to me when I sit down in front of a computer screen to write.

Every day I give thanks to what happens to me when I write. It's a continuous gift, it seems to emanate simultaneously from inside and outside of me, and I don't have a good name for it. It is a kind of flow, an energy, a spirit, a sense of my writing being a nexus of connections for which I am only the channel or medium. I can't explain it. And probably I shouldn't want to. But I give thanks to *it*, whatever and wherever "it" is.

On these pages, I'd like to thank the people and places that helped shape this work. I do have names for them. On a daily basis, I appreciate the time and space made for my writing by my wife, Sandra, and our son, Nicolas. Sandra also reads and edits my work and tells me when I'm being "too academic." Together, she and Nic laugh me back to a kind of mid-level sanity when I take things too seriously, or forget that we only have one shot at being a family and that my writing may be part of that but it is certainly not all of it. While I am thanking family, I'd also like to express gratitude to my mother- and father-in-law, Martha and Clarence Bray, who regularly travel several hundred miles, often passing up casino opportunities, to help tend Nic and us when our work schedules become overwhelming. And I'd like to thank our family dog, Carey, who does wonderfully what dogs do best, which is to remind us that lying down patiently beside us, and urging us to walk with her through the autumn leaves, are acts of pure love.

I'd like to thank my friends and colleagues at the University of North Carolina at Greensboro, who have helped make my life as their department head easy enough to accommodate research and writing, and who act as if being an ethnographer is a normal thing for an adult to do. Among them are my willing early-draft readers, Pete Kellett, Craig Smith, and Joyce Ferguson, whose comments have refined what I have written and added dimensions to it that would not have been possible without those conversations. I'd also like to thank Jody Natalle,

Heidi Reeder, David Dunlap, Sally Alvarez, Sharon Bracci, Robbyn Matthews, Lori Lindberg, Anne Flora, Paula Pilson, and Diana Dalton, for being my colleagues at UNCG, and for helping to make what I do there continuously interesting and challenging. Tom McNish, my undergraduate research assistant and master of the electronic search engines, gave me information I otherwise would not have found. And I'd like to thank Janice Smith and Chad Boyd for supporting all that we do in the department, and for helping me track down persons, rights, and permissions.

I am fortunate to have a very supportive writing community available to me via e-mail, annual conferences, "blind review," and occasional personal visits. With these people I share my writing joys and academic frustrations, discuss my ongoing work, and serve as well as a receptive audience for theirs. They have made me feel, individually and collectively, far less alone; they have made me better-read and more informed and have, in so many ways, reconnected me to the discipline during times when I felt I was completely out of touch, or neglected, or forgotten. They are: Eric Eisenberg, David Payne, Elizabeth Bell, Mark Neumann, Art Bochner, Carolyn Ellis, and so many of their students and ex-students at the University of South Florida; Patricia Geist, Peter Janis Andersen of San Diego State University; Stew Auyash of Ithaca College; Nick Trujillo of California State University–Sacramento; Annette Markham of Virginia Tech; Rita Whillock of Southern Methodist University; Paul Kohl of Luras College; Bryan Taylor of University of Colorado–Boulder; Steve May of University of North Carolina–Chapel Hill; Christine Keisinger of Southwestern College; Carl Lovitt of Clemson University; Jim Anderson of University of Utah; Patricia Riley of the University of Southern California; Ron Wendt of University of North Dakota; Dennis Mumby and Robin Clair of Purdue University; Dwight Conquergood of Northwestern University; Lexa Murphy of DePaul; Lyall Crawford of Weber State University; Linda Welker of Eastern Kentucky University; Larry Frey of the University of Memphis; Steve and Lindsley Smith, Jan Rushing, and Tom Frentz of the University of Arkansas; Roger Aden of Ohio University; David Procter of Kansas State University; Mara Adelman of Seattle University; Maria Cristina Gonzalez of Arizona State University; Jin Brown and Pamela McWherter of University of Alaska–Fairbanks; Ron Pelias of Southern Illinois University; the whole of the Alta Conference on Interpretive Approaches to Communication from

1987 to 1991; the participants in the Seminar on Narrative Ethnography at the National Communication Association in Chicago in 1997; and the participants in the Seminar on Shopping as Communication and Consumption at the National Communication Association in New York City in 1998.

I owe a great debt of thanks to two people at AltaMira Press: Mitch Allen and Jennifer Robin Collier. I also express my gratitude to Mark Woodworth for his careful editing and Lisa Bravo for managing the production of the book at ImageInk.

Finally, I want to thank my many students over the years, several of whom are now listed in the paragraphs above, for helping me grow as a teacher and writer through their reading, conversation, and work in various ethnography classes. I got into this line of work to become a teacher, and their accomplishments serve as constant reminders of how rewarding that can be, and also of how much I still have left to learn about it.

1 | On Becoming an Ethnographer in the Academy

*The only time I know the truth is when it reveals itself
at the point of my pen.*

NORMAN MAILER
Quoting Jean Malaquais

Writing the New Ethnography is the material, textual manifestation of a
long and complex process of my becoming a writer, a process in which
I am still actively engaged. Its ethnographic slant has been fashioned by
a way of working, a way of entering the world every day, which privileges asking questions about others in cultural contexts constructed and
understood by a self whose presence is very much in the text. Dan Rose
calls this process "living the ethnographic life" (1990), but mostly I just
think of it as *becoming who I am.*

For me, ethnographic fieldwork and the writing that comes of it is
less a formal method of inquiry than it is a disciplined attitude and
conversational style that I have learned to make into a way of life. In
this way, I am fortunate. Universities have paid me to live this way.
Many colleagues and students, and in some cases the public, have read
and responded passionately to my writing. I have had the personal satisfaction of having "been there" at the front of the interpretive turn in

communication studies, and now have fine memories of the individuals and conversations that made that turn possible.

But I don't kid myself. Mine has been a life enriched and rewarded by doing those things I probably would have done anyway. If not in academe, then as an investigative reporter. If not that, then maybe as a novelist. If not that, then probably as just another guy somewhere, scribbling a diary or journal that one day he hoped to turn into a book about the times he has lived through, the things he has experienced and witnessed, the people he has loved. In many ways, I've just been lucky to be an academic, to have come into the field at a time when the sort of writing I wanted to do was emerging as a method of inquiry. And in other ways, "lucky" is a word that others apply to me because they only see the work that turned out well. They don't see the mistakes, the failures, the projects that still are incomplete, the articles and books that were rejected.

I don't think I consciously "decided" to live and write this way. I'm not sure anyone does. To become a writer in a genre called ethnography is a choice that more accurately finds you, and then defines you. You may want to be a writer. But you have to find something worth writing about. You have to acquire an ability to write about it, which usually means studying the texts, the styles, the heroes and heroines that came before you. You have to practice your art, as does any other artist, which, in my view, means you dedicate at least a part of each day of your entire life to nothing else. While this personal struggle to find your voice and to say something meaningful is going on, you have to learn to take criticism. You have to learn to listen to all of it, respond to some of it, and ignore some of it. You have to cultivate an audience for your writing. You have to go to many places, talk to many people, market your work much as any other hawker of commercial goods does, sell yourself and your work as commodities.

You have to do all of these things *and* live with yourself.

Live with yourself in a context of others.

Now, let's assume that you begin your life's work, your quest to do all of these things, while you are a university or college student. You may major in English, or communication studies, or journalism, or anthropology, or sociology, or whatever. You are drawn to a discipline as a fly is drawn to light. You circle it from a distance, but find yourself inexplicably attracted to its sudden brightness, its heat. You can't turn away. You find yourself enjoying conversations made out of this discipline's jargon. You delight in your newly acquired vocabulary. You begin to see things differently, using the vocabulary you have acquired to frame your experiences. You begin to be consumed by a desire to learn more about this way of framing life. You spend actual money on books that you are *not* required to read.

You may then find yourself in graduate school. You discover that your purpose there is to learn how to "do research" and "contribute to the field." You find those challenges strangely appealing, even though you still have a hard time understanding exactly what they mean.

Every day, you are scribbling. You are trying to find the right words to describe a concept, method, practice, moment, feeling, activity, strategy, relationship, or community. You are reading. You are living. Among the writing and the reading and the living, you begin to define yourself. As an *academic.* Perhaps even as an *intellectual.* As a person whose job it is, as my friend and former student Bryan Taylor once put it, "to build a head."

Probably this will strike you as funny. I know it did me, until I thought about it. Then it made a rude kind of comic sense. Since then, it has taken on the aura of truth to me.

Kenneth Burke says you can approach life as either a comedy or a tragedy (1989). I think that is true. Some writers learn to roll with the punches, while others languish in the suffering. Either response pattern directly influences what we write about, and how we write. That I write with a sense of humor, and reveal my own and others' vulnerabilities; that I approach each new learning experience as a novice or beginner; that I take occasional risks with prose—these are all connected to the ethnographic life as I lead it. To my life as I know it. To my view of the world, as I see and experience it.

Your choices may be different from mine.

Your life certainly will be.

At some point it will become clear to you that new ethnographers have an obligation to write *about* their lives. I say "obligation" because new ethnographic texts require that your observations and evaluations of others be firmly rooted in a credible, self-reflexive "voice," which is to say a believable, compelling, self-examining narrator. In life's conversations, whom do you trust—the person who never discloses her or his own feelings, who has no interesting life stories to offer in exchange for the details of yours? Or do you trust the person who emerges in the talk as someone living a passionate and reflective life, someone willing to share with you its joys, its pain, its speculations, its ambiguities?

The problem with the answer I personally have given to these questions is that sometimes readers mistake my desire to produce a credible voice for the production of too much self-ish prose. I spend too much time talking about myself, and not enough time talking about others, or contexts. Maybe this is true. For some of my readers it surely is. I can accept their criticism because I am still learning how to find a balance between the story of life as I have lived it and the stories of others' lives that have been spoken into existence, within and against mine. I am still learning how to become a writer. Criticism helps me.

Even though it seldom feels good.

NOBODY IS BORN A WRITER. It is an identity we invent for ourselves and then try very hard to live with, and within. It is always part fantasy and part detective story.

The fantasy is when we imagine ourselves to be a "writer," usually as a result of having already written. There we are, successful and toasted. Surrounded by people who admire our words. Maybe the fates of nations change as a result of what we, and we alone, can articulate about the human condition. Maybe we are rich. Maybe we dedicate ourselves to helping those less fortunate than we are. Maybe we give in to a lush life of personal self-indulgence and intoxicating sexuality.

What*ever*. It's *a* fantasy.

The detective story is all about learning to read and to follow the clues that get you to—and through—the storyline. Learning to read clues *into the weave of contexts*. Learning the histories and conversational flows of a discipline. Figuring out how things add up. Being a good detective is about using observations and interviews to elicit information and then using the information to establish motives, patterns, and connections. It involves spending a lot of time just watching people. Talking to them. Waiting for awareness. Reflecting on the meanings of talk, patterns of behavior, women, men, love, money, work, family, God, history, the future, as well as the here-and-now of life.

That sort of thing.

This is *not* fantasy. It is a necessary process of constant discovery, of invention, of reversal, and of synthesis. Professors would probably like me to say it is hard work. Hard, *disciplined* work. Which it is. But it is also *fun*, lots of fun. If you like this sort of "work." Which I do.

I *enjoy* fieldwork. I look forward to hanging out with new people, visiting unknown places, engaging in observations, interviews and conversations, rituals and rites that I have only read about and some that I have never even heard of before. I am a pushover for new experiences. I love thinking about what it all means. I cherish those moments.

So for me, living an ethnographic life *is* fun.

WRITING AN ETHNOGRAPHIC LIFE is fun too. Just a different kind of fun.

Unlike fieldwork, which is about adapting yourself to the swirl and mix of a social world, writing is a *solitary* activity. You do it best when you do it alone.

And it takes time. Anything that takes time also requires patience. Patience is a hard virtue to acquire because you have to *do* it to *acquire* it.

Writing also requires a place in which to do it. Sometimes it takes years just to figure out where that is, for you. And the organization of that space is likely to be sacred. The energies have to be right. *Just* right.

Writing is all about *ritual.* Some writing rituals are personal ones, such as writing only in the morning or late at night; or writing while drinking coffee, or listening to music; or not shaving until you finish a final edit.

Some writing rituals are textual, such as my personal habit of reading and editing what I wrote the day before, as a warm-up exercise to perform prior to writing anything new. Or my bad habit of writing long sentences that the next day I have to break down into smaller ones. Or my personal goal of writing a section a week, a chapter a month, a book a year.

Some rituals are idiosyncratic. Scott Fitzgerald, for example, said that he never had sex while writing because he believed it drained his creative fluids. See what I mean?

◻   ◻

To live the writing life as an academic is to agree to live within a culture of criticism. No giant deal, because really, everyone in every walk of life has her or his own source of criticism, risk of rejection, source of negativity, and occasional pain. Look at it this way: Prizefighters take fists on the chin, academic writers just get hit with words.

But academic life is a life of *constant* criticism.

Constant criticism is too much to take for some of us, some would-be academic writers, to endure. You've got to know this going in. Think of our subculture this way: We are a tribe whose principal activity is producing texts. Tribal ritual has it that we must submit our texts to others to evaluate, and that these evaluators must judge what we write "blindly."[1] We seldom get paid money to write, or review, or publish our texts; it is just *expected* of us.[2] Moreover, it is hard to get good reviews and even harder to get published. By a kind of secret consensus among the tribal elders, nobody's first draft is *ever* good enough. The best we can hope for is an encouraging letter from an editor that asks us to "revise and resubmit." This process of revising and resubmitting can involve several rewrites and resubmissions, until we reach either clarity or insanity.

The message is clear: What we write is *never* quite good enough. This is a hard way to live. A hard way to craft a confident, writerly self. Particularly if you love language, and texts, and the academic life, to begin with.

On the other hand, most scholars will agree that getting feedback and learning to work within a critical community are important ways in which we learn to improve our writing, and certainly to refine our thinking. With very few exceptions, everything I've written has improved with the input—the feedback *and* the criticism—of others. But at times a punch on the chin would have probably felt better. From where I stand now, as a senior scholar with a decent record of publications, one of the best things I've learned from living in a critical community is *resilience.* By acquiring the skills and strengths associated with the writing–feedback–revisions process, I have become a stronger *person.* I have become someone who is better able to cope with, and even to rise above, many of life's uncertainties, sudden changes, and rough demands.

---

1 The notion of a "blind" review has come under some attack recently. For example, some scholars argue that it is not hard to figure out who is the author of a scholarly work; all you need to do is consult the listed references. Others argue that an author's name ought to be open to scrutiny during the review process, since so much of our work, our professional credibility, is based on our record of published research—in short, that a name should be associated with a line of thinking. Still others argue that reviewers should have accountability too, that the author ought to be able to judge the merits of a reviewer's comments based on her or his evaluation of the reviewer's work. And still others argue that "blind" reviews are necessary in the sciences and social sciences, but pretty much beside the point in the humanities or criticism.

2 Another way to conceive of it, however, is that for every refereed journal article I've published, I've received some form of merit increase in pay; for every scholarly book, I've increased my chances for promotion, which, in most institutions, carries with it a pay increase. So this reasoning is not entirely true.

The writing life is not an easy life. Nor does *where* we do it always help.

We exist, we write, and we do research, within institutional structures known as schools, colleges, or universities. There, we must teach and perform community service in addition to writing. Our teaching and service are also peer-reviewed, which becomes yet another source of potential criticism and continuous improvement. In the case of teaching, this means colleagues or department heads appear in our classrooms regularly to evaluate how well (or poorly) we are doing this part of our job. They might drop in while our students are "on," or not. While *we* are "on," or not. The students also evaluate us. At most institutions, student evaluations occur at least once in every course, every semester. Documents must be prepared that testify to our teaching abilities each year for annual reviews; in some schools with public postings, they are available around the globe via the Internet. Within this cultural context, any hint of praise or accomplishment is usually balanced with "suggested improvements."

The message is clear: No matter how well we perform, our teaching, too, is *never* quite as good as it *could* be.

And then there is our academic hierarchy, the whole "status thing." It begins while we are still in grade school, where the promise of a better life, more freedom, and on and on, is always narratively positioned in the next higher grade, or at the next level of education up.[3] Elementary schoolers yearn for middle school, middle schoolers for high school, high schoolers for college. At each level the promise is never really fulfilled, but still we dream of better things to come. After college comes a master's degree; then, for some of us, a doctorate. After years of professional training that usually exceeds those endured by lawyers and physicians, we are appointed only as an *assistant* professor, and at low pay. After doing those things that are required of us (which are never fully spelled out), our materials are submitted to various levels within the institution for further study and evaluation by those faculty members and administrators who are superior to us in rank. If we are deemed worthy, we are promoted to *associate* professor. Years later, after a great deal more labor and external suggestions made for

---

3 This is an educational application of an insight provided originally by Earl Shorris, in his work on the politics of middle management (1984). For a more detailed account of the historical development of status hierarchies, see Eisenberg and Goodall (1997), Chapter 3.

improving our personhood, writing and publishing record, reading, personal habits, perhaps even our clothing or our friends, we become a candidate for another round of institutional critique. If we pass muster through this screening, we are called, finally, *Professor.*

Or we could go "up" for dean. Provost. Chancellor. And so on.

Ours is a status hierarchy that burns a human fuel of constant evaluation and critique. It is a symbolic order that reminds us that no matter what we do, it is never enough—and that we can always do better.

Beyond these sources of criticism lie the added dimensions of institutional skirmishes and subculture warfare that typically pit discipline against discipline, method against method, art against science, business against the humanities, and so on. Arguments, in some quarters, are far less likely to occur than slurs, innuendo, ad hominem attacks, or slander. True dialogue—which we teach as a communicative virtue—can seem virtually impossible. A culture of criticism thrives on finding fault with every person, every argument, and every thing (including itself). One result is that very little nurturing or helpfulness goes on among or across the ranks of college faculty. Under such turbulent everyday working conditions, some interdisciplinary colloquia or departmental meetings should probably be held in gladiatorial arenas, with the panelists and department members armed and visored and with a crew ready to carry out the dying. To win, or to fight to the death of one of the competing ideas, seems too often to be a favored academic sport. Because we adversarial academics are all cut from the same basic cultural material, we are supposed to *enjoy* this, thrive on it.

If we were *not* academics, and if this were *not* an endorsed set of cultural and tribal activities, we would likely be called masochists and sadists and remanded to the care of people who are licensed by the state to talk us back into sanity. Into a condition of mind in which our humane purpose is to care for, and about, each other. Our reality is indeed socially constructed, but for some reason many of us have decided to make of our reality a series of critical prisons, in which we are both inmates and the guards.[4]

What I have written so far leans heavily toward a negative view of criticism and its uses in our academic culture. But fortunately, it only tells part of the story. On the positive side are generous scholars who

---

4 My adoption of this particular prison metaphor is drawn from Wallace Shawn's play *My Dinner with Andre.*

view their task as journal editors, reviewers, and colleagues as one of mentors rather than sparring partners. Who engage in academic dialogue. Who try to help rather than hinder the efforts of others.

So it isn't editors in general that are the problem. Like the proverbial bad apple, it's the rare, but evident, bad editor who all too often ruins a young writer's life. Their weapon is "only" words, but their choice of words, when read by that aspiring writer, often feels like upper-cuts to the chin.

PARDON ME. I sometimes speak my mind.

There are cultural signs of hope, however. For me, one direct sign of potential change in academic culture is the willingness of some brave academics to turn the critical lens back on our institutions.[5] To examine our cultural practices just as we would any other tribe's. To write about the emotional ups and downs that accompany this otherwise "privileged" way of life. To write, openly, about the cultural politics of publication, tenure, and promotion decisions. To disclose and analyze what actually happens during faculty meetings and what the subtext reveals. To discuss the role of gender, of race, of class, of sexual orientation, in all that we do. To question what we have for so long simply taken for granted.

These are clearly a writer's solutions, but we all work where and how we can. More importantly, the ability to write about the personal experience of academic life is one of the ways in which the new ethnography can make positive contributions to knowledge and create differences in people's lives.

❐   ❐

What I am trying to do in this book is to lay open the process of becoming a writer—an ethnographic writer—*within* a university culture.

It is impossible for me to get "all" of it, and it is equally wrongheaded to try to apply the entirety of my generalizations to any specific case. Nevertheless, I hope that what I *do* offer will be helpful. I don't think it is right to provide instruction about the writing processes associated with composing the new ethnographies without also inscribing the institutional contexts in which what gets written is evaluated and its author judged.

---

5 For ethnographic examinations of their lives as "institutional subjects," see especially Bochner (1997), Ellis (1995), and Richardson (1995). For a sociological treatment disguised as a dictionary, see Nelson and Watt (1999).

Most readers of this book will be people who have taken—or who are contemplating taking—the "interpretive turn" in ethnography. This means, in part, that most readers already see a need for (or are at least open to) alternative forms of qualitative research and writing. But not everyone in academic culture sees such a need. Politically, the interpretive stance and openness to alternative forms of inquiry and representation is another source of potential academic critique. Publishing interpretive work has never been easy, because the alternative forms of expression challenge the accepted formats and styles of account giving and report writing that most traditional academics value and that some hold sacred.

The key to gaining wider academic acceptance for interpretive work is, I believe, to combine "solid fieldwork" with "good writing." These phrases mean that no matter what stylistic strategy you deploy to represent what you've done in the field, what you say about what you did there must be written—at minimum—in an intelligent, timely, professionally competent, and interesting manner. Beyond these criteria (which, as you will see in Chapter 6, require further critical reflection), many ethnographers these days believe their work should be empathetic, caring, therapeutic, and compassionate. All of these labels are laudable goals. They are writing goals that sound obvious, right?

But the obvious is often deeply ambiguous as well.

Consider the criterion "intelligent." This means "smart," right? But how do you write a "smart" ethnographic story? How do you "do" smart, on the page? What constitutes smart in fieldwork? Name the last smart passage you read in a scholarly journal. Now ask a colleague to read this passage and respond to the questions. Does your colleague agree with your choices, with your interpretation of what is smart?

Or consider the criterion "timely." This means that what you write about has to be current. But this assumes that what's current hasn't changed much since the last article or book you read. Which assumes you have been reading the right stuff. Which is to assume there is such a thing. Or, that the people you read and revere are doing it. Try this experiment: Ask someone in your department who is not interpretively oriented to answer the question about what is current in the field. Compare your answers. What can you learn from these differences? What can they teach you about your field of study? About publishing in the field?

Now consider the criterion "professionally competent." This phrase means that your fieldwork will be thoroughly and ethically conducted.

It also means that your writing will be done according to the manual of style appropriate to the journal or publisher to whom you are submitting it, and it will be free from typos, grammar errors, improperly numbered footnotes or endnotes, and the like. All of which is necessary, but seldom sufficient, evidence of a professionally competent piece. For example, you can write perfectly well about the tediously mundane and find your work rejected on the grounds it is not professionally competent. You can write about something that someone else has already covered but that you failed to find in your literature search. You can write a piece only to discover that in the mind of the reviewers and editor, you should have used another framework or measurement technique to make sense of your data. Again, the phrase "not professionally competent" can cover a variety of interpretive possibilities.

Finally, the phrase "competent" can mean that your writing (and, by implication, your work in the field) must be free of all possible references to what is intensely personal or emotional or that involves sexual innuendo or description. Which is to say, any word, sentence, paragraph, or stylistic choice that is likely to cause readers (even *a* reader) to feel uncomfortable or empathetic, laugh or cry, get mad or be offended, sit up straight or squirm.

What about the term "interesting"? Everyone knows the research questions you ask must be interesting. Your fieldwork should be done in an interesting place. Your writing of the questions and about the fieldwork must be interesting. But interesting *for whom?* After all, different audiences find different questions, subjects, and styles interesting. Aren't we really talking about appealing to members of your particular discourse or interpretive community?

And what can be said of the newer ethnographic criteria? The call for work to be "evocative," "empathetic," "caring," "therapeutic," "emotionally honest," and "compassionate"? Are these goals, these criteria, any less ambiguous or subject to less critical argument than our traditional ones? *No.* For each goal expresses a value that elevates a way of telling a story or an expected (or hoped for) reading outcome. And reading outcomes are always determined by readers, who themselves have internalized standards, goals, and preferences for the prose.

So, as you can see, even though the seemingly innocent phrases "solid fieldwork" and "good writing" are transparent, it is critical *how* they are interpreted within a particular critical and evaluative *community,* for a particular *audience.*

In the following section, I'll share with you a story about how I learned to appreciate the power an audience has to define evaluative standards for written work. It's also a story about differences in audience members' preferences for styles of prose and the relationship of those differences to the social and professional choices we all must confront when we are trying to become writers. The story has a moral too. See if you can figure it out.

◻   ◻

The setting for this autoethnographic account is State College, Pennsylvania, and the year is 1978. Imagine me, your narrator, as a doctoral student in what was then called Speech Communication. I was 26 years old, a white male with blond hair, hopeful blue eyes, wearing what was at that time a very stylish "outlaw" mustache. I was six-feet-two and weighed 180 pounds. Against the better judgment of some faculty members in my department, I had elected to use "creative and biographical writing" as my research tool (instead of statistics or two foreign languages); thus I enrolled in creative nonfiction, fiction, and biographical writing classes.

The writing seminars were designed to be akin to workshops, supposedly on the model of the famous University of Iowa Writer's Workshop. Essentially, this model asked each student to write something each week and turn it in to the instructor a few days prior to class. The instructor duplicated and distributed the material ahead of time to each member of the class, and selected one or two pieces for in-class discussion. The discussions generally consisted of careful, line-by-line dissections of the chosen pieces, with critical commentary supplied by the instructor as well as the students. Pieces of writing that showed some merit were revised and reconsidered later in the semester; those that didn't make the cut were discarded. The goal was to have one finished piece of work at the end of the term.

These classes were *not* for the meek. Discussions of work were vigorous, critical, and, at times, *very* personal. Critiques of writing were detailed and no attempt was made to improve students' self-esteem. The avowed purpose was to help make each of us into a professional writer, and, as we were constantly reminded, professional writing is a tough and highly competitive, highly personal, business. Unlike other graduate courses I'd taken, nobody cared if I had a good idea but executed it poorly; in a writing workshop there was no difference between ideas and their execution. Similarly, the writing process was the avowed way in which ideas—as well as characters, plots, and themes—were created; there was no separation of research from writing. You wrote *as* a method of inquiry.

I learned a lot about writing, and about myself as a writer, from participating in these classes, but I was also learning about *cultures of writers.* As with any social grouping, differences and hierarchies emerged in our seminars. Individuals whose work was regularly singled out for discussion achieved status, while students whose work was regularly overlooked lost status. Having status meant having a voice in discussions of other students' work. There were also the usual collegiate cliques based on differences in lifestyle choices, majors, and perceived levels of personal attractiveness.

Collectively, these groups and hierarchies became identified with target *audiences* for our stories. Predictably, some members of a class would "love" some stories and deride others, usually based on their ability to identify (or not) with the main character and theme. There was a powerful social pull to identify yourself with one of the in-class cliques, for that way you would have an audience for your work. If you were struggling to find an identity as a writer—and I was—it was easy to associate social success, and fit within an in-class clique, with having attained an audience for your writing. Instructors didn't necessarily agree with the critiques offered by these cliquish in-class groups, of course, but to have your work cause disagreement, or controversy, between these groups…well, that was a badge of honor.

I came dangerously close to confusing the bestowing of that badge with becoming a writer. Here is the rest of the story.

TWO TYPES OF WRITERS attended every writing seminar. We called them the Writers and the Poseurs.

The Writers were always few in number, and, as a group, not particularly stylish in dress or deportment. They looked and acted ordinary. In the beginning of our time together, none of them wrote especially well. Reading their work, it was hard to see a future bestselling author among them, or even a person who could scrape by selling his or her own work. But as they evolved throughout school and after it, their work acquired distinctive storylines, and many of them developed a voice as individuals. Those who did usually wrote every day. They edited what they wrote. They wrote again. They passed their work around for comments, for discussion, for criticism. They talked about what they were writing, the joys and challenges of it.

The Writers were hungry for a *participative* audience. But they were also learning about themselves. Writing, especially the personal writing that characterized our seminars, does that to you. It provides a medium for self-examination. The writing process encourages you to closely revise and edit your work in ways that sensitize you to how much like a fine instrument and tool language is, how multifoliate are its shades of meaning. It also teaches you to respect the differences between words and realities, for as fine an instrument and tool as language is, it is not fine enough to capture all of what *is,* or even very much of it. The results of this style of learning among my classmates—learning by writing, by editing, by revising—are as various, probably, as the fingerprints of the students exposed to it. But most of us learned to appreciate language more fully, to take less about it for granted, and never to assume, ever again, that our identities were somehow beyond or above it.

The Poseurs in the class outnumbered the Writers. A few prettier people always dressed and acted as if they "had written"; they were flocked about and imitated by lesser poseurs, pulled in by the gravity of their displays, much as moons are pulled into predictable orbits around distant planets.

During my time in school, the official costume of the capital-P and small-p would-be writers was anything dark, so long as it was black. Some of them also smoked, *beautifully.* Others had the eyes our culture associates, improperly, with an inner purity, while still others had a vacant blankness we associate, rightly, with the loss of any sense of innocence. Several of them were deeply into the muses offered by recreational drugs or alcohol. Many of them claimed troubled pasts, and a couple of them would have very troubling futures. They all routinely uttered "fuck" in class, and wrote explicitly about obsessed sex, back when it was still a bit of a risk to openly do so. When they spoke, it was mostly to whine or complain. When they turned in their stories, just reading them made most of the rest of us feel uncomfortable. They appreciated that.

They were hungry for the satisfactions of language too, but mostly they would settle for *the look* of being hungry, played out for an audience of each other.

AT FIRST, WHEN I JOINED THE CLASS, I didn't know what type of writer I was.

I admired the Poseurs, I think. Not so much for their beauty, or their attitude, or even their stylish black clothes, but for their general dark recklessness, the dull radiant energy of it.

I had, by that time, failed at writing for too long a stretch to feel reckless about it anymore.

I was twenty-five or -six, then twenty-seven, and writing was my one true passion. I just wasn't very good at it. I had developed discipline: I wrote every morning. With it came my everyday failure, for my work had been rejected by nearly everyone, often with diminishing degrees of politeness. No agent would take me because I hadn't published anything beyond a few poems, and no publisher would look at my work because I didn't have an agent *and* because I had published a few poems.

I could have felt oppressed and marginalized, but I didn't know the words for it.

I had recently lost a father I never really knew, and had given up on ever being the sort of son my mother wanted me to become. I left a supposedly good job selling advertising because it didn't allow me time to write, and became a short-order cook in a diner in a coal-mining village called Philipsburg, in central Pennsylvania, to eventually accumulate enough money to return to school. I worked from 5 A.M. to 3 P.M. six days a week. I left the diner, *Jerry's Place,* and walked home to my second-story apartment in an old, dark green Victorian dwelling, where I would shower off the stink of grease, sweat, and cigarette smoke, put on clean clothes, sit down at my typewriter, get high, and write. I lived, mostly, on Campbell's tomato soup mixed with whole milk, in addition to whatever sandwich I could assemble out of leftovers at work.

I made just enough money to pay my meager bills, and to smoke.

I had very vague ideas about whom I was writing for. I think it consisted mostly of imagined women whose assumed sadness and general longing (or horniness) my words could cure. Women who would undress for me because I was a writer. And who would then, sometime later, disappear. In my mind, there apparently were enough of these women to constitute an audience, somewhere.

It's pretty clear to me now that I was lonely living in Philipsburg.

It is also clear that I was confusing sex with writing, and imagination with audience.

Nevertheless, at the time I didn't know that. I wrote every day. My lust, my desire to become a writer, was disciplined, at least in *that* way.

Sometimes I had to wait until payday to afford the postage to mail a story to a magazine. When they were inevitably returned, either unread or with a form rejection letter, I felt a little ashamed and increasingly stupid. By the next summer, I had saved some money and applied to graduate school at Penn State. My intention was to study conversation, mostly because I thought it would teach me how to compose better conversations in my stories.

Being a lonely failed writer living alone in Philipsburg just wasn't working for me.

So, within the bittersweet surround of this highly personal context, the P/poseurs' sexy black recklessness attracted and bothered me.

The other group I thought of as "the Writers." These were young women and men—not very many of them out of the whole of the class—who had attained "voice." I could tell that the professors respected their opinions. So, too, did some of the Poseurs. The Writers' stories were generally a cut or two above the norm, but not always. On one level, I wanted to join their elite band, but I wasn't yet good enough. All of them had published work. Or, at least, I thought they had.

Then, one day, one of the Poseurs got a story accepted for publication in a major literary journal. He brought the letter into class and showed it around. We all claimed to be very happy for him, as this level of recognition would clearly lead to even better things. As it did.

After class, some of the members bad-mouthed him in predictable ways. He was a gay blade, and this story obviously appealed to the editor, who was, himself, notoriously gay. This was true, but was probably irrelevant. Somebody else said the whole story wasn't *even* fiction, for god's sake, it was a rough transcript of a night the writer had told her about a couple of months ago. Another student said if *that* was true, we ought to hang out with the writer for a change. At least we'd have some fun. This brought the usual round of cheers and derision.

But no matter what we said, the fact was that he had done it.

I went to see my writing teacher that semester, a man named Phil Klass. Under the pen name William Tenn, he had been an early producer of serious, literary science fiction back in the fifties and sixties. He had the face and general build of a wire-haired fox terrier, if you add a wild head of tall white hair to that image. He was a native New

Yorker who viewed his life as a college professor in central Pennsylvania as the outer limits of eccentricity. He always came to class harassed, rushed, and just slightly pissed off.

As a teacher, he was intense and demanding, occasionally inspiring, but always fair. He told wonderful stories about writers and writing, and being close to those stories made us feel a kinship to the art. The only story he told us about himself was singularly memorable. He had once attended a Big Literary Party in New York. This gathering was a relatively new experience for him (at that time), because he had just published his first novel. Despite years of supporting himself as a writer who sold whatever he could (mostly pulp stories to sci-fi magazines), his face was not one that was well known. But he was still surprised when he entered the room and was introduced to someone who was posing *as him.* "Hi, I'm William Tenn," the guy offered.

Phil decided to play along. After all, how often do you get a chance to watch others respond to someone claiming to be *you?* "Good to meet you," he replied, "I'm Phil Klass."

He related a few of the resulting comic incidents of that memorable New York evening, mostly for laughs. But as always, Phil was performing for us at the level of metaphor and metonym, and there was a larger point for us to grasp. This time it had to do with the difference between the *identity* you create as a writer, and the *person* you know yourself to actually be. On the page you could create any identity you wanted, but off the page you had to live with the person you were. The question is: If you met yourself at a party, would you like who you were?

It was a question, I thought then, aimed squarely at the Poseurs. I didn't know then that if it *was* aimed at them, it was also aimed directly at *me.* For in Klass's eyes, I was a poseur. Not even with a capital P.

As an editor, he was both meticulous and relentless. He believed that a writer had to suffer to be sufficiently motivated to write well. But I didn't know that any more than I knew he thought I was a poseur, when I entered his office to complain.

"Life isn't fair," I began.

"So?" He looked at me as if I had just said the most obvious of things, which, of course, I had. His bushy white eyebrows reached up into the nether reaches of his forehead.

I explained about the Poseur's story getting published. I whined about my own failures. I was pretty sure, in fact I knew, that everyone realized I was a good writer, and so on. So why didn't I get my work accepted?

The question hung there, low storm clouds over a precipice.

"Listen," he told me, "if you think you are living in a world where virtue is rewarded and good triumphs over evil, you are probably reading a goddamn romance novel." He grinned. He liked what he had said. It showed. Then he turned back to his papers. Either he had nothing else to tell me or he had better things to do. Either way, it was a clear invitation to leave.

I stood up and replied, nonchalantly, "Yeah." Then, I shrugged, like the Poseurs did in class.

He nodded, as if confirming his suspicions about me. "Right," he said.

It was starting to rain outside, and I felt it was getting colder in here.

The next week, Mr. Klass stuck in my mailbox a story without a title or author page.

I read it immediately.

It was about this young man who, like many hunters in Pennsylvania, practiced his shooting skills in the off-season, using a technique called "plinking." The basic idea was to set up some cans or bottles in the woods and use them as targets. "Plink" was the sound made when a bullet struck one of them.

The story was told in what I then called "contemporary Hemingway," meaning it was constructed out of short sentences and short sections, with the focus almost entirely on action. It was a page-turner, something most of the Writers and all of the Poseurs overtly and fashionably shunned as "mass-market trash," so, of course, I had to be a little put-off by it.

It didn't have the then-trendy feel of either a postmodern or a minimalist tale. There were no deeply ironic referents, as we had been taught to admire in Barthelme. Nor was the conversation pithy and bittersweet, as in Carver. There wasn't any hint of magical realism, as in García Marquez. It lacked drugs, sex, and rock 'n' roll.

It was *just* a story.

I wondered why my teacher had given it to me. Maybe he was telling me I should aspire to "mass-market trash." Or maybe he was just sharing a good story with me. Naw. He always worked his students with life metaphors. I was confused.

Then I turned the page.

Young man goes plinking, and suddenly finds that someone else is out in the woods, only *he*—the young man, not the tin can—is the target. From there on, "plinking" goes on to become a signature tale of the hunted man, wherein fear begets violence. By the end of it, I was completely inside this hunted world, and totally annoyed at myself because of it.

I wasn't supposed to *like* writing like this.

Yes, this *was* a lesson directed to me. Like the young man in the story, I approached my writing as a kind of "plinking." I was shooting cans of insignficance to anyone, preferably any woman, who would listen. I didn't understand that writing was a personal quest, a way into my self, and into my culture. I, too, was afraid. Oh, I *knew how* to write, all right. I had studied it and studied it. But I hadn't yet used it to confront anything more substantial than a made-up tale that vaguely resembled something out of Kafka. My writing was derivative and formulaic. It was distanced from who I was and from the life I was living. I was afraid to take real risks with my writing or my conversations. I never wrote from the perspective of dramatic reversal. Nor did I have my characters ever really *learn* anything troubling or difficult about themselves through the action in the story. Push that fact a little further and the truth was, I could write university-approved sentences, but I hadn't learned yet how to tell a story to a noncaptive audience.

But *damn*—this guy, whoever he was, could write sentences and tell a story!

I went to talk to Phil Klass about it, about my mixed reactions, my confusion. Of course, my talk was just another metaphor for my own sorry failure. He told me that the author and I had shared the same seminar the previous spring. He asked: Don't you remember him?

I said, quietly, "No."

My teacher smiled. "David Morrell?"

Still nothing.

"See," he said, "life isn't fair." He lit a cigar. "A young man writes a story like that, which *I* think is a great story, which *you* think is a great story, right—"

"Right," I nervously agreed.

"Yeah. And what happens to him? He gets torn up by his so-called *academic* peers for telling a great story."

"Really?"

"Really." He blew smoke in my general direction. "But David doesn't give in. He got a teaching job at Iowa. I think he's turning this story into a novel. Mark my words, Goodall: David is a *writer*." He spoke that last word as if it were sacred. "In the end, everyone who knows a good story when he reads one will appreciate that." Then he grinned. "And those that don't, *fuck'em*!"

David Morrell went on to a distinguished writing and teaching career. I think of him as a regular guy in that class, one of the Writers, not one of the Poseurs. He was a guy who wasn't just "plinking," not just hanging out wearing the right black clothes, not just complaining or bragging about his sex and drug life. This was a guy who used writing as a process of inquiry, who wrote to learn about himself and, in turn, could use what he learned to write stories *for an audience.*

I knew then that even though I lacked the clothes, the affected attitude, and even the social success to show for it, I had been acting and writing like one of the Poseurs.

It didn't matter that I wrote every day.

I didn't have an audience. At least not an audience beyond the Edenic women of my own imagination.

I didn't have self, either. I hadn't used writing to learn what or who my self was.

I could write sentences. But I still didn't know how to tell a *story*.

▢   ▢

I include that account in this book for three reasons.

The first and most obvious reason is that *the performance of writing is relational.* If you want to become a writer, you need to write stories that other people want to read, to relate to. It's not enough to want—as all poseurs do—to "have written." It is not enough to acquire the various clothing and accoutrements of the so-called "artistic life." It is not enough to just sit in on writing classes, hoping to soak up some kind of mysterious message that will suddenly transform you into a writer. And it is not enough to simply tell a story about something that happened to *you*. You need to use the process of writing to find a storyline *and* then have the discipline to work it into a narrative others want to engage. This means you need to create—out of the raw materials of lived experience, imagination, and reading and talking with others—some *pattern* in that storyline that is symbolically rich *and* significant for an intended audience.

You must learn to engage readers in an evolving conversation.

The second reason for including my story in this chapter is to underscore this truth: Audiences read stories not so much because they identify with the initial conflict as because they feel at one with the process of self-discovery and transformation caused by how the conflict is worked out. The characters in your story *have to learn something* out of what happens to them. They must *grow* into an understanding and maybe change, forever, because of it. They must get deeply in touch with something vital within themselves.

Good writing, like good conversation, is transformational.

The pattern you help the reader to discover must contain some basic human grammar, out of which readers can find the blood link to their own experiences, their own reading and talking, their own constructions of how persons and things become meaningful through everyday actions. This is more than simple identification with the character or plot; it suggests a closer identification with the way in which the story that is told *could well be their own*. This is what teachers of writing often mean when they say that the story "must draw readers in and keep them there." In a very real sense you are building a life-experience metaphor *large enough to contain both of you*—writer and reader.

The third reason for including my story is to illustrate how *a pattern in a story can generate a larger context in which all patterns, all constructed forms of lived experience, can symbolically converge.* Morrell's story was less about "plinking" than about the common human need to overcome an impossible situation ("life is unfair, right?"). Thus, the challenge is to create a way of understanding and being in that situation that *transforms* it and us. When I read "Plinking," I found myself identifying with the nature of the struggle and learning from both that nature and my totally absorbed personal identification with it. The character's struggle to survive was my struggle too. The terms of my struggle, in life, were different. But through the story I saw how closely their themes, their patterns, were the same.

Great writing is naturally *dialogic*. It is a medium, a message, that furthers our journey.

Writers write to discover, and to further themselves, *and* they write for audiences *outside* of themselves. They have stories borne of personal experience that don't end with just retelling the personal experience, but instead are designed—through conscious, stylistic deployments of language—to connect readers to larger patterns of lived experience and cultural meaning. Writers learn to find storylines by paying attention to their selves in relation to the details and patterns of everyday life, and reading large the potential for connection. It is through the process of writing that we connect those details and patterns back to our selves and, through the magic of language, to something else. Which is to say, we connect our accounts to the larger story, to the bigger plot, to the discovery of our part in the nature and purpose of persons and things. That is the mystery, and that is the quest, that for a writer is always *there*.

Writing Experiments

1. Write a personal account of why you have decided to study communication (or sociology, or anthropology, or administrative science, and so forth). In it, try to narratively connect significant life experiences to your academic goals. What does this say to you? What does it teach you? What could it teach a reader about you? Write out your answers, please.

Now go back and describe, as accurately as you can remember it, one actual communication exchange that formed one of those significant life experiences. If it was a conversation with a teacher or parent, try to write it out as it happened. If it was a private reflection, try to capture the mood and flow of your thoughts at that time. Think about how you ought to account, on the page, for silences, absences, implied meanings. Consider what you might be able to write to more fully represent or evoke the *feeling* of this experience.

Now read your account *aloud*. Listen to the attitude you embody, the rhythms and cadences of your voice, the way you accentuate particular cues and skip lightly over others. What does your *voice* do to add a sense of humor or seriousness to a particular exchange or passage? How can you better express that in writing?

2. Write a brief autobiographical account of yourself using only (or mostly) proper nouns. For example, here is my entry from *Casing a Promised Land* (1989b):

Places: Martinsburg, West Virginia, 8 September 1952. Rome, London, Cheyenne, Philadelphia, Hagerstown. *Schools:* The American School, St. Dunstan's, Carey Junior, Roxborough, South High, Shepherd College, University of North Carolina at Chapel Hill,

Pennsylvania State University. *Jobs:* lifeguard, short-order cook, political activist, musician, psychologist's assistant, waiter, account executive, college professor, consultant. *Favorites:* blue, Raymond Chandler, golden retrievers, Italian or Szechuan, Herbert Blumer, Miller Genuine Draft. *Current status:* happily married, gainfully employed.

What kind of person do you think emerges from these (mostly) nouns? Now look at the list of nouns *you* made to describe your life. What do these nouns say about you? What (besides the verbs) gets left out?

Now think about the last time you had a conversation with someone new. How much of that conversation resembled a listing of nouns? Do nouns encourage talk? Or do they not? What images do they conjure?

3. Develop a richer autobiographical account by connecting your responses from items 1 and 2 with the personal reflections I've asked for. Before you begin to write, consider what theme you are trying to develop. What do the events, the persons, the conversations and conjectures, in your life add up to? And yes, I know your journey is still incomplete. But what theme emerges so far?

If you are really stuck, if you don't know your theme or can't figure it out, just begin to write. The activity of writing can lead you from one sentence to another, from one experience to another, and eventually get you to an "*aha!* moment." What you write won't be your story, but it may help you figure out what your story ought to be. And maybe how to write parts of it.

But there is more to it than "just writing." To accomplish this task requires you to think "up one level" from these raw data to find a *theme* for your life story. Think about the representational issues involved in that for a while. Think about it in the company of your favorite beverage. Have two of them. Maybe talk it over with friends.

Here's another technique you may want to try. In between the *aha!* moment and the actual writing of your story, jot down the theme on a piece of paper, and then provide—from your data—the supporting *motif* structure and what it suggests. Some people work with clusters and circles, some with clear connecting lines. A motif is anything—in this case the noun'd events, persons, and places—that supports or explains or leads readers to an understanding of your theme.

If you find this task difficult, try considering the text of your life as if it were a novel you're reading. What are its chapters? What in each chapter helps move the story along? What gets in the way? What doesn't matter?

Now edit your nouns, your theme, your motifs, and your story. Who are you?

For Further Reading

The works listed below will help you extend and apply the material in this chapter.

Kreiger, S. 1991. *Social science and the self: Personal essays on an art form.* New Brunswick, NJ: Rutgers University Press.

Langellier, K. M. 1989. Personal narratives: Perspectives on theory and research. *Text and Performance Quarterly 9:* 243–276.

Okely, J., and Callaway, H. 1992. *Anthropology and autobiography.* London: Routledge.

Richardson, L. 1997. *Constructing the academic life.* New Brunswick, NJ: Rutgers University Press.

2 | *Finding the Story in Ethnographic Words*

We breathe in air, we exhale stories…

WILL BLYTHE
Why I Write:
Thoughts on the Practice of Fiction

I took "the ethnographic turn" during the summer of 1984.

It was the year I earned tenure at the University of Alabama in Huntsville. I received the official letter one afternoon late in May. A surprising thing happened. I opened my tenure letter, saw in the first line that I had been granted tenure and was promoted to associate professor, and found myself incapable even of *forcing* a smile. Instead, for a long, suspended moment, I stood there with the letter in my hand and a sense of loss in my heart. The humid air was as thick as syrup, warm and sticky as the road to hell, and perfectly still. I looked down at the letter and read the words again, as if maybe I had missed something on the first reading, something that would make this moment *feel* good. That didn't happen. I had come to a desired destination, but I wasn't happy about it.

Why? The question was my own. Its echo, in that suspended moment, defined my life.

The answer did not take long in coming to me. Everything I had done to win tenure, every word I had written to gain a promotion, no longer seemed worth it to me. I had won a place in academe, but had lost my soul.

My soul as a *writer*.

The Faustian bargain I had struck was a simple trade-off. I had traded the creative prose I wanted to write, the stories I wanted to tell, for traditional academic prose that was then the standard for journal and book publication. To earn my tenure stripe, I gave up just about everything I had learned at Penn State about creative writing, about using writing as a form of inquiry, and about the complexity inherent in representations of self, others, and contexts. I had sat down four years before at my self-correcting typewriter (ironically accurate term, don't you think?) and wrote what my academic readers expected to see.

Which was not entirely a bad thing. After all, traditional journal scholarship enjoyed a ready-made audience. Those audience members, divided as they were by divisional lines and methodological preferences, nevertheless formed several large interpretive communities. Writing for one or two of them was what was expected of a scholar. Research wasn't easy. Crafting academic prose was hard work. "Submitting" to a journal or publisher (another interesting expression, wouldn't you agree?) was always a gamble. Rejection of what I had submitted was a sentence that condemned me as much as what I had composed. The only available help was to write and submit again. A sentence from an editor that read "revise and resubmit" came to be, for me, a rhetorical source of relief, of "self-help." Like the gambler I'd become, it was the emotional equivalent of winning just enough at the table to stay in the game. For a gambler, this translates into placing yet another bet on the thin but vain and addictive hope of winning it all.

So there I stood on an otherwise ordinary day in May, having won it all. Academically, my writing self was pronounced to be clinically clean, and completely corrected. I had used that backspace/delete key so often in the past four years that I had effectively erased creativity and passion from my writing. I had given in to the prose demands of my profession. But I knew, in that long, suspended moment, that I wanted my passion back. I needed to write creatively again. I wanted my soul, my soul as a writer, to be reborn.

I also knew that I wanted to remain in my profession. The tension between my desire for creative expression and my need for a life within an academic culture was dialectically real but personally confusing. Was there a way to resolve this? Could there be a way *to write myself out* of this conundrum?

I decided, on the way back into my old house on Humes Avenue, that what I needed to do was find a new *storyline.* To do that, I reasoned, would require rethinking the rhetoric of communication studies scholarship. It would require rereading and new reading and refiguring and new figuring—all the research skill sets coming into play. Most of all, it would require connecting the storyline—whatever it was to be, wherever I would locate it—to the ongoing scholarly conversation I had recently joined in organizational communication.

I needed to be able to use this new storyline to articulate a gap, a "presence of an absence" (Barthes, 1972), some lack of something in our disciplinary construction of knowledge, some uncommon place from which to speak. I needed to call into being a way of writing about communication and organizations that could interest others in our field, and sustain me. Maybe because I had been reading Raymond Chandler novels, I believed this task would require approaching my personal conundrum as if it was a *mystery.*[1] Maybe because I had been hanging out with an ex-detective, I came to define my role in the mystery as a scholarly detective. All of which is to say that I needed to use all of the resources of my scholarly training and personal life to engage, and hopefully to resolve, this scholarly problem.

You must use rhetoric to defeat rhetoric, Socrates advised.

---

1 Raymond Chandler had something to do with it, but my application of the term "mystery" to ethnography originates in the writing of literary critic Kenneth Burke: "Mystery arises at that point where different kinds of beings are in communication. In mystery there must be *strangeness*; but the estranged must also be thought of as in some way capable of communion.... The conditions of mystery are set by any pronounced social distinctions, as between nobility and commoners, courtiers and king, leader and people, rich and poor, judge and prisoner at the bar, 'superior race' and underprivileged 'races' or minorities.... All such 'mystery' calls for a corresponding rhetoric" (1969, p. 115, emphasis mine). It also borrows from the French dramatist and philosopher Gabriel Marcel, in that "mystery" is a fundamental orientation toward participation in the existential drama and phenomenology of everyday life. Viewed this way, "mystery" encourages us to see ourselves as connected to others, whereas a "problem–solution" orientation separates us from each other by emphasizing differences in reasons for behavior, choice, and speech (see Goodall, 1991, pp. x–xvi, for extended discussion).

Yes, and you must use the *material of your life* to find the *material for a story.*

    ◻   ◻

I began my investigations as any detective does, with an inventory of what I already knew about the case. This was a mystery whose rhetorical clues were contained in our scholarly narratives, which meant I should be able to locate traces of them in *my* scholarly work.

I began, as Gregory Bateson advises, by looking for basic patterns in the culture under study. Because I was searching scholarly literature in the communication culture, and because my aim was to discover something about the way that literature was composed, I turned my attention to an analysis of the *form* of scholarly work. What I saw was that the basic prose formula for what I—and *so* many others—had written as traditional scholarship followed a predictable pattern:

- Introduction
  - Gain the attention of the audience by identifying the general issue I plan to pursue within an existing body of literature.
  - State a thesis or argument that I plan to prove or demonstrate.
  - Provide a preview of the main claims to be advanced in the body of the essay.
  - Offer an inducement (that is, what the reader derives from reading the piece).

- Body
  - Review and critique the relevant literature to establish credibility as a researcher.
  - Clearly identify the existing "gap"—the problem—in the literature.
  - Fill the "gap" with a solution, such as a new argument and relevant supporting evidence.
  - Include an application of the new argument to a piece of discourse, a narrative, a conversation, or the like.
  - Derive "important" or "significant" new findings or conclusions from the study.

- Conclusion
  - Review and summarize the essay, emphasizing the relevance of the new idea to an ongoing line of inquiry.
  - Make suggestions for future research.

It was obvious to me, as I am sure it is to most of you, that this form for expressing scholarship is very much like the standard format taught to students for making a problem-solving *persuasive speech*. Or, at least this is what we in the communication field endorse as a standard format for that assignment.

It occurred to me that the most persuasive speeches I'd heard outside of a classroom were *not* delivered according to this standard formula. Martin Luther King Jr.'s "I Have a Dream" speech, John F. Kennedy's inaugural address, and various sermons, lectures, campaign speeches, and depictions of passionate public address in popular films were definitely not delivered according to the approved format. Uniformly, they were more creative, and, in most cases, poetic. The speakers spoke less from prescription than from their hearts. They treated their audiences as partners to the speech, not passive receivers of it.

Hmmmm.

How could this insight, simple as it was, apply to written forms of scholarship? Could there be an analogy between alternative forms of public address and alternative forms of qualitative writing? My hunch was, *there was*. Like any good detective, I followed the leads provided by the clues. In this case, I went out in search of it.

Which meant I went into the library.

One clue inevitably leads to another. Then to another. And so on. Some don't pan out, others do. What I was searching for, I thought, required me to retrace what I perceived as a bifurcation of persuasive forms in public address. But I was wrong. As long as I perceived scholarly writing as *only* a form of public speaking, and alternatives to it as some one thing that was disconnected from my personal history and experiences, this mystery would only deepen. I was imprisoned by a conceptual framework of my own rhetorical making.

I was searching for a literal comparison when I should have been looking for a *metaphor*.

METAPHORS CONNECT SUPPOSEDLY DISSIMILAR PHENOMENA. I was trying to link essentially similar genres: forms of public scholarship with forms of public speaking. What I should have been doing instead was comparing public speaking to other forms of human communication, and then comparing those other communicative forms to creative forms of writing.

It may strike some readers as odd that I would conceive of writing and speaking as dissimilar phenomena. They are both forms of expression that rely on language, right? Someone writes, someone reads; someone speaks, someone listens? The obvious intelligent answer is "yes." But you have to remember that the communication discipline originated by splitting off from English on the grounds that instruction in speech was essentially dissimilar to instruction in writing. Since 1915 our profession has had an academic and political stake in defining itself as a distinct field and especially, fundamentally, to keep maintaining that speaking and writing are very different activities. Because I never had a reason to question this distinction, I suffered from accepting it. Eventually, when I came to the end of yet another long day in the library making no progress because the question I was asking made no sense, I realized the error of my ways.

That move was liberating.

Writing and speaking were *similar* phenomena. Viewed this way, "languaged" this way, the insight made me recall a line from a lecture in graduate school—from Herman Cohen, I think—to the effect that one of our discipline's founders conceived of public speaking as "enlarged conversation." Was it James Winans or Herbert Wilchelns?[2] I couldn't recall. But the line had direct application to this mystery. Once I myself had uttered the notion, I could think of creative scholarly writing as a form of *conversation*. Enlarged conversation. A form of personal address rather than a public address. An ongoing, dialogic, interpersonal process rather than a "hypodermic needle model" speaker–message–audience process. I would later complicate my thinking on these issues, but for the time being I was content to work with the refreshing simplicity of them.

Analogically conceived of in this fashion, my way into a new, scholarly storyline turned more on using writing to express what is up-close and personal than it did on insisting that it remain distanced and impersonal. Good conversation is a mutual journey of discovery that instructs and delights; good conversational style in writing should do the same things. Credibility, in conversation, is not limited to the sources you cite as authorities; it also sums who you are as a person. Can you be trusted? Are you likable? These, too, should be applicable to scholarly writing.

---

2 It was James Winans. See his *Speech-making* (New York: Appleton, Century, Crofts, 1938), p. 3.

I *liked* this metaphor of creative scholarship as conversation.

But I still had a long, long way to go. I was assembling some intriguing clues, but I had not yet found a way of connecting them. I had to reread scholarship in my discipline, and in my subdiscipline, to find a way into the ongoing conversation that would make what I wanted to say about creative scholarly writing palatable to my peers. I had a clue about the storyline; now I needed to read for clues to the *gap in the literature* that my storyline could connect to.

    ❐   ❐

I tell you this story because it is intended to be an analogue to your own experiences. Telling it often helps my students in a beginning ethnography seminar to feel less anxious about creating a plan to guide their own research and writing. They, like you (I assume), too often secretly believe they lack something—call it a "research question gene"—that they actually have. Most of us come to phrasing what it is that we write about by combining personal experiences with close reading in professional journals and books. Saying it that way makes it sound linear and clean, but it seldom is that. As my story reveals, I have stumbled into some very good ideas by following some very bad ones. The personal experiences that brought me to writing new ethnography were painful, and the close reading I committed to often left me better read, but not really any wiser.

Still, you have to trust *the process.* You have to believe that somewhere in the material of these two mysterious stories—the life story and the research literature story—you will find a clue that leads to a connection. You will locate a gap in the existing literature. You will come into a way of asking questions about it that leads to the creation of a storyline. You will, eventually, write *your* way out of *your* personal conundrum.

But you have to *trust* the process. And the process begins with locating a gap.

To locate a gap in any scholarly literature requires that you read *a lot.* In every field, every discipline, every subdiscipline, a printed conversation is occurring between and among scholars that forms most of what is published in scholarly journals, yearbooks, and books. To figure it out, you need to be able to identify the major and minor players, their positions on the issues, and why and how they agree and disagree. Remember, as Bryan Taylor told me, you are "building your head."

To learn who the players are, begin with the *most recent* essays published in the leading national, international, and regional journals. Read the essays. Go to the references. Target the specific references written by scholars common to *all* of the essays. Think of this exercise as one in which the outcome will be something like a map of the territory, or, if you prefer another metaphor, a family tree.

Make a large wall chart (or these days, a computer file) of these names, relationships to institutions, and their arguments, more or less like William Faulkner did with the characters for his stories. Go back through at least five years of publications, preferably ten, more if you can. Where new players emerge, create a space for them. See how their arguments figure into the general conversation. Pay special attention to *the beginnings and endings* of each essay or chapter, because in the first few paragraphs the authors will identify the key ideas, and in the last few paragraphs they will tell you how this essay should be read and used.

In this part of the process of finding the storyline, your job is to notice *patterns*. You will notice patterns of citations, then of themes, and then of specific issues. You will notice patterns of language usage, ways in which key terms are defined. You will notice patterns of professional controversies and institutional expertise. All of these findings will become personally and professionally important. Remember, *trust the process*. Approach your task as a cultural study. If you follow my advice, believe me: you will notice patterns in our culture. *Meaningful* patterns.

You will also learn some personally valuable lessons. For example, you will learn that most authors use pretty much the same references in most of their work. This is because they, too, are engaging in an ongoing conversation, trying to tie their words to the larger stories being told. It is also because, out of all the reading and rereading we do, we all end up with a few favorite books, articles, and authors. The personal message here is fairly easy to decipher. While you need to read widely in your field, you will need to become a *very close reader* of a few *foundational* books and a few regularly cited articles or chapters. These are the references that everybody who is anybody in this specific area uses. These are the arguments, the lines of thinking, that not only build an evolution of understanding but form a prose parameter around a theory or an idea. From the foundational readings, you should be able to piece together—in an additive, year-by-year, fashion—the recent work done on those readings, authors, and ideas. Why focus on the "recent"? Because scholarship is an ongoing process, because when "contributions" are made to a field it implies that the field moves on to something else, and because there is no point in repeating what someone else has done.

You will also notice something else. Most new writers break into the field because they have read something very closely that other scholars either have never read, or haven't read that way or that closely. This, too, is a pattern. The personal message for you is to read widely enough to be able to find a new book (it's usually a book that does it) that has some analogical application to what's going on in the conversation in your field.

You will notice other patterns, too. For example, these days there is distinctly more *cross-disciplinarity* in and among ideas and major players. This means that not all of the foundational or even important work is contained in one discipline. It also means that each discipline has its own part of the overall conversation, its own major and minor players, and its own distinctive theoretical or methodological identifiers. An analysis of ethnography in the field of communication studies, for example, reveals that most of the references to most of the essays published in most of our journals regularly make use of sociologists, psychologists, philosophers, organizational studies scholars, anthropologists, and literary critics. In some cases, you will find published articles in our sponsored journals with *no* references to any work done in the Communication field. In others, you will find that a majority of the citations are drawn solely from our national and regional journals. And this seeming disparity is all right. Scholarship is about *ideas,* and ideas are rarely limited to one discipline or subject. The important point isn't where an idea comes from, it is to remember what you are reading, and using, it *for.*

You are reading for the *storyline.* You may not be sure what you are using it for, at least not yet. But that is all right. Be patient. Ideas, and uses for them, often take time.

You are also reading to find out what is *collectively written* about an idea, what *individual voices* have to say about that collective idea, and for an *opening* that you can address. This is what I mean when I say that most traditional scholarly essays are built on a *problem-solving* public speaking model, wherein the "problem" exists primarily as a "gap" in the existing literature and the reason you write is to offer a "solution" to it. In my own evolutionary quest to write from an alternative metaphor, I still find the concept of a gap relevant.

Let me explain why by giving you a current example.

ONE OF THE ONGOING CONVERSATIONS in ethnography (and more generally, among the humanities disciplines) concerns the idea of "representation." In a strictly literal sense, "representation" refers to the ability of language to capture—to re-present—an existing external reality. When viewed this way, representation is an issue in ethnography because it asks scholars to reflect critically on how well, or how poorly, language is adapted to that particular task in fieldwork (see Welker and Goodall, 1997).

For example, let's say you are keeping a research journal on the conversations of teenagers who hang out in shopping malls. You have labeled this form of cultural exchange "mall talk." You go to malls regularly, listen to what is being said, and make notes on the words exchanged, the actions, behaviors, and clothing of the participants, as well as the overall contextual "feel" of the mall itself. Here is an excerpt from your fieldnotes:

> "Like, wow, man…you *know?*"
>
> "You bet, dude. These so-called *merchants*…heheh…these merchants, man, want us mall rats outta here!"
>
> "But they want our *money,* dude." The boy looks down and kicks at the floor. "It's just not fair."
>
> "They just don't want us hanging around." A pause. "Walkin' around, like we do."
>
> "*Check it out,* man. That fluff chick's hair is really *zook*ing!"
>
> "Wow." The boys watch the girl walk by. The girl pretends to ignore them.
>
> "What would you do with *that,* dude?" There is a shared laughter among the boys.
>
> "Yeah, and I bet the merchants don't care if *she's* just walkin' around." More laughter.

From a strictly literal point of view, what do these fieldnotes *represent?* Is there a commonly shared "mall reality" *that these words capture fully?* Probably not. My guess is that you would agree there are many experiences in malls, and this particular slice of it is only that: a slice. This is what is meant, in part, by the claim ethnographers make, that all representations are *partial* depictions of reality (Van Maanen, 1995).

Even with that caveat, do the words *accurately* and *completely* capture the experience they report on? Tougher to answer this question, isn't it? After all, you and I weren't *there* when this exchange occurred.

More to the representational point, the *writer's focus* on the shared talk among the boys obscures what the young girl with the big hair is experiencing or thinking about. It also excludes the perspective of the merchants, who are depicted in the boys' talk as a group lined up against them. In part, this is what ethnographers mean when they say that all representations are *partisan*. They are partisan because they generally represent only the point of view of the teller, and only reveal, or capture, that which the teller of the tale wishes to focus on.

Finally, what do we learn about "mall talk" as a result of reading this description? While it is true that there are some interesting and even creative uses of language—"fluff chick," "zooking"—there is little *news* in this excerpt. Young males have always discussed young females, and vice versa. Boys typically hang out—on street corners, in diners, in malls. Their talk has always been reflective of the cool jargon of their times. We know these things to be true because there are many, many studies over the years that demonstrate it, analyze it, place this form of talk within a specific time, place, and culture. If this excerpt becomes a candidate for inclusion in an article, then, *it must show something that isn't well understood,* or that hasn't been fully articulated. Sure, it represents a slice of life in a local mall. But what else does it do? What does it show us, or teach us? If we come away from the representation *with more questions than answers,* then ethnographers say that this representation is *problematic.*

So, in summary, not only is this representation partial and partisan, but it is problematic, too. Now here's the kicker: *All representations are partial, partisan, and problematic* (see Eisenberg and Goodall, 1997, Chapter 2). From a strictly literal perspective, there is no available language for a representation that is capable of achieving some Archemedian, all-knowing, all-seeing, godlike point of reference (see Anderson and Goodall, 1995). Words are representations of reality, but reality is far more complex—more full, more radically diverse, and more whole—than any representation of it.

The second representational issue for ethnographers is what Stuart Hall has identified as using representation as a "replacement for" a reality (1997). This is a *connotative* use of the term "representation" that has distinct *political* ramifications. Hall uses film footage of the British Olympian Lynford Christie as an example of how this form of representation works. When Christie won his Olympic medal, viewers saw a black man carrying a British flag across the track.

Hall explains that for many people throughout the world, this image was doubly puzzling. It was puzzling because most people associate—represent—"British" with white people, and because blacks are seldom represented carrying a British flag. Thus, Hall explains, the whole idea of what is represented by the term "British" was called into question for many viewers. It was as if Christie's image was a *replacement* for what they assumed to be true. The image of a black man with a British flag did not re-present a reality that existed, for clearly the image captured the reality itself: Christie won the medal and carried the flag. The *work* done by the image was to replace what constitutes "British" with another image. And in this way, that image was *political.* It changed the way some people worldwide could think about what it means to be British.

For cultural studies scholars in general and some critical ethnographers specifically, the idea that representations are political statements is important. For example, a lot of what we think of as "knowledge of the world" is really knowledge of the Western, white man's world. During the last quarter of the twentieth century, scholars in many fields have been attempting to recover knowledge from what they refer to as "underrepresented groups." Feminists, for example, often research and write about ordinary and extraordinary women in history from all lands and of all colors and creeds that have been ignored, neglected, or abused. By placing their stories alongside the existing historical accounts, we gain a fuller appreciation for the complexities, as well as the injustices, of prior, more partial accounts. We also learn that these recovered women's stories often challenge what we have taken for granted, assumed to be true, or simply overlooked. Such representational scholarship is inherently political. As political as were the preexisting Western white man's accounts.

Similarly, scholars who study gay or lesbian leaders, persons, communities, and discourse often do so in a effort to recover what has been "left out" of the mainstream construction of knowledge in a variety of fields. The same political work is also done by scholars who want to bring into public light the lives, the work, the struggles of African Americans, Jews, Native Americans, Hmong immigrants, Japanese geishas, Israeli youth, Palestinian freedom fighters, and so on.

My point here is that the idea of representation is both an intriguing idea, or concept, as well as an issue that warrants a lot of new scholarship devoted to collecting and telling stories about people, places, and things that never before attained scholarly interest or legitimacy. The "crisis of representation" is often cited as a reason why we should encourage alternative forms of scholarly writing as well. After all, if you can argue that underrepresented groups should be represented in the scholarly literature, you can also make a plausible case for underrepresented forms of scholarly expression also needing space in scholarly journals. Not everyone will agree with you, and no editor will grant space to you just because you claim you ought to have it. Scholarship—and forms of its expression—are controversial and journal space is hotly contested. But there is a respectable gap under the general conceptual heading of "representation." If you are skillful, you can use this gap to help make your case.

Back in 1984, when I was experiencing my personal crisis of representation, I lacked the terminology to make such a case. To locate that terminology, to find a way to articulate what I wanted to do within the context of scholarship, was a major source of my detective quest. By the way, this lack of available terminology occurs to all of us, so you shouldn't be ashamed of it or daunted by it. Part of the process is learning to deal with it as an intellectual challenge, not as a problem or deficiency in character. It just means you have more work to do. More reading and writing to do.

Let's assume for a moment that the idea of representation intrigues you. You want to bring the concept into your research. What do you need to do? First, as I have mentioned earlier, you need to thoroughly familiarize yourself with the players, evolution of thought, and current controversies about it. But where should you begin?

As I write these paragraphs, in the spring of 1999, my recommendation is to begin with the Stuart Hall video called "Representation" (1997). In addition to the brief treatment I have given it, the video provides rich details and images that will stay with you, and that will guide your understanding as well as confront you with some of your hidden biases. I also recommend reading an edited book by John Van Maanen called *Representation in Ethnography* (1995). Van Maanen brings together in one relatively slim volume the views of leading ethnographic theorists and practitioners on the singular concept of representation in fieldwork. It contains a list of references that ought to help you organize your search for the "family tree" of ideas that shape what we think, now, about representation. Go to them, read them, begin making your chart. Finally, conduct a keyword search on "representation" with some other key terms commonly associated with it (for example, fieldwork, authorial, writing, culture, and whatever specific area of research you are pursuing) using the computer catalog resources at your library. If you need help learning to use these information technology resources, ask to speak to the research librarian in your field. Use the printout of titles (and abstracts, and in some cases the full text of the article) to add to your chart.

At some point in your reading, reflecting, and charting, you will begin to see an emerging scholarly story—or stories—about representation in the area of your specific research quest. You will have found the basic *disciplinary* storyline. And if you are lucky, you will begin to see there is a gap—something missing or something not being told or something that is completely wrongheaded—that you want to address. You will be motivated to join the conversation.

Welcome!

◻   ◻

Now let's get down to how you learn *to write* that disciplinary storyline, fill that literary gap.

Before I go any further, however, I want you to think about the *gendering* of advice about writing traditional scholarly essays. To rely on a problem-solving model is to gender the writing about scholarly issues in a particular way—in a *masculine* way. As most people who teach and write about gender and communication will attest, a masculine communication style is characterized by trying to solve problems and reporting on—re-presenting—a reality they believe to be relatively fixed and stable. A more feminine communication style is characterized by an emphasis on rapport-building with listeners, in which there is a distinct preference for processing information (for example, reflecting, personally, about meanings) over problem solving (Tannen, 1990, 1994; see also Trenholm, 1996).

But the gendering of scholarly writing is deeper, and more problematic, than easy generalizations such as those cited above. As Carole Blair, Julie Brown, and Leslie Baxter argue, women's voices—and feminine styles of writing—are typically "disciplined" (1995). By their use of the term "disciplined," they mean "made to accord with" masculine standards for appropriate topics for research, the conduct of the inquiry, and the prose style used to represent and report it. For example, for many years academic research literature simply did not address any issues related to human emotions. Carolyn Ellis, one of the pioneers in an area now called "emotional sociology," used fieldwork and autoethnography to explore this unexamined yet powerful aspect of life. But to do so, she had to confront a decidedly male bias against talking about our emotions, much less studying them.

This is because the conduct of inquiry was (some would argue it still is) decidedly gendered in a masculine way because of the dominance of a *scientific* approach to research and model building. This model for scientific research is "masculine" in orientation because it assumes there is a knowable, external reality that principled (read: disciplined) inquiry can observe, identify, classify, and report on. It further assumes that knowledge should be additive; to know something of scholarly value is to add to an existing body of facts another fact, then another, and then another. The result will be a generalizable model, theory, or explanation. And the explanation, because it is generalizable, should predict future actions within that domain.

Because, within the sciences and social sciences, this is what research reporting is *about*, and what research is supposed *to do*, this model preferences a *formula* for writing a scholarly article. The formula is appropriate to scientific inquiry because findings *are* additive and knowledge *is* cumulative. Such work isn't about "creative" expression. Rather, it is about the common quest for *truth*. This reasoning is why scholarly journals—particularly in the sciences and social sciences—are gendered as masculine. They report the results of principled inquiry within a tradition of knowledge building that is aimed at representing *truth*. Even the recognized stylesheets that every journal article and book must adhere to reinforce this code of scholarly conduct (see Bazerman, 1987).

But what if truth is gendered in a *feminine* way? Or in a cross-gendered way? What would an "appropriate" research topic or question be? How would the *conduct* of a study differ? What alternative forms of written expression would fairly represent these important differences?

I ask these questions because it helps explain why, in 1984, my detective quest eventually led me to take "the ethnographic turn," and perhaps even why I dared to take it only *after* receiving tenure. While I agree in principle with Blair, et al., it is also true that the "disciplining" of a voice and of a reporting style also influences how *men* write in the academy. In my own case, I was trained as a creative writer and as a biographer—skill sets that emphasize a close, personal connection between the writer and that which he (or she) writes about. I learned to work in genres of writing that suggest that if you move a reader to tears, or to laughter, or into a deep internal struggle with their taken-for-granted assumptions, you have done a good thing. I acquired habits of research, and of being in the world, that prize close observation and engagement of others, and of contexts, that are *always reflected back to the writer's self.*

After all, *I* am the one authoring this account, am I not? My credibility as a writer depends on how well I *develop a relationship* with my reader, which is largely determined by the *character* I reveal on the page. In terms supplied by the rhetorical theorist and critic Kenneth Burke, my persuasiveness is based on the ability of readers *to closely identify* with me, my perceptions of others, and my descriptions of contexts, within an overall story structure that moves from *desire* to *satisfaction* of that desire (Burke, 1989). My job as a writer is to:

■ Vividly and dramatically arouse a reader's interest in my topic
■ Deploy language to shape the account into a coherent narrative unity that resonates with the life experiences of the intended reader
■ Move the reader to a sense of completion, to a conclusion that satisfies or satiates the reader's original quest for the experience of reading, or knowledge, or both

What I had been doing since receiving my doctorate, how I had been writing throughout the tenure process, was more akin to the scientific, problem-solving model widely endorsed in the scholarly community as the "proper" form of expression. My training as a biographer, and as a creative nonfiction writer, was distinctly at odds with my discipline's view of writing—specifically, with the kind of writing appropriate to the construction of "legitimate" knowledge.

For example, in 1983 I authored a *Quarterly Journal of Speech* essay based on my dissertation about the interpersonal communication of Zelda and Scott Fitzgerald (Goodall, 1983b). Despite its presence in a humanities journal, the writing still reflected a masculine preference for solving a theoretical problem (the title is "The Nature of Analogic Discourse" instead of "Talking Love to Death"). The institutional politics of publication (I had to submit to publication standards to gain tenure and promotion), and every discipline's recognized need to limit space for individual articles, dictated that I narrow the whole of my dissertation into a brief, bare-bones, essay. The two hundred pages from my dissertation that carefully and methodically developed material from the Fitzgeralds' lives became two or three paragraphs in the published article. The thesis, from which the title is derived, was taken from a footnote in the dissertation. The writing in the essay assumes an off-putting, highbrow, academic tone, which is nowhere apparent in the style of the literary biography I wrote as the dissertation. This essay is clear and compelling evidence of how well I had become "disciplined."

I have no doubt that if the Fitzgeralds had lived long enough to read this essay, the whole point of it would have struck them as comically ironic. Their lives *prove* some academic theory—you must be joking! But more importantly, the writing in it would have presented a problematic representation of them, to them. Probably it would have confirmed for them the truth of Scott Fitzgerald's statement: "Biography is the falsest of the arts" (cited in Goodall, 1980, p. 14). However, the same charge could be made against *any* writing that tries to re-present, or to "stand in for," the lived experiences and personal meanings of people who have lived in the past. Biography may be "the falsest of the arts," but that claim doesn't necessarily mean that the knowledge gained from representations of lives in it isn't true. Nor does it mean that the writing of a biography, which is an attempt to bring order, coherence, and meaning to a life, isn't an act of knowing. What it *does* mean is that representation is an issue for biographers as well as for ethnographers, for philosophers as well as for literary or rhetorical critics.

I can say critical things about writing biography. Can we agree that the same criticisms could be—perhaps *should* be—articulated about scholarship in general? Isn't one of the insights brought about by the term "crisis of representation" also an apt description of writing *any* scholarly essay?

Perhaps you should consider writing about this problem in your field of study?

EVERY NOW AND THEN during my Faustian-bargain days, my resistance to these disciplinary sources of representational domination would show itself.

I would write an evocative description, turn an interesting phrase, make use of a dramatic metaphor, but journal editors doing the job the discipline expects of them routinely used red ink to mark through these passages. Some of them even apologized for so doing. But in the end, the disciplining of Dr. Goodall, what he was allowed to represent, was very much the central issue in my academic Faustian bargain.

I had found another clue to the disciplinary storyline, but I had also found it *troubling*. It wasn't so much that there wasn't a gap that I wanted to address with an additive bit of knowledge. Nor was it an argument about a topic that I had a particular issue with. It was larger than that. It had to do with my personal experience of being a teacher, a teacher of communication.

My subdiscipline was organizational communication. I believed that what I was learning—certainly what I was teaching about humans communicating in organizations—was largely a *mis*representation. The reason for the misrepresentation had largely to do with the questions we were disciplined to ask, the conduct of the disciplined inquiry we were encouraged to pursue, and, most importantly, the genres of writing we were limited to and constrained by.

Yes, I had found another clue to the gap. I knew how to read it. I certainly lived it. I just didn't know what to do about it.

I "DISCOVERED" ETHNOGRAPHY almost entirely by accident.

I hate to admit it, but it's true.

In all of my writing classes at Penn State I never once heard the word "ethnography." By academic osmosis, I somehow knew that ethnography was something anthropologists (and some sociologists) did, which was about as intriguing to me at the time as the kind of writing physicists and mathematicians did, which is to say, not at all.

Ironically, I studied for my doctorate in the same department Tom Benson taught in, and I wrote my dissertation in the same year he published "Another Shootout in Cowtown" (1980). This essay—very controversial in its time—was the first extended piece of interpretive ethnography published in our field. But I never took a course with Professor Benson, and I never knew he was writing interpretive ethnography. Why didn't I? Because my major advisor, Gerald M. Phillips, forbade it. At that time, Phillips and Benson were officially, departmentally, at war. I was told, in no uncertain terms, that if I chose to take a seminar with "him," I wouldn't be welcome in my advisor's office.

Gerry Phillips was a brilliant, complicated, compassionate, wonderful, but at times an extremely frustrating, man. I liked and admired him, but I also understood the power he held over me. I didn't want to anger him. Nor did I want to test him. I felt I needed his approval. So I didn't take a class with Tom Benson. Which was, I now think, a real shame.

It is probably also a shame that in all my communication studies courses in one of the best schools in the discipline, I was *never* required to read any work by Gerry Philipsen, a scholar who truly opened up the field of communication to ethnographic inquiry in the mid-1970s. But, to be fair, I was in a rhetoric-and-communication-theory-heavy department with strong, traditional views on the conduct of scholarly inquiry. Such "radicals" as Philipsen were not read because there was so much else to read, and so much "disciplining" of us to do.

I was already way out on a lonely departmental limb by declaring my research tool to be creative and biographical writing. So I didn't want to push anyone too much. I just wanted to graduate. Get a job somewhere. Continue to pursue the writing life.

Besides, these scholars I was privileged to study under were Big Names in the field.

They knew what was going on.

Why rock the boat?

THIS FEELING, THIS DISCURSIVE EMPTINESS, worked on me throughout the summer of 1984 and well into 1985. Because I hadn't read about "representation," I didn't even have a good name for it.

These were the clues I could name: Part of what was missing in our literature could be called "the human stories" of communication in the workplace, which was clearly a rhetorical byproduct of the distanced, so-called objective, positivist-endorsed method of acquiring information from people.

Another part of this representational crisis that I couldn't name was the way positivist scholars wrote about their so-labeled "subjects." People at work were represented as if they were no more complicated than crops in a field, or cows in a pasture. By focusing on managers' and employees' behaviors, we turned what we called research "subjects" into behavioral "objects." Later I would encounter, during a lecture at NASA, an operational definition of a human being that recalled my uneasiness about positivist research models: "Humans are sacks of behaviors suspended by a calcium skeleton and driven by something called cognition" (cited in Goodall, 1989a). I thought, then as now, that this dominant method of inquiry was responsible for mistaking symbol-users for soybeans, and for misreading meaning-based, interpretive beings for "sacks of behaviors." In both cases, the product and the operational definition were amenable to statistical reporting, but sadly lacking in their ability to re-present or evoke what people experienced at work or used communication to accomplish.

As I said earlier, the final and damning part of my personal representational crisis was the nagging doubt I had about the relevance of most of what I taught my students about organizations and communication. I mean, could you *really* expect a software programmer to pragmatically do a better job communicating with his or her boss, clients, coworkers, or customers by applying *systems* theory? "Yes, Ms. Jones, I see that the negative feedback loop that I mislabeled as a throughput is really the answer here."

What answer would that be, exactly?

And whatever might be the question?

I even *liked* systems theory. I tested adults on their knowledge of it.

But I didn't as yet have a name for this ineffable "other thing," this alternative explanatory qualitative framework, this new way of doing research, this creative genre of writing, that I knew, just *knew,* had to be better. So I kept reading. I kept reading for clues.

ONE DAY, THUMBING THROUGH back issues of journals in the library, I found an essay by Michael E. Pacanowsky and Nick O'Donnell-Trujillo (1983). The essay was only then a year or so old, but reading it was an awakening. Among other things, it made me wish I had subscribed to *Communication Monographs.*

In it, these scholars told a story that posited "culture" as oppositional to, and a kind of narrative remedy for, the language and research methods associated with "systems." They used the study of an organization's culture as a way to challenge both the dominant social science paradigm for conducting research *and* the dominant traditional scholarly essay format for reporting it. *All right!* I damn near cheered!

These authors told me that all of my anxieties could be dispelled and my dreams of finding a way to tell the human story of organizational communication could be accomplished by refocusing my attention on ceremonies, rituals, rites, artifacts, uses of humor—what they called "cultural performances." The basis of studying and writing about these "cultural performances" was something called "ethnography." They included a set of references unique to me in our literature, places for me to go to find the narrative roots of this alternative storyline. I was, in truth, *uplifted* by this news.

But, admittedly, I was also a little jealous of it. I mean, *hell,* somebody had beat me to it. In my typical masculine argumentative way, I resented the news that was liberating me. At least a little bit. At least at first.

I then did what every scholar learns to do when textually confronted with new and useful information. I went downstairs to make a copy of it. I wanted to own it. Walk around with it. Show it off to others. If this was a stage and I was a player, this would be my time for "strutting and fretting upon it," like some frumped-up dandy suddenly drunk on a new lover's promise. "See *this!*" I wanted to say to soooooo many people, "somebody else thinks like I do!" But I was in a university library. Such displays of joy, such jollification of the research spirit, weren't tolerated. So I slunk quietly down the stairs wearing what must have been a wide, stupid grin, dancing, rejoicing, and confronting my accusers only in my head.

It was the best ten cents a page I *ever* invested. For less than the price of a mocha latte, I had words in my hands that could change my life.

I had found my personal organizational communication Book of Genesis.

◘   ◘

For reasons that will become clear to you a little later in this chapter, I want to switch frames (and voices) now. I want to go back in time to recover some history of ethnographic text-making and storyline-finding. I want to do this so that you understand that the personal and professional influences on ethnographic work have always been located deep in the lived experiences of the particular woman or man. And I want to do this because part of the obligation in becoming an ethnographer is to listen to these stories, these arguments, to expose yourself to the wisdom literature that has shaped the field.

In one sense, I am doing this shape-shifting now because this is what I had to do when I read the Pacanowsky-Trujillo article, examined their references, and discovered that there was a literature with which I needed to become familiar, if not intimate. If I was going to understand ethnography, I needed to read in it. Try to make sense of it. Connect one dot in its lineage to another, then another to another, and finally come up with a coherent narrative about my connection to it. If I couldn't do these things, chances were slim that my desire to speak to the field, to help to right what I perceived as wrong with writing about organizational communication, could be any more than a kind of uninformed, undifferentiated, academically barbaric bark or howl.

My guess is that you will need to do this too.

HERE IS THE NARRATIVE BEGINNING[3] of—as John Van Maanen aptly expresses it—"the Book of Genesis" (1988, p. 10) for ethnography:

> Imagine yourself suddenly set down surrounded by all your gear, alone on a tropical beach close to a native village, while the launch or dinghy which has brought you sails away out of sight. Since you take up your abode in the compound of some neighbouring white man, trader or missionary, you have nothing to do, but to start at once on your ethnographic work. Imagine further that you are a beginner, without previous experience, with nothing to guide you and no one to help you. For the white man is temporarily absent, or else unable or unwilling to waste any of his time on you. This exactly describes my first initiation into field work on the south coast of New Guinea. I well remember the long visits I paid to the villages during the first weeks; the feeling of hopelessness and despair after many obstinate but futile attempts had entirely failed to bring me into real touch with the natives, or supply me with any material. I had periods of despondency, when I buried myself in the reading of novels, as a man might take to drink in a fit of tropical depression and boredom. (Malinowski, 1922, p. 4).

You can interpret this passage *as writing* in at least two ways.

Approached as a *representational form,* the writing leads me in the general direction of Edward Said's critique of it as a prime example of *colonialism.* Said (1983) points out that the origin in consciousness for many modernist authors (such as Proust, Eliot, Woolf, and Conrad)—as well as, we can infer, ethnographers such as Malinowski—is the historical presence in Europe at about that time (early twentieth century) of dark-skinned others who "challenge and resist settled metropolitan histories, forms, modes of thought" (p. 223). The need to understand these strangers brought with it an imperial need to control them, hence intimately connecting rhetorical forms of cultural representation with

---

3 Close readers of Malinowski will note that I am, in fact, not beginning at the actual beginning. I have chosen to quote this passage—labeled in the text as III—because here is where the actual storyline begins. The brief two sections prior are, in my view, rhetorical warm-ups before the narrative pitch.

civilized (read: Western whites') forms of order and modernist (read: Western whites') rationality. If, as Said has it, we "think the narratives through together within the context provided by the history of imperialism" (p. 224), we see that in literary form, the rhetorical exigency for desire begins in the *perception of strangeness* and the rhetorical satisfaction ends in *narrative control* of the story.

This is admittedly pretty heady stuff. But the stakes for understanding the politics and consequences of representational choices are also high. No ethnographer worth her or his salt wants to be called a "colonizer." It is also important to recognize that since the very beginning of modern ethnography, personal feelings and perceptions, a storytelling form, and an intellectual quest have been the rhetorical and narrative cornerstones of an ethnographic narrative.

Notice that even in this early passage, Malinowski reveals personal information about his character. He finds that his material and contextual conditions—of being a stranger in a strange land—led him to read novels. And that these novels were "like drink." I can, myself, understand precisely what he means here. I can, and do, associate myself with these circumstances, and recall many times when novels have been both my comfort and my drug of choice. From these metonymical associations, I get closer to Malinowski as a person and as a narrator. I find that we share common personal experiences, perhaps even common problems. Again, I am rhetorically and narratively induced to identify with the author through this tale, which, as I reach that point in the story, I realize is one that I am also actively involved in. This is what literary theorists call "co-constructing a text," and "coauthorship of meaning." It is also what communication scholars call "building empathy," "identification," and "relational coordination." In my give-and-take with this passage, I am acting very much as a conversational partner.

Another association begins to shape and color my understanding. When we compare what Malinowski read (as evidenced in his *Diaries*) with his assertion that—like drink—they helped him deal with his despondency, we find a confluence of desire for an experiential storyline with the material manifestation of literary adventure tales (especially Conrad). In these adventure tales, a white male hero typically finds himself struggling for meaning among a group of darker-skinned natives (especially in *Heart of Darkness*). Malinowski's imagination—always key to ethnographic texts—was, indeed, a Western white man's *literary* imagination. The ways in which he organized and gave meaning to his lived experience in the field would, I believe, necessarily follow.

I am reminded of two related claims by two quite unrelated thinkers. Margaret Mead once posited (in Manganaro, 1990) that "the writing of anthropology [was] something that only the gifted could do: in that respect the writing of social science became equated with the composition of the literary artist" (18). Similarly, the linguist Harvey Sacks (1970) wrote that in "doing the business of being ordinary" a person had to be "entitled to extraordinary experience" in order to live "an epic life." These two notions coalesce, somehow, to produce a common rhetorical and narrative thread. Many observers—most notably James Clifford in his "On Ethnographic Authority" (1983) and George Stocking in *Observers Observed* (1983)—suggest that it is the "personality" of the author that gives credibility and power to a particular ethnographer's tale. This ethnographic personality "transforms the research situation's ambiguities and diversities of meaning into an integrated portrait" (Clifford, 132).

Let's consider the ethnographic "personality" as a narrative and rhetorical *construction*. Essentially, it is a *strategically deployed self*. It defines a "character" through his or her "voice." The personality of this character acquires shape, force, and meaning through representations of questions and concerns, actions and passions, personal and professional life. Readers come to think of the narrator as similar or dissimilar to them, as credible or not. Judgments are made about intelligence, familiarity with concepts, communication skill, travel, even about the causes of their evident good fortune. All of these character and personality attributes are made based on the *rhetoric* of a narrative. Which is to say, the *rhetorical choices* of the author.

Although wrapped in the prose of modern scientific rationality and familiar—to the reader—professional and personal sensibilities, Malinowski's personality in acquiring cultural knowledge is one of someone who is clearly extraordinary, or even gifted. No matter what the nature of the culture or experience, he skillfully acquires—and stores away—the lessons of the field in ways that show the triumph not only of scientific rationality but also of he himself. Indeed, this may be what Mead meant by a "gifted person." Viewed narratively, to be "gifted" means being *entitled to have extraordinary experiences with which to author an epic life*. For this reason and in this way, the ethnographic *personality* is always—and, if Sacks is right, *necessarily*—heroic.

But beyond the narrative deployment of a personality, something else seems to be going on. Is part of what we think of Malinowski—about his status as a hero, about his extraordinary life—driven by the rhetorical *form* of the story he tells?

I AM NOT SUGGESTING, by the way, that the desire to live an ethnographic life is *necessarily* the desire for a heroic life. What I *am* suggesting is that the character of the author—what Clifford calls the "personality"—is shaped by his or her responses to what are represented as cultural exigencies. Surviving for a year or more as the lone white man among a group of non-English-speaking natives was, in Malinowski's time (the early decades of this century), an extraordinary life experience. That he acquired knowledge of their culture, that he fit in well enough to learn quite a bit about his hosts—these, too, were considered extraordinary feats. But most importantly, that Malinowski chose to write about his experiences—chose to re-present them—in ways that drew from *adventure tales* is the mark not only of his view of himself as a character in this drama, but also of the *power of a rhetorical form to shape a reader's understanding.*

When searching for ethnography's storyline, you should not fail to read these narrative details as clues. As Dan Rose (1990) observed, we learn to write ethnographies by reading them. Given that Malinowski's story about his time with the Trobiand Islanders established the connection between the adventure tale and the ethnographic account, it is a good idea to ask: What is the rhetorical nature of this pattern of storytelling, this adventure hero's story?

Aristotle observed that classical drama—by which he assumed the ideal was tragedy—follows a basic pattern, or form, of storytelling. An opening scene would reveal the conflict between the main characters, whereupon the "rising action" would episodically reveal the playing out of the conflict to an inevitable "climax" in which the original conflict would be resolved. From this point to the ending of the dramatic action would be a short period of *denouement,* in which major and minor figures in the drama attempted to account for the meaning of what had happened, thereby establishing the consequences of such actions.

Does this sound like the basic narrative pattern for an adventure story, too? It does to me. This narrative pattern is culturally versatile. It describes the basic plot of most detective stories, thrillers, "coming of age" tales, autobiographies, and even romance novels. You can locate this pattern in films, television dramas, and plays.

Aristotle recognized this structure as a cultural contract between performers and audiences. Arriving at the amphitheater, audience members "knew" what to expect. What played out after that—what moved the experience from desire to satisfaction—was the development of a deeper, more intimate *relationship* between the author and the audience, a relationship mediated by the audience's ability to *identify* with the plot and performances on stage.

From this elementary dramatic structure, the "basic form" of story-telling in the West evolved. So, too, did our anticipation—what Kenneth Burke calls "desire"—for the *storying,* not only of staged drama, but also of the uses of rhetorical and narrative enchantments to evoke and shape imagined possibilities for culture and identity. Burke, in *The Philosophy of Literary Form* (1966), asserts that "form *is* the appeal," by which he means precisely what he says. Any reader in the West is drawn into the *form* of a story prior to being induced into its particulars. From the patterning of form, we acquire the rhetorical boundaries of *genre.* And from genre, we learn how to make evaluative judgments about the relationship of the given text to its idealized form. Hence, form *is* the appeal, as Burke would have it, but form is also the moving force that culturally propels what a story must do, from its origins in myth to its articulation in consciousness.

Consider that in modern anthropology during Malinowski's and Mead's era, the standard of excellence for ethnography consisted of a series of set-piece chapters, each one marking the author's passage from innocence to experience and then to knowledge. The early conflict between the anthropologist and his/our lack of understanding of the natives and place moved through a series of encounters, or learning experiences, much as the rising action of a play moves, scene by scene, toward its inevitable climax. The climax for the fieldworker was two-fold. First, there was an eventual acceptance of the identity of the eth-nographer among the natives that sets up rhetorical conditions for positing summary knowledge claims about the nature and culture of the other. Second, the final chapter provides an opportunity for a genre-specific *denouement,* in our case a summing up of what had been learned and what work is left to do.

From a reader's perspective, the original desire to know about another culture was satisfied when the "dramatic" conflicts between their culture and the ethnographer's own were worked out. The ability to do that within this Aristotelian form, the ability to work out such dramatic cultural conflicts, is narratively the work of an extraordinary person, a hero, a gifted narrator.

John Van Maanen (1988) points out that this period of the ethnographer as hero was relatively short-lived. When gaining academic legitimacy from questions about the role of ethnography in the demise of native cultures, and about the influence of the ethnographer on the lives of those he or she studied, the hero type was transformed into other characterizations of the narrator/ethnographer. And with this alteration came new forms of ethnographic writing.

In 1988 Van Maanen published *Tales of the Field: On Writing Ethnography*. His book is a hallmark in the history of ethnography. In it, he accounts for the relationship between narrative and rhetorical *form* and the historically situated standards for ethnographic *content*. He uses the changes in "textual conventions" to describe an academic evolution in writing ethnography characterized by three distinct styles of "taletelling": the *realist* tale, the *confessional* tale, and the *impressionist* tale. Table 2.1 summarizes the narrative and rhetorical characteristics of these tales.

Van Maanen established a way for readers of ethnographic work to categorize and evaluate *the narrative form and rhetorical style* of what they read. It also provided writers of ethnographic texts with a historical appreciation for why and how changes in ethnographic authority were aligned with corresponding changes in academic and cultural values. Perhaps most interestingly—at least for our purposes in this book—was Van Maanen's characterization of a new category of "impressionist tales." These tales were early experiments in new ethnography. As you can see from Table 2.1, many of the textual conventions of impressionistic writing still apply today.

An interesting question these days concerns the relationship of form, or genre, to the construction of knowledge in the new ethnographies. How has the influence of alternative genres for writing scholarship shaped what counts as cultural knowledge? How has the more overt inclusion of the personal voice influenced what we think of as a scholarly contribution?

These issues will reappear throughout this book. They are issues *you* ought to grapple with, discuss with others, and write about.

TABLE 2.1: VAN MAANEN'S CLASSIFICATION OF ETHNOGRAPHIC TALES

REALIST TALES *"Doctrine of Immaculate Perception"*	CONFESSIONAL TALES *"Self-Absorbed Mandates"*	IMPRESSIONIST TALES *"Present the Doing of the Fieldwork"*
CONVENTIONS *Experimental Authority and Interpretive Omnipotence*	**CONVENTIONS** *Personal(ized) Authority*	**CONVENTIONS** *Textual Identity and Dramatic Control*
■ Single author, dispassionate, third-person voice ■ No-nonsense accounts of "the facts" ■ Godlike posture toward those studied ■ Absence of personal details about the author from the text ■ Assumption of "good faith" ("whatever the fieldworker saw and heard is more or less what similarly well-placed and well-trained participant/observer would see and hear") ■ Writer has credentials as a scholar with institutional affiliations	■ First-person narratives that establish intimacy with the reader ■ Strives to persuade reader of the human qualities and frailties of the fieldworker ■ Writer develops the attitude of a student toward members of the culture studied; task is to learn from the culture rather than interpret it ■ Writer/fieldworker attempts to normalize her or his presence in the activities of the culture ■ A general etiquette of acceptance by the natives ■ Displays empathy and involvement with issues in the members' everyday lives	■ Standards for text construction are literary rather than disciplinary ■ Form of the narrative is dramatic recall ■ Story stands alone without elaborate theoretical framing ■ Productive use of maximally evocative language ■ "Shows" rather than "tells about" the experience ■ "You-are-there" feel to the telling of the events; a kind of "organized illusion" of participation in the culture ■ Tension is built, then released; the surprise ending is not given away but may later be found in earlier clues ■ Events move back and forth in time to give rise to later understandings
Traditional Scientific Report with Argumentative Form	*Confessional Form (with emphasis on the fieldworker's point of view)*	*Artistic License to Experiment with Narrative Forms and Rhetorical Structures (emphasis on fragmented knowledge)*
■ Documentary style, focused on details of everyday life ■ Use of powers of observation to direct the writing and interpretation ■ Rigid categories of analysis ■ Avoidance of the abstract	■ Inclusion of autobiographical details ■ Story focuses on the character-building conversion of the writer from an academic who sees things one way to a sympathetic participant who sees things another way ■ Shifting points of view, depending on the activities engaged in or described	■ Cultural knowledge is slipped into the story rather than separated by category ■ Narrative displays the learning process used to acquire knowledge of the culture and people
Natives and Cultures as "Observed Subject"	*Natives and Cultures as "Naturally Occurring"*	*Experimental Characterizations of Natives and Cultures*
■ Makes continuous use of accounts and explanations by members of the culture ■ Includes myths and stories	■ The text provides a sense that the account is reasonably uncontaminated by the author's intrusion	■ Writer's individuality is expressed; she or he becomes a character in the story rather than its teller

REPRESENTATIONAL LESSONS CAN ALSO BE LEARNED from analyzing the influence of *modern argumentative logic* on early anthropology texts.

Kenneth Burke (1935) teaches us that "a way of seeing is also a way of *not* seeing." In other words, our construction of knowledge is based on literary, or mythic, patterns that reveal some ways of knowing to be privileged and that obscure others. Our way of telling the story of the Western white man among darker-skinned others established patterns of signification that were rooted in a dominant cultural desire for finding—or for making—a common story among all humankind. Differences that mattered internally to the culture, but that didn't contribute to the form of the text, were viewed as "alien" in the field and (pardon me) as "extra-textuals" at home. We know this is true of Malinowski and Mead; we can assume that it has also been true for those who came after them, studied with them, and were rhetorically influenced by the tales of their fieldwork.

As Van Maanen's classification clearly points out, ethnographic stories have always been rhetorically sensitive cultural performances. The writing of ethnographic texts, in general, fits the reading expectations of its intended audience. To "write well" means that the writer adapts her or his materials to a literary form consistent with the audience's expectations. Such adaptation in ethnography means that sentences are crafted out of the raw materials of remembered experiences, fieldnotes, artifacts, and surmises, within an overall structure of meaning derived from the anticipation and satisfaction of the basic form. The result is audience affirmation of a narrative and rhetorical kind. "Form *is* the appeal" (Burke, 1966).

This "wry codicil" provides a soundbite summary for what we have been learning so far: good writing is "good" because it conforms to an audience's *formal* expectations. We see why journal and book editors want to prescribe proven prose formulas for scholarly work. But is this all there is? Surely *not*. What happens when someone comes along and *breaks* with tradition? How did ethnographers, in Van Maanen's typology, move from "realist" to "confessional" to "impressionist" tales? How can we explain ethnographic work that is "edgy," or even "ground-breaking?"

KENNETH BURKE OBSERVES THAT we also learn about the defining power of rhetorical forms when something odd occurs that challenges them, namely "perspective by incongruity" (1989). What makes a reading experience "odd" is that something "stands out"; it *departs* from expectations, surprises us, challenges the textual authority of a given form. In the recent history of ethnography, one excellent example of this occurred when Vincent Crapanzano (1986) read Clifford Geertz's then-edgy, then-genre-breaking essay "Notes on a Balinese Cockfight" (1973).

Geertz's essay recounts the story of a research trip he and his wife, Hillary, took to the island of Bali. In typical fashion, early on the ethnographers are at odds with their subjects and region and are treated, as Geertz says, "as wind" (in Rabinow and Sullivan, 1987; p. 196). They aren't trusted in the local Indonesian community. They are lied to, and deceived. Then one day, as they get mixed up accidentally in a police raid, they find themselves in a cockfighting arena. Geertz is amazed by the relationship of "men to their cocks" (p. 200), of the rules regarding betting, and of the curious symmetries formed around the central arena. Because he has run from the police and personally witnessed a cockfight, Geertz gains the trust of locals, for whom these activities are routine expressions of their daily lives. He then develops a highly literary, first-person account for Bali culture based on his observations, experiences, and surmises about the *meanings of play* that are represented in a cockfight. He experiments with the form for scholarly expression, as well as its content. He ends the piece triumphantly, confident that he has acquired knowledge of what was previously a cultural mystery.

Beyond the storyline (which is only partially represented here), Geertz's essay is clearly an attempt—and a supremely successful one—at creative nonfiction writing. Unlike traditional scholarly essays that at that time adhered to formulas, this piece of scholarly work was a *story*. It was vivid, it was dramatic, it includes ironic reversals of fortune, it has a playful title and headings. It displayed a sense of humor. It was profound, yet accessible—a real academic page-turner.

Vincent Crapanzano's claim is that this essay—whose literary merits he unabashedly admires—could have been written *without any of the events in the story having actually happened*. In fact, he doubts many of them did. He argues that Geertz's interpretive story—a radical departure from the then-accepted literary form of the realist tale—is so narratively charming, the form of it is so rhetorically compelling, its language is so metaphorically powerful, and its style so literately fashionable, that *it must be* a fiction.[4] It *can't be* ethnography. The

---

4 Would it have been any less valuable a tale, an interpretation, if it was labeled a "fiction?

assumption here, I suppose, is that ordinary experience, for an ethnographer, is necessarily less literately epiphanic, less metaphorically charged, and certainly less textually "worked over."

Makes you wonder if there are textual limits to representing an extraordinary life, doesn't it? Even so, Crapanzano was surprised by this piece of writing. It challenged his received notion of ethnographic form. It "messed with" his beliefs about ethnographic content. Perhaps something that was so pleasurable to read couldn't be considered academic writing. He seriously entertained the notion that Geertz may have made the whole thing up. His evidence for that charge is the *perspective* this essay affords on other ethnographic writing. Geertz's text offers us something other than argument, something other than what is expected, something, as Burke has it, that gets borne out through "perspective by incongruity."

THE ISSUE, HERE, OF COURSE, is both the *departure* of Geertz's text from the realist form as well as its *arrival* on the ethnographic culture and academic literary scene.

Interpretive methods arrived with the publication of this essay. Interpretive methods were different; they provided "perspective by incongruity." In part, this was achieved in the *attitude* of the writer toward the writing. For the interpretivist, the world was not "given"—not an external thing to be reported accurately, but rather something "constructed" out of *interactions* with it (see Denzin, 1989). Culture was not something "out there" in the field to be discovered, uncovered, and *then* written about. Instead, culture was *what happened at the moment the writing was performed.* Questions were asked that set into literary motion a series of rhetorical events on the page that involved (and enlarged or complicated) the linguistic relativity of a person whose goal was to write into coherence "a meaningful order of persons and things" (Sahlins, 1976). The writer's appropriation of nonacademic literary devices, inclusion of knowledge drawn from popular culture, direct address, and word plays are rhetorical and narrative endeavors designed to initiate a different kind of *relationship* to his or her reader. And, through that relationship, to produce a *different kind of knowledge.*

The fieldwork method that was key to these new writing experiments became known as "radical empiricism" (Jackson, 1989). It was "radical," because the writer's personal lived experience in the culture was taken as the first organizing principle of the text. The writer was not simply to represent what he or she did, but also to reflect on both it and the meaning of such reflections in the conduct of the study. And it was called "empiricism" because close observation, participation, and analysis established *what* was to be written about, but not necessarily *how* it was to be represented. Genres of writing, as Geertz would himself later point out (1983), became "blurred."

Concurrently, the ethnographer's dependence on knowledge constructed primarily from observation—from the eyes and ears—was questioned. What about knowledge gained by the other senses? Don't humans acquire information—indeed, understandings—from the multiple influences of all the senses working together? Shouldn't ethnographers strive to represent the active presence of these sensory influences more accurately? As Paul Stoller's *The Taste of Ethnographic Things: The Senses in Anthropology* (1989) summarily posited, ethnographers need to consider a more full-bodied approach to textual construction, albeit one that is still mediated by language.

As a result, or perhaps as a literary and cultural by-product of these issues and textual controversies, another kind of intellectual awareness was brought into scholarly focus by the emerging interpretive, or narrative, turn. At the School of American Research in Santa Fe, New Mexico, during the (cruelest) month of April 1984, a group of ten innovative ethnographers, anthropologists, and cultural and literary historians met to discuss "the making of ethnographic texts" (see Clifford and Marcus, 1986, p. vii).[5] If ever there was a moment in contemporary ethnography when the realist ethnographer's world was turned upside down, when a discipline was shaken up by a series of scholarly discussions, this was it. Two key texts resulted: the April 1985 issue of *Current Anthropology,* and the now classic volume, edited by James Clifford and George Marcus, *Writing Ethnography: The Politics and Poetics of Ethnography* (1986).

It is impossible to capture the many moods and various themes of these reports of their discussions. But suffice it to say that the participants' comments were framed by the then-current debate about the loss of modernist sensibilities that influenced the rise of postmodern and interpretive textual constructions, as well as the influence of a

---

5 The participants were Talal Asad, James Clifford, Vincent Crapanzano, Michael Fischer, George Marcus, Mary Louise Pratt, Paul Rabinow, Renato Rosaldo, Robert Thornton, and Stephen Tyler.

new style of critical reading. More important was the expressed realization, perhaps long suspected but nevertheless clearly revelatory at the time, that the *way in which texts were written*—the *rhetorics* of their construction—could no longer be assumed to be a direct, unmediated reflection of the fieldwork experience. It was, as Marcus phrases it in the last pages of *Writing Culture,* "the introduc[tion of] a literary consciousness to ethnographic practice" (p. 262).

Thus, the materials for the new ethnographic class of impressionists and interpretivists were *the shape and pattern of lived experience as shaped and patterned by the ethnographer's personal, political, and poetic experiences, choice of narrative forms, and uses of language.* Textually, this cultural turn in the discipline of ethnography tends to make the writing done in its name virtually indistinguishable from writing done in the name of *literary journalism* or *creative nonfiction* (Denzin, 1997; Goodall, 1989a; Van Maanen, 1988). In fact, it legitimates it. So, too, does the interpretive stance open the academic door to alternative forms of representing lived experiences. Impressionist tales—fiction, drama, poetry, dance, personal letters, film, and even Internet-based hypertexts—written from appropriated forms for new scholarly expression, vie for scholarly attention and publication space.

This turn toward interpretivism and impressionism created problems within academic circles. For some denizens of the realist camp, there was a perceived loss of *authority* and a professional crisis of *identity.* No longer could the authority of an ethnographic text be assumed, because no longer was it rhetorically or politically possible to transparently depict a culture and people. With this loss of textual innocence would also come a loss of professional identity and status within the academy. Interpretivists, whose arguments admittedly lacked the authority of a scientific warrant, were, in many places, accorded the second-rate status of dentists among our doctorate class. Impressionists were accused of abandoning the disciplines that supported and trained them; in some cases, they were asked, Oughtn't they try to get appointments in creative writing departments? And asked: If what these new ethnographers were authoring should be judged by aesthetic standards used for works of literary journalism, creative nonfiction, fiction, or even poetry, what was their true *scholarly* contribution to knowledge? And: What new intellectual equipment are we giving our colleagues and the public to *think* with?

Among traditionalists, these fears supported a frequently expressed sentiment at conventions: When representation is in crisis, truth probably lags not far behind. For the new ethnographers, this "crisis" among traditionalists was interpreted as a resource for potential liberation. After years of struggling with feelings of quiet incompleteness that suggested that the gap we ought to be addressing was within that which we held most sacred—our theories and methods—we new ethnographers began experimenting more openly with new ways of framing questions, conducting inquiry, and writing. We began turning our gaze *away* from those whom we were studying to the *processes* we used to study and write, and within that turning, we came full circle, back to *ourselves* (Tedlock, 1991).

    ❐   ❐

I want to complete this chapter by rounding off my "interpretive turn" story. This is the part of our scholarly adventure/self-discovery story where the metaphorical detective reveals his methods, arrives at his conclusions, and neatly wraps everything up in front of his listeners.

The Pacanowsky-Trujillo article began to teach me to think about organizational communication differently, and to frame what I was observing and experiencing differently. For example, instead of viewing organizational communication as a form of *behavior* amenable to systems analysis, I began to examine the patterns suggested by bits and pieces of that behavior as *practices* given as *cultural performances* (deCerteau, 1984). Instead of looking at a routine exchange of conversation between employees, say, as an episode of this or that kind of categorical talk, I began to see that the *everyday practices* and *what was being said* were both evidence of culture's imprints and the product of an organization's and individual's *meanings*. I found I could examine how everyday symbols and signs; shared talk and coordinated actions; cartoons, dreams, and even the colors of cars in parking lots—all collaborated to produce meanings that contributed to a unique, if diverse, sense of the workplace. I was encouraged to learn the practical, everyday bases of *performances* of selves, with and among others, in specific contexts.

All of these sources of narrative change and methodological inspiration were intellectually exhilarating. They gave me new things to read about, to talk about, and to teach my students. The article provided me with resources for conducting inquiry: new questions and fresh tools. But these interpretive intellectual gifts were little more than warm-up exercises. The real news, for me, was in between the lines of that article.

It was the encouragement to read *against* the grain of all that I had experienced, read about, and learned. It nudged me toward finding a way to combine theoretical and narrative insights. Organizational theories had provided me with behaviors to categorize and analyze; rhetorical theories had taught me about language, influence, and audiences; ethnography had provided me with an understanding of the story form and the role of the personal voice in writing about lived experiences. What remained was a way to link all of these theories, ideas, and methods. This one article opened the proverbial door to an intense self-examination that would turn into self-reflexive notes in my fieldbook. As I completed readings, and rereadings, of the Pacanowsky-Trujillo article, and as I began scribbling in my notebook, I *began to know* what that was.

It felt like the final clue to the initial mystery of my future as a writer within the culture of academia. It was nothing less than the salvation of my writerly soul.

Its enchantment can be summed up in an ambiguous word: *culture*. I wanted to write about cultures in organizations. But it was *how I would write about culture* that was truly a personal breakthrough. My task, my vision, was to write *stories* of and about organizational cultures. Finally, I had found a way to write myself back into the scholarly conversation without compromising what I felt, and what I knew in my heart, to be *right*. Right for me, right for my discipline, right for my students.

Transforming my emerging vision into a textual reality in the area of organizational communication—what John Van Maanen called "a rather stuffy field" (personal correspondence, 1989)—proved more difficult than I imagined. It was one thing to argue theoretically about the value of stories in scholarship; it was quite another to write stories that passed muster *as* scholarship. I had solved one mystery and found one storyline, only to discover that I was already wrapped up in a quest for another one. The real work of transformation was yet to be done.

That work was to become writing stories that succeeded on two levels simultaneously—as accounts of communication and culture, and as personal, self-reflexive, narratives. Where these two stories would meet, at the narrative intersection of self and others—that was my new challenge.

It was the challenge of writing the *new* ethnography.

Writing Experiments

1. Select an investigative report from a current issue of *Esquire, The Atlantic, Harper's, The Oxford American,* or *The New Yorker.* Read it and ask: how did the writer develop her or his storyline? Where did the idea come from? What current cultural conversation did it grow out of? What rhetorical techniques—narrative, dialogue, dramatic conflict, reversal, and the like—are used to develop the storyline? How do these techniques keep a reader interested? What arguments are presented, and how are they warranted? What are its heuristics?

Now compare and contrast an article on a similar topic in one of your scholarly journals. Ask the same questions.

Compare and contrast *the styles of writing* in each of them. What are the differences? What are the similarities? How do the authors construct their stories for their targeted audiences? What role does language use play in them? Which account do you find more compelling? More personally appealing? More useful? What did each of the essays teach you about the topic? Were there differences in what they taught you that were based on the deployment of a literary style?

Construct a brief three-to-four page review of these essays for *The Journal of Contemporary Ethnography* (yeah, I know, *JCE* doesn't publish reviews of essays—just books—but overlook that, okay?). What will you say about each of them? How will you represent them to your colleagues? What recommendations will you make?

2. Research an idea you have for a fieldwork exercise. You will probably be doing a fieldwork exercise in conjunction with the next chapter, so think of this as preparing yourself mentally for what you are about to enter. Ask yourself what your research is teaching you about developing a storyline for this idea. What is the ongoing scholarly conversation that your research and writing needs to tie into? How can you make use of the material in this chapter?

Spend some time in the library and on-line, researching your potential topic. As detailed in this chapter, make a chart of the major players, themes, and the outstanding issues.

Rough-out a draft of a literature review based on your reading and personal reflections. Pay attention to how you structure your case so that you can enter this ongoing scholarly conversation with *a research question.* The research question ought to address the gap to be addressed and filled in.

80

Think about alternative ways of *framing your literature review.* Would it be best to set it up with a story that is used to detail what we claim to know, and what we don't yet know, about this topic, event, or episode? Or would it be better to provide a more traditional, additive style of reviewing previous studies in a particular tradition, pointing out at the end where the gap in the literature is, and what you propose to do about it? Or would it be better to compare and contrast lines of research between competing scholarly views on your topic? Remember, each strategic choice will establish a type of relationship with your reader. It will also shape how your reader understands what you want to do and will say something about who you are as a researcher and a writer. Sketch out at least three different approaches to writing your literature review, and talk them over with your class and instructor.

3. Write the beginning of an essay that doesn't make overt mention of any of the research you've done, but makes conscious *use* of it. In other words, *tell a story drawn from personal experience* that reveals—or is derived from—the scholarly issues you plan to develop, or imagine a scene in which certain key research issues play out. You may want to render your work as fiction, creative nonfiction, poetry, or drama.

Now ask three members of your class to read it. Without telling them anything about the issue you are pursuing, or the research you've done, gain their responses to it. Do they see what you are trying to do? Do they read what you've written as worthy of a "scholarly" journal or book chapter? What recommendations do they make to improve your writing? What do their suggestions say to you about how your account influenced them?

For Further Reading

Reading the material listed below will help you extend and apply what you have read in this chapter.

Manganaro, M. 1990. *Modernist anthropology.* Princeton, NJ: Princeton University Press.

The introductory essay by the author provides an outstanding overview of the history of ethnography as written through an examination of the narrative and rhetorical evolutions in it.

Pacanowsky, M. 1988. Slouching towards Chicago. *The Quarterly Journal of Speech* 74: 453–467.

Mike Pacanowsky was a pioneer in experimenting with alternative forms of writing communication studies. Read this essay and analyze the writing in it. Does it conform to Van Maanen's "confessional" tale? Or, perhaps, would you classify it as more of an "impressionist" tale?

Philipsen, G. 1975. Speaking "like a man" in Teamsterville: Culture patterns of role enactment in an urban neighborhood. *The Quarterly Journal of Speech* 61: 13–22.

Gerry Philipsen was a pioneer in applying traditional ethnographic methods to communication studies. Read this early essay and analyze the writing in it. Does it conform to the standards Van Maanen articulates for a "realist" tale?

Tillmann-Healy, L. 1996. A secret life in a culture of thinness. In *Composing Ethnography,* edited by Carolyn Ellis and Arthur Bochner. Walnut Creek, CA: AltaMira Press.

Lisa Tillmann-Healy is a new ethnographer with a unique voice and compelling writing style. Read this story and analyze the writing in it. Does it conform to Van Maanen's "confessional" or "impressionist" tales? Or is it a new hybrid? Is the category of an "impressionist" tale large enough to accommodate her style in this essay? Or is the writing in this piece aimed at establishing a new form?

3 | Representing Ethnographic Experiences: From Fieldwork to Fieldnotes to Stories

The strange idea that reality has an idiom in which it prefers to be described, that its very nature demands we talk about it without fuss—a spade is a spade, a rose is a rose—on pain of illusion, trumpery, and self-bewitchment, leads to the even stranger idea that, if literalism is lost, so is fact.

CLIFFORD GEERTZ
Works and Lives:
The Anthropologist as Author

A new ethnography is a story based on the represented, or evoked, experiences of a self, with others, within a context (Goodall, 1991). Its theme is the persuasive expression of interpreted cultural performances.

The story's narrative and rhetorical supporting structure (for example, its form or genre, episodes, passages, conflicts, turning points, poetic moments, themes, and motifs) are constructed out of ordinary and extraordinary everyday life materials that, from a reader's perspective, allow meaningful patterns to emerge and from which a relationship develops. What makes these patterns "meaningful" is the writer's ability to piece together the everyday life events—conversations, thoughts, observations, practices, sensual events, musings—as if he or she were reading clues to a larger *mystery* (Goodall, 1989a; 1991; 1996). What encourages a relationship between writer and reader to develop is the reader's ability to connect his or her life, her or his experiences, both to the everyday life events *and* to the larger mystery.

This representation of what ethnography "is," however, is more the story ethnography tells once the writer has reached the end of the last line on the final page of the manuscript. It is the view from how it shapes up, or attains meaning after the tale-telling is over. It is the summary perspective arrived at when the article, chapter, or book *has been* written and read.

Most advice about *writing* ethnography is given from the vantage afforded by reaching the end of the process, which is really the other side of the actual writing. Probably because, from the completion of the story, everything leading up to it somehow now makes sense. But in this chapter I want to return to the beginning of an ethnographic writing project. Which is to say, I want to return to *the everyday contexts in which "things happen" that get noticed and recorded in the field.*

This is a chapter that covers a *lot* of ground. I have divided it into sections with the intent of helping you organize your reading into manageable segments. I could have divided these sections into separate chapters, but I want to show how *interconnected* each part of the ethnographic process is. Accurately representing that process seemed to me to require placing all of the material in one chapter. As the title indicates, I will use that material to show how you *begin fieldwork,* write *fieldnotes,* and then use the fieldnotes to *construct a story.*

FIELDWORK AND FIELDNOTES are generally considered the "raw data"—the grammar—of ethnography (Sanjek, 1990; p. 6–8).

In ethnographic practice, wide and meaningful differences govern how this "raw data" is collected and recorded (such as in a diary, in a journal or professional notebook, with a tape or video recorder, or from memory, or combinations of them all). The general principle is that each ethnographer, in his or her own way, learns, develops, or evolves a preferred style of being in the field and, with it, a preferred fieldnote practice emerges. For most of us who practice the new ethnography, this usually means some combination of:

- Hanging out with others in their local contexts
- Engaging in verbal exchanges with them
- Sharing and learning about their everyday practices
- Digging back into our own—and their own—memories for likely antecedents to current practices
- Jotting down notes, or tape recording interviews, when possible

- Returning to our offices/homes/rented rooms to write out representations of field experiences
- Engaging in armchair, after-the-fact self-reflection, analysis, and editing of the fieldnotes into a narrative

For those of us new to this craft—and at some point we were *all* new to it—the writing of fieldnotes is usually a source of great mystery and several uneasy questions. What should we pay attention *to,* in order to write *about?* What and where should the veritable lines of "real life" in our stories *emerge from?* Where do we find the words for experiential reconstructions of conversations, observations, and everyday practices? How, in short, am I supposed to "do" fieldnotes?

If you are reading quickly, please *slow down.* The underlying theme of this chapter is all about slowing down.

Slowing down so that you can *really pay attention* to what is going on. So that you can hear *in* and *through* this text, not just "look at" or "see" the words on the page. So that you can learn where and how to apply your own quotation marks, underscoring, choice of fonts, and italics. So that you can understand the implications of white space, of silence, of the presence or absence of a rhetorical gesture.

What are the basic elements of a fieldwork grammar that teach us *what* to write about? *How* do we render it sentence-able? How should we frame it for our intended readers? What are the basic "things that happen" in the field that we should pay attention to? How should we proceed from those hurriedly composed sentences and recalled fragments to patterns of meaning, thematic stories, theoretical and practical conclusions?

These questions frame, and haunt, the work of this chapter.

Please read the opening paragraphs again. *Slowly.*

(If you are asking yourself: "Where do 'opening paragraphs' stop?" then you are reading at the proper rate, and with an ethnographic attitude. If you are not sure why that question is a necessary one, then please consider that anything meaningful has a definable shape—a beginning, a middle, and an ending. Asking about endings is one way to trace the meaning back to its origins, and thereby to have captured a form through which interpretation is made possible.)

Now read the whole of this thing—these utterances, this thing that is happening right now on these opening pages—once more, this time *aloud.*

Why aloud? Because I want you to *hear* the implications involved in moving an interpretive experience from the eye to the ear. I want you *not* to think that just because you have *looked* at the words in these paragraphs you *know* what they mean. The process of interpreting experiences—including reading experiences—is more complex than that. There is a craft about it, an art to it. It requires self-examination to locate where your interpretive frames come from, as well as sensitivity to the possibilities for alternative meanings that move you into new understandings. It requires a tolerance for differences, and for ambiguities. It requires a studied ability to take language *very* seriously.

Why am I acting like this? Why am I directing you in this way?

Because fieldnotes are less about what you initially "see" and "experience" than they are about *connecting* those fieldwork details to larger and more self-reflexive issues. Which is to say that what fieldnotes represent is one part recorded observations and experiences and two parts interpretation, or how you learn to *hear in* and *through* all of that.

What Is a Fieldnote?

Allow me to work at a less poetic level for a while.

Let's take as our starting point the idea that "ethnography is a written representation of culture" (Van Maanen, 1988). Let's further consider "culture" to be "the production and consumption of everyday life," as well as how everyday life is *accounted for* and *storied* into "meaningful orders of persons and things" (Sahlins, 1976). Our task, then, is to learn to take fieldnotes on simply what gets done—the verbal exchanges, nonverbal performances, and array of practices—in everyday life. (Notice how the word "simply" infects the previous sentence with a kind of grammatical virus?)

If it were possible to translate verbal exchanges, nonverbal performances, and the array of practices directly into an ethnographic account or story, writing fieldnotes would be what James Agee once described as capturing "the cruel radiance of what is" (Agee and Evans, 1941, p. 11). Capturing and re-presenting the radiance of "what is" sounds like an ethnographer's task, doesn't it? Sounds like what fieldnotes are for, right?

Unfortunately, it's *not.* Fieldnotes are—as you learned in the previous chapter about all forms of representation—partial, partisan, and problematic. Your goal may be to capture the big "what is" of a culture, but your tools for accomplishing that are not capable of completing the job. Language is symbolic, research is perspectival, and your narrator is not omniscient.

Furthermore, nothing we can know about a culture or about ourselves is free from *interpretation*. Fieldnotes based on experiences, thoughts, hunches, hypotheses, dreams, interactions, and observations are *head-work*. We do the work of interpretation and writing with symbols. This is why writing fieldnotes is best conceived as a *grammatical* activity with an experientially *rhetorical* basis. You write what you have been *attracted to* and *convinced by*. You write what you have read as *meaningful*; you interpret what you have read as a meaningful *pattern*. The story you write will be part of the larger story of who you are, where you've been, what you've read and talked about and argued over, what you believe in and value, what you feel compelled to name as significant.

Writing fieldnotes is a deployment of language whose overall purpose is to linguistically imprison a series of motions and actions for the purpose of making a scene, or an episode, or a turning point in this unfolding human drama. Its aim is also to attribute in words what is unsaid, what is unspoken, or what casually but perceptibly drifts, like smoke among strangers, in between what is, what might be, and what appears to be.

Fieldnotes, once written, *mediate* between lived experience and ethnography (see especially Jackson in Van Maanen, 1995, pp. 36–78; for a fuller treatment of the range and complexity of this concept, see Sanjek, 1990). This means that fieldnotes are neither direct translations of experience, nor a final text. As such, they occupy an interesting literary and professional niche that has fascinated and confounded ethnographers for some time (see Emerson, Fretz, and Shaw, 1995).

To teach aspiring ethnographers to write fieldnotes begins with teaching them to take *detailed* notes.

I recommend keeping a personal diary or a professional notebook, or both.

A *personal diary* is a record of what happens to you in everyday life. It tends toward the intimate, and it is generally not intended for public consumption. A common entry might include the date of an entry, details about your day, a conversation that was strangely meaningful, an episode that was ecstatic or troubling, and some random reflections on what it all means to you. The value of a personal diary is that it often contains information about your deepest, most private, experiences, as well as same-day (or same-week) analyses of the meanings of those events in your overall life.

For an ethnographer, keeping a personal diary is one way to access highly personalized information about *yourself* as data. The downside, as Malinowski would have discovered if he had lived a little longer, is so can others.[1]

A PROFESSIONAL NOTEBOOK IS A RECORD of what you observe, hear, overhear, think about, wonder about, and worry about that connects your personal life to your professional one.

A common entry might include a statement about something you've read and its application to an event or episode you've observed or lived through in everyday life. Examples of interesting conversations, or displays of costuming on a local street, or a well-turned phrase you may have overheard on the way to class—all of these small bits of data are potentially useful to the practicing ethnographer, particularly when they serve as resources for analysis or critique.

For ethnographers, having a record of everyday life—which means having a place to record what you "hear in" what happens—is vital. It is a way to practice writing the events of everyday life, every day.

If you are an ethnographer who makes productive use of professional notebooks, you will usually incur the following advantages:

■ You will have an *evolutionary and development record* of what you were thinking about and experiencing that can be very useful in terms of checking later developments in the field against this "working knowledge."

■ You will have a *personal account of how what you were reading influenced what you were thinking about and doing* in the field.

■ You will have established, for later analysis, a *grammatical map of the mental and emotional territory* you were working out of and with while in the field.

---

1 I am referring here to his posthumous volume, *A Diary in the Strict Sense of the Term* (1968). In it, his personal musings about his daily practices, feelings about his subjects, and worries about what he is really up to tell a very different tale from the one represented in his ethnographies.

As an example, what follows is an excerpt drawn from the professional notebook of Michael E. Pacanowsky (1988):

From his notebook: Gregory Bateson, *Naven,* 2nd ed. (Palo Alto, CA: Stanford University Press, 1958). Heinneman suggested I read this book, and it's the first book I've come across where the author treats the mode of writing as problematic. His first chapter is entitled "Methods of Presentation."

> *If it were possible adequately to present the whole of a culture, stressing every aspect exactly as it is stressed in the culture itself, no single detail would appear bizarre or strange or arbitrary to the reader, but the details would all appear natural and reasonable as they do to the natives who have lived all their lives within the culture. Such an exposition may be attempted by either of two methods, by either scientific or artistic techniques.*

The power of artistic technique, according to Bateson, is its ability to impressionistically imbue all details of cultural life with an "ethos" that is causally active in the culture and that makes the incidents of narration pregnant with the emotional tone of the culture such that without this tone these incidents would be culturally impossible.

Implications: The genre of scholarly writing must always be understood to be a choice—it is not a given. It need not go unquestioned. All scientific descriptions of cultural ethos, because they are explicit, have to be incomplete (although the current social scientific mind gets excited if it accounts for 16 percent of the variance). Fictional descriptions, by the very nature of their implicitness and impressionism, can fully capture (can I be so strong?) both the bold outlines and the critical nuances of cultural ethos. Before I get too taken away by this find, thank you Heinneman, I have to remember—after writing these observations, Bateson tacked on 300-some pages of additional prose, fully managing it without once descending (ascending?) to fiction (1988; p. 454).

Pacanowsky uses this entry in a published essay to provide details about what he was thinking about while he was examining the relationship of his work and writing to then-established standards for published scholarship in the discipline of communication. It accomplishes two purposes: (1) it establishes the writing of a professional notebook as an integral part of his development of the eventual essay, and (2) it allows the reader to see, as Geertz phrases it, "what the devil [he] thinks he's up to" (1973) while he is composing it.

But "reading an entry" in a professional notebook is very much like observing "what is happening" in the field. In addition to interpreting the writing as "representing the mental and emotional territory" going on within Pacanowsky's head, we are also left with clues to how this passage served to render sentence-able his experiences with *Naven,* as read against the background of his professional life. In this sense, the interpretable life of an entry is often as complex as the lives it seeks to capture, and to represent.

Read over that entry again. Where do you find traces of what Pacanowsky was "hearing in" what he read? Look closely at his choice of words, the grammar or code by which he constructed this entry. Notice how the whole of it is framed by a particular passage that spoke directly to Pacanowsky's concerns about a perceived (read: constructed) distinction between "facts" and "fictions," about differences between artistic technique and scientific descriptions, and about the implications of these distinctions to the genre of ethnography?

What about the role of "Heinneman" in the entry? Don't you think Pacanowsky's language surrounding that name is a textual clue about his relationship to this figure? How should we read the "thank you Heinneman" line? With what emphasis would you speak the words "thank you"? What emotional baggage does the writing of that phrase within the context of that paragraph bring with it?

Now how did *you* decide *that?*

FIELDNOTES OFTEN MAKE USE of writing done in diaries and professional notebooks. But they should not *just* be that.

Whereas the focus of diaries and professional notebooks tends toward self-reflexive accounts of the life of the *writer,* fieldnotes are generally intended to capture and represent the lived experiences of *others.* While it is true that most seasoned contemporary ethnographers blend the two forms of writing into one document (thereby blurring the genres in a practical way), achieving an inward/outward balance of data from lived experiences can confuse beginning students.

The usual problem is that beginning ethnographers tend to be influenced by the literary style and rhetorical content of the last book or article they read. If the reading was done in the emerging genre of "autoethnography," the balance between inward/outward tilts rather dramatically toward the *inward.* We learn a great deal about the personal reconstructed and autobiographical history of the author, but very little about how that history connects to the lives and accounts of cultural others. The result can be an overly self-ish text that may have great personal value for the writer (and this should *never* be discounted) and perhaps even some provocative value in generating dialogue, but that doesn't achieve the goal of *balancing* the inward and outward representations.

Why *should* you balance them? The reason is that while there is consensus at the level of theory that representations of an "other" are necessarily contained *within* a self's worldview and are present in every representation, the perceived scholarly value of work that is largely about the "personal" is still contested. The usual charge is that writing that focuses closely on the self, on one's experiences, is either egocentric or solipsistic, or both. For example, I was recently taken to task in a major professional journal review of the revised edition of *Casing a Promised Land* for being "too autobiographical," which seemed to me to be ironic given that the subtitle of the book announces itself as an *autobiography!* Similarly, when Linda Welker and I coauthored a retrospective account of her staging of a performance of that same book (Welker and Goodall, 1997), we were criticized for being "unethical" because one of the authors—me—was reviewing a performance of my own work done by the other author. That I might actually have something to say about its representational qualities, its evocative force, or even that I might able to credibly answer questions about my own motives for writing the book, seemed to this well-regarded critic "beside the point of true scholarly work." In his view, the less known about the writer's self, the better.

That I find fault with his view is obvious. That I rail against the narrow-mindedness of the journal reviewer is equally obvious. But my larger point is that ethnographic writing that is perceived as overtly personal is likely to be targeted for criticism by scholars who simply reject its value out of hand. What they may formally embrace in theory may repel them when practiced. And this is a risk that beginning ethnographers, as well as seasoned ones, should be aware of.

On the other hand, if the beginning ethnographer's reading was done in more traditional, otherness-oriented text, the balance tilts *outward.* We learn about the lives and accounts of others (depictions and accounts of which are vital to the development of a skill set for any ethnographer), but to the virtual exclusion of autobiographical information about the self who produced the text. The result is often the creation of an authoritative, omniscient narrator—a modernist textual god—whose observations we are supposed to trust simply because they appear to be born out of a kind of "immaculate perception" (Van Maanen, 1988).

Learning how to *balance* the two potential foci is, I think, critical to the professional and personal development of the writer. Why? Because learning to balance rhetorical sources of creativity with the inevitable sources of rhetorical constraint is an important aspect of *mature* writing. By "rhetorical sources of creativity" I mean writing that emerges from the confluence of deep, personal self-reflection, epiphany, the use of rhetorical and narrative devices, and the poetics of expression (Atkinson, 1990; Denzin, 1996; Goodall, 1989a). By "sources of rhetorical constraint" I mean representations that rely on skilled observation and analysis, those rhetorical techniques capable of establishing the *credibility* of the ethnographic writer and the *vraisemblance* of the scenes and accounts depicted (Atkinson, 1990; Todorov, 1977). Together, these narrative and rhetorical forces coalesce in the report to induce in readers the conviction that the writing is indeed factual and authentic.

For these reasons, I ask students to keep either a diary or a professional notebook (in which they record self-reflection about their own experiences in everyday life) *and* a set of fieldnotes (in which they record their observations and analyses of others). As they become accustomed to creating texts that blend and balance the two resources, I encourage them to use whatever method of recording their lives and observations/analyses that works best for them. By then, in most cases, they have already begun doing that.

❐   ❐

Question, Professor: You told us to go out and record the facts we observe in everyday life. What is, ethnographically speaking, "a fact"?

Good question. Excellent, in fact.

Facts are *interpretations.*

They represent conclusions drawn from *partial* truths, *partisan* perspectives, and *problematic* methods of asking questions. Facts are interpretations derived from forms of learning or discovering, and from ways of knowing and being in the field. As such, facts are *social representations* (Rabinow, 1986).

When I say this, the looks on the faces of my students have "HELP" inscribed indelibly upon them.

I have just produced a series of words that, for many of them, has shaken the very foundations of what they believe, what they have learned in other classes, what they probably count on to get through the day. I have told them that the world they take for granted as "given," *isn't*.

For some others, it is as if I have simply confirmed a long-held suspicion.

And for a few, it is little more than a statement of the obvious.

In each one of these responses lies a potentially rich personal terrain that I encourage them to explore in their diaries. But in the meantime, what I have said about facts ups the ante on successful fieldwork writing.

I use stories to elaborate. Particularly when tensions are high.

I tell them about a scene I admire in a film called *My Dinner with Andre*. I like the scene because in it Andre, a film producer (played by Andre Gregory), is reporting to Wallace Shawn, an actor, about "an experience he has had recently." He says something like this:

> I was in New York and New York is an interesting place, you know, because almost everyone you meet there is claiming to want to get out. But they never leave. You know why? Because their view of New York is constructed like a prison, in which they are both the inmates and the guards.

I explain that ethnographic facts—like this constructed language prison called "New York"—are assembled out of fragments of lived experience and reflections on their meanings. Andre's statement, then, is *factual*. He said it. The words are real. However, while most academics take the social construction of reality seriously *as theory*, it is often difficult to apply that theory to social life without seriously disturbing our most cherished—and therefore, guarded—beliefs about how things and persons "are." Thus, Andre's statement, his metaphor about the prison-house of language, *is also an interpretation*, a way in which he constructs the reality of persons and a city, the way he finds meaning in it.

Facts *are* interpretations.

The second story is one assembled and told by my students. I organize a simple perception exercise around an overhead screen depiction of a busy intersection in an imagined city. It is a pencil drawing. It might be a representation of New York City. It could be San Francisco. Or even Omaha. Point is, there is a lot to look at "going on" in it.

There are tall buildings with people at the windows, there is a newsboy hawking papers on the corner, a couple of young men standing by a storefront door, someone else turning into an alley with something in his hand. Two women are speaking to a police officer (whose gender is uncertain) in the middle of the intersection, where we see the immediate aftermath of a two-car collision, complete with leaked fluids on the street and several gawkers. Just beyond the wreckage is another vehicle, parked but dented. Was this car involved in the accident? We can't really tell. At least, we can't tell from the evidence. Not from the facts, as we observe them. Not from a static, after-the-fact, representation of a "happening."

What I do is ask each student to write down a description of what she or he sees and thinks about when exposed to this street scene. I give them about five or ten minutes to do so. Usually, I leave the room, because seldom are fieldnotes recorded with your professor in the room.

When I return I ask each student to read aloud what was written. Can you guess what I hear?

In most cases the students give fairly accurate representations of the persons and things in the street scene. This is a boy on a corner, there is a police officer, here are wrecked cars, and so on. But in almost every case, they attribute *action,* or *cause,* sometimes *consequences,* to the accident. To the person turning into the alley with something in his hand. To the kind of day the police officer has had. And so on.

What they have done is *apply imagination and inference* to a static cultural scene. They have constructed its factual meaning by interpreting the individual fragments available. They have organized the scene into a story, and in most cases the form of the story is represented as a little drama with a beginning, a middle, and an ending (in some cases, not; what I sometimes get is a factual list of everything that can be seen. I then ask about whose *order* the list is in). With conflict that demands resolution. With large and small parts for each of the players. With emotion. With attitude.

I repeat, facts *are* interpretations.

One other lesson is derived from this exercise. It is a lesson that is especially useful for ethnographers who are learning to appreciate, and to deal with, how deeply *personal* their interpretations are, as well as how *diverse* possible interpretations of the same scene by different viewers may be. I usually start the discussion by saying something mundane like "We learn a great deal about *ourselves* by looking at how we interpret a scene." I then engage them in a discussion that compares individual perspectives on the scene based on choices of language used to represent it, nuances of tone, why certain aspects of the scene were dominant for some viewers and absent from other's depictions. I ask "Where, in your personal history, did the words for this description *come from?*" The lesson is obvious: Descriptions of the outward world come from deep inside of us. Because each of us has been shaped and informed by different deeply personal experiences, our descriptions of the same scene are likely to be as distinctive as they are personal.

Facts are *personal* interpretations. Examined reflexively, they show us not only *how* we see the world, but also *why we interpret it* as we do.

"WHAT SHOULD I TAKE fieldnotes *on?*" asks a student in every class I've ever taught on ethnography, usually right after the exercise on perception and facts.

Built into that question is a rough acceptance of the truth revealed by the exercise, combined with a new anxiety about the actual practice of fieldnote *writing*. The basic assumption at work in the student's question is that a fieldnote is a written recording device that is capable of simply transferring "what is" (even if it *is* an interpretation) to a page. When viewed this way, the question "what should I take fieldnotes on?" can be answered pretty easily. I tell them: Take notes on *everything* that happens. *All* of it. Don't miss *a single thing*.

When I answer this way, I "hear in" what my students are *not* saying something like this: *That Dr. Bud. There he goes again.* Or less polite possibilities, depending on the student and her or his tolerance for perceived ambiguity.

But I respond that way for a good *pedagogical* reason. And because of something that happened to me a number of years ago…

◻   ◻

During the mid-1980s the study of organizational narratives was becoming "hot stuff."

In part this was due to a lot of people reading the same Pacanowsky-Trujillo piece that turned me around, and that I described in the previous chapter. But there were other scholars advancing the cause of organizational narratives as well, in disciplines as distinctive as administrative science, organizational sociology, medicine, occupational therapy, and industrial psychology.

Fueled by my reading of the aforementioned article, I made the classic pedagogical error of asking a small group of my advanced students "to go out and collect organizational stories," which, in my youthful enthusiasm and general naïvete about cultures, I assumed were "out there" to be "collected," like butterflies. I then told them we could "analyze" the narratives back in the classroom. Next week.

I was a fool and this was a big mistake. But I didn't know that yet. I had to learn it, from experience.

One by one my students filed into class the following week with looks that ranged from mildly frustrated to completely unhappy. When I asked them why they looked so downtrodden, one of them responded: "You told us to go out and collect organizational narratives. We didn't *hear* any."

I learned from that student's honest expression that the problem they encountered was partly caused by my lack of better instructions. It was also partly based on what was a posited, rather direct, if not fearless symbolic correspondence, between the interpretivist's *word* and the interpretivist's *world.* I had failed to tell them that narratives were *socially constructed* out of the raw materials of lived experience and observed phenomena. I had failed to mention that no matter how much theoretical service we give to the old general-semantics idea that "the map is not the territory," we usually go out into the world and act as if it really *is* the territory.

These students went out to hear *stories.* They didn't hear any. What they expected to encounter was something like what they knew a story was or could be. In their collective quest for stories, they missed the opportunity to take fieldnotes on what they were encountering: people talking to each other, engaging in practices, and the like, over the course of a day. As I explained to them, what they were encountering (but not writing down) was part of many ongoing stories, the final shape, editing, and interpretation of which would be up to them. In this way, they would be *making a story* out of the stuff of those routine exchanges between and among persons.

But that is often too large a lesson to unleash all at once.

So, instead, I have learned to rhetorically nudge them toward it. I let them "hear in" what happens if I take the question—"what should I take fieldnotes on?"—to its logical limits. I have learned how to demonstrate, using all the available strategic ambiguity I can muster, the impossibility of answering the question *any other way.* If you assume that there is something "out there" to take fieldnotes "on," then you end up confirming a vision of the world and its re-presentation that can never be satisfied by fieldwork practice or linguistic constructions.

If you set out to hear a story, and you don't hear one, does that mean there is no story, or does it mean that your linguistic construction imprisoned your perceptions? Moreover, if you set out to take fieldnotes on "what is," *what else could you do* but write down *everything* that happens, in all of its complexity?

If students are still perplexed, I add some practical dimensions to my initial framing.

Does "everything" include what others are thinking? How are you going to gain access to what they are thinking? Can you climb into their ears, take a look around? Be injected into their bloodstreams?

Does "everything" include what they are feeling? If so, how are you going to access or record that?

Would it include the interplay of biology and culture on the moment? How do you write that?

Or do you propose to draw an imaginary—but rhetorically manageable—boundary around the limited scene you are capable of observing and experiencing, by ignoring some of that cruel complexity?

Does that mean you then don't locate that scene within all of what's happening at the same time in the city? The state? The nation? The world? History itself?

Whose history, anyway? What about *her*story?

Put simply, you *can't* observe everything, which means you can't write down all that occurs. If your goal is a grammatical correspondence between the practices of everyday life and a text of those practices, you are, in fact, doomed to failure as an ethnographer.

Perhaps you should consider a career in the behavioral sciences. Pardon me.

I ask students to "hear in" what they are saying in response to that question, to "hear in" all of the assumptions they are carrying with them. Then, when the inevitable rhetorical light collectively goes on, I help them learn how to *rephrase* their question.

THE QUESTION OUGHT TO BE: "What *can* fieldnotes represent or evoke?"

This is a much clearer and better question because it fits the tool to the job. It admits the limitations of the tool and opens up the application of it to what can be accomplished. I like that sort of speaking, that sort of construction. Don't you?

I believe fieldnotes can record and represent or evoke three varieties of experiences:

1 *Verbal exchanges* between or among persons
2 *Practices* within a physical world of persons and things
3 *Implied, inferred, or interpreted connections between and among them* that are owned and accounted for by the writer

Let's examine each of these in more detail.

Verbal Exchanges

Verbal exchanges—interviews, exchanges of information and gossip, conversations, debates, arguments, negotiations, dialogues—are, for a communication-based ethnographer, the *substance* of our first principles about what matters in the social construction of cultural realities. Verbal exchanges are the *organizing focus* of everyday experience, and as such, these exchanges represent a fundamental way to create fieldnotes.

There are three stages involved in creating and reflecting upon fieldnotes about verbal exchanges:

1 *Write* down precisely what gets said (including nonverbal cues and pauses) between the speakers.
2 *Code* (that is, determine the generic type) the conversation for analysis (see below).
3 *Reflect* on the meaning of the conversation as a "type" of communication (the coding), as an episode with the evolving story you are encountering, and (perhaps, if it seems appropriate) as it interacts with your personal experiences.

Below is an example, drawn from my fieldwork with the rock 'n' roll band Whitedog (Goodall, 1991). The scene depicted was one that I noticed recurring when we members of the band got together for rehearsals, or for stage performances. The setup was always the same: Dave, our "Roadie," would do something he was asked not to do. The band members would assume Monty Python–ish accents to assess what punishment he should receive, the preferred one being the implied threat (never carried out) to "choke him." This episode attained a ritual status for band members. The following scene—a typical conversation—opens when Mike Fairbanks (aka 'Banks), our lead singer, enters:

"Hey man," I say.

"Hey man," he replies.

"Hey man," Drew says.

"Hey man," he replies.

There is an easiness in rituals like this. There is much comfort living in them.

"Dr. Bud, did Dave follow all the rules?" This from 'Banks, right on cue.

In my best Monty Python fake-peasant British accent I say, "All but one, sir. All but one."

'Banks rears his eyebrows, joins in on the accent. "And which one might that be, sir?"

I pretend not to want to say. "It was a very small rule, actually, sir."

"Quick, man, let's have it."

I cover my face with my arms in a tragic gesture, say only, in a small accented voice, "the one about touching the board, sir. That one. But only that one."

"I must choke him, you know."

"Oh, but I wish you wouldn't, sir. Not this time. He's been, well, pitiful, sir, ever since I caught him. I chastised the bastard meself. I shouldn't think he requires choking, not today, sir."

"I don't know. I still feel the need to choke him. It is a rule, you know."

Drew walks over, joins in the merriment. "I think it was such a small rule that you should overlook it this time." Drew puts his hand on 'Banks's shoulder. "Do it for us, sir, for the good of the band."

"Oh, very well then. For the good of the band."

'Banks points a finger at Dave, who, during this scene, has been perched sulkily on a barstool, Silver Bullet in hand. "You've been very bad," says 'Banks. "Do you repent?"

"Oh hell yeah," says Roadie Dave. "I fuckin repent. I mean it. I really do."

We all break up in laughter.

Dave looks at us, "What's so funny, guys? Huh? Huh?"

This only brings more laughter, Cindy and the barman this time joining in.

Dave shakes his head and does his very best Sad Dave look. "I'm just an asshole, I guess."

He looks pitiful, then hopeful, but is a WHITEDOG nonetheless.

"Well, he may be an asshole, but at least he's our asshole. Isn't that right?" This from British Drew.

"That's right," says 'Banks.

And that's the end of it. (Goodall, 1991; pp. 235–236)

Coding: I wrote this scene from memory one night on a barstool, but the episode happened so often that its particulars were well established. The beginning of the interaction involved a *phatic communion* introduction made up of the simple male sign of recognition, "Hey man." All members of the band (but not the Roadies) present at the time were involved. The band leader—'Banks—initiated the exchange, always, as a sign of his status in the band hierarchy. The exclusion of a Roadie was a way of marking status in the band in comparison to the "help," and I rarely witnessed any violations of this construction.

The initial conflict was established when 'Banks would inquire about any band rule violations committed by Dave, the Roadie. Because Dave always did something he wasn't supposed to do, and because on several occasions his rule-violation caused problems for the band, this was both a necessary and ritualized form of address. The use of the Monty Python–ish accents by the band members (but not the Roadies) allowed for a playful, analogic interaction that revealed the violation while dramatically placing our band's lived experiences on par with those from the band played by the film troupe. 'Banks, as the band leader, was the person called on to determine the Roadie's fate, and—according to band traditions—that punishment was always supposed to be "choke him." On many occasions, 'Banks would actually pretend to do so, thus inscribing the scene with a kind of male macho performance of self that both elevated, and commented on, 'Banks's actual power in the band.

The scene reaches a dramatic climax when 'Banks is talked out of choking Dave. In this way, band members—especially Drew, the lead guitarist—established their analogic power to mediate the scene in ways that mirrored the power and status they actually had within the band.

The *denouement* phase of the ritual interaction views Dave accepting the band's decision, "repenting," and then doing or saying something that reaffirms the relatively low level of intelligence he actually displayed among band members. This reaffirmation of his guilt was immediately followed by our reaffirmation of his membership—albeit bounded by his lower status as a Roadie—in our band.

Reflection: This scene is an example of how white, middle-class men "do" the business of male ritual bonding via (1) phatic communion and a sequencing of (2) dramatic action (in this case, *stylized aggression*). The scene and conversation depicted are drawn from a rock 'n' roll band in a nightclub, but are in many ways generalizable. Verbal recognition establishes the initial contact; a manufactured conflict organizes and situates the talk as one dealing with power and status, with an observable preference for physically violent (in this case, playful) resolution; and the actual exchanges are punctuated by laughter, sexual innuendo, and profanity. Yep, this is white boy stuff, through and through. And the band calls itself Whitedog. Indeed.

The level of playfulness exhibited by the exchange of talk is itself a way of marking race, classes, and gender. White males typically take on the accents, the voices, of cultural others to engage in verbal play. Often the styles of voice and accent reflect a "put-down" of the other race and/or class and/or gender, and often the put-down is sexually charged. Do all white boys act this way? No. But enough of us do to warrant the stereotype.

On a more optimistic level, the creativity exhibited in the exchange is remarkable. The use of voices drawn from film characters, the active willingness of the participants (even Dave) to engage in the ongoing drama, and the overall comedic portrayal of a rule violation point to the extraordinary resources that these men brought to bear on an otherwise ordinary situation. This ritual was experienced as a kind of lift out of the tedious task of setting up the instruments and the stage prior to a performance. It was, then, a form of ritualized ecstasy that helped them to make the transformation from nonprofessional musicians and individuals doing specified mechanical tasks to the elevated roles of "band members." It solidified stage identities and encouraged everyone to experience that night as fully, as richly, as *un*ordinarily as possible.

My feeling during the ritual was one of anticipation and general fun. I was looking forward to what I would soon be participating in, helping create. As a band member, I enjoyed a middling status (rhythm guitarists usually do), so even though I could have interceded on Dave's behalf more directly, I felt it was not "my place" to. That role was reserved for Drew. I also had a sense of our *performing* this ritual for the audience of Cindy (the club manager) and the barman. Our success, in part, would be measured by how quickly and fully we could draw them into our little drama. This was one way in which we created an audience for ourselves—something that I think is *essential* for any stage performer to master.

Finally, I am struck now by the *comedic* choices we made, when we could just as easily have performed the ritual as tragedy. I wonder what this says about us? Maybe we saw ourselves—or at least at that stage in our band's evolution—as having more in common with stand-up comics than with "serious" actors. We were still playing *covers,* despite our strong preference to playing our original music. Maybe this ritual is a sign of that. Maybe having this much fun is a comment on our collective interpretation of our assumed or desired worth in comparison to what we are actually doing. Maybe in our world, laugher is a kind of tonic we take against a fear of our true mediocrity, our status as just another pretty good bar band playing somebody else's music.

Or maybe not. Maybe I am making *way too much* out of this. Maybe we were just having a little fun, and our ritual is one way we did that. Rock 'n' roll has always been about playing the fool to the king, right?

CONVERSATION, AS YOU HAVE JUST WITNESSED, is the organizing term I loosely apply to a wide variety of face-to-face (and mediated) verbal exchanges. When writing fieldnotes, it's a good idea to be able to make finer distinctions between and among types of such exchanges. Allow me to work with you on the nature of conversations for the next little while.

Clearly there is a wide range of possibilities for the actual purpose, conduct, and exchange dynamic of potential conversations (for instance, see Agar, 1994; Goffman, 1959, 1967, 1974, 1980; Hopper, 1992, 1998; Pearce, 1989; Shotter, 1993; Shotter and Gergen, 1994). When coding conversations, I begin with a rudimentary, modernist typology whose representational basis is then tested against the various complexities, and challenges to the typology, encountered in the field.

The first representational move I ask students to make is to conceptualize forms of verbal exchanges as existing on a continuum between "phatic communion" and "dialogue." Like this:

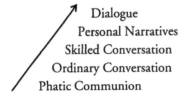

Dialogue
Personal Narratives
Skilled Conversation
Ordinary Conversation
Phatic Communion

I then develop other forms of verbal exchanges that can be charted between the ends of this continuum. I maintain that verbal exchanges can be "coded" or described, as:

■ *Phatic communion, or ritual interaction:* Phatic communication refers to the "Hi, how are ya?" (or, in the above case, "Hey man") class of routine social interactions that are themselves the basic verbal form of politeness rituals used to express social recognition and mutuality of address (see Watzlawick, Beavin, and Jackson, 1967; Philipsen, 1975, 1976, 1992; Goodall, 1996). Some interpersonal researchers also use phatic communion to describe the initial stage in relational formation, characterized by question-asking and -answering sequences designed to determine common interests or concerns (see Knapp and Vangelista, 1992). Typically, phatic communication exchanges are used to reveal cultural patterns of:
  • Hierarchy and status
  • Race, class, and gender differences and distinctions
  • Turn-taking sequences and the rules that enable and inform them
  • Risky shifts or unexpected turns that elevate the level of exchange
  • The influence of commodity capitalism on the structure, content, and meanings attributed to surface investments in. conversation

■ *Ordinary conversation (discussion, gossip, or information exchange):* Patterns of questions and responses that provide the interactants with data about personal, relational, and informational issues and concerns, as well as perform the routine "business" of verbally acquiring, describing, analyzing, evaluating, and acting on information in everyday life. To see and "hear in" what information persons exchange with each other can be helpful in understanding the communicative basis of their relationship. For example:
  • George Casper Homans (1961) posited that in all human relationships the key concept of "equity" is derived from routine exchanges of goods, services, sentiments, and time. Such information can be analyzed at both the *digital* (what gets exchanged) and *analogic* (what it says about the relationship) levels (Goodall, 1983b).
  • Organizational communication researchers (see Eisenberg and Goodall, 1997, Chapter 8, for review) typically describe business

103

and personal hierarchies and power through analysis of routine exchanges among superiors and subordinates, peers, employees with customers, employees with suppliers, and so forth.

■ *Skilled conversation (conflict management, argumentation, and/or debate, negotiation, interviews):* These exchanges represent a "higher" or "deeper" level of information exchange/discussion, usually attributed to professionally trained communicators, negotiators, ethnographers, and commentators (see Senge, et al., 1994). This conversational exchange features an elaborate and interlocking, mutually understood, means to arrive at a mutually organized, but not always predetermined, end. For example, conversations that feature an exchange of conflicting views, charges, or constructions of meaning are important emblems of how a culture structures rules (and violations) for managing or resolving disputes. As a type of conversation, these engagements can:

• Be caused by, or emerge naturally within, a discussion or routine exchange
• Be ritualized within a relationship pattern, such as the relational "double bind" (see Watzlawick, Beavin, and Jackson, 1967)
• Be ritualized within civic forums for the airing or resolution of differences, as in structured formal debates

■ *Personal narratives:* Conversation can be marked by the presence of individual or mutual self-disclosure, wherein the episodes of disclosure are used to situate, coordinate, detail, and explain or retell pivotal events in a personal or organizational life. These storytelling episodes are generalized as "narratives" and may be recorded, transcribed, and analyzed methodically (see Kellett, 1999; Kellett and Goodall, 1999; Mumby, 1993; Riessman, 1993; Taylor, 1997).
■ *Dialogue:* Conversations (fairly rare) can reveal a kind of spiritual or unordinary "meeting" in which the talk moves from exchanges of information and the coordination of new understandings to a higher level of spontaneous mutuality (see Buber, 1985; Eisenberg and Goodall, 1997; Senge, et al., 1994). When this happens, the interactants typically report that the dialogue "transcends" the ordinary boundaries of self and other as well as topical continuity, producing a lived experience of ecstasy (see Goodall, 1996).

Using this continuum, let's explore an example of how fieldnotes taken in an informal setting can be coded using the material above.

Here's my fieldnote entry on an exchange of talk I overheard in a Hardee's restaurant just outside of Central, South Carolina:

G1: "Soooooo, let's talk about you?"

G2: "Welllll, my Daddy's one of the richest men in the upstate."

G1: "How nice..."

G2: "Yes. Well. When I was twelve, my Daddy bought me a fine thoroughbred racehorse so I could ride across our 5,000-acre farm."

G1: "How nice..."

G2: "Yes. And well, when I turned sixteen? My Daddy bought me a brand new red Corvette convertible so I could drive out to our farm from home in Charleston to ride my horse."

G1: "Well, how nice..."

G2: "Yes. And, well, just last month? Daddy bought me an airplane so I could fly from Clemson to Charleston every weekend, where I left my red Corvette that I can drive to our farm to ride my horse."

G1: (Silence, and an icy smile)

G2: "Now tell me about you?"

G1: "Okay. Well, my Daddy's always believed in sending us to the finest schools."

G2: "Is that right?"

G1: "Yes. So I went to one of the finest boarding schools in New England, where I graduated valedictorian of my class. I came to Clemson because this is where my Daddy, and his Daddy before him, came to school."

G2: "And what did you learn in that fine boarding school?"

G1: "Well, for one thing, I learned how to say 'How Nice' instead of 'Fuck You...'"

You may stop laughing now.

I use this fanciful exchange to point out that in most conversations there are a wide variety of possible *interpretive* invitations. The key, for any ethnographer, is to find a theoretical/critical framework through which to reveal the deeper meanings of the exchange.

In this exchange, for example, one framework is *dramatic form:* The "rule of three"[2] that tends to apply to North American joke-telling also works to frame the participants' understanding of the dramatic build to a climax that is so much a part of their conversation (Goodall, 1983a).

---

2 This refers to the fact that in our culture it is always the third event that includes the punchline.

Another is the role of *surprise in sense-making:* The presence of a dramatic reversal at the end of the exchange signals both a move to reverse the status via the element of surprise and an insult (Louis, 1980). Additionally, the exchange may be viewed from a perspective on *interpersonal power* by applying a resistance-to-domination framework to the reversal tactic (deCerteau, 1984; Scott, 1990). And, of course, the whole conversation can be framed as a thoroughly *gendered* exchange (Tannen, 1990, 1994; Wood, 1996).

There are many ways to understand "what is going on" in talk. What I have provided is a way of analyzing the meaning from an *outsider's perspective,* from an *observer's* critical vantage. However, another ethnographic technique is to ask the interactants what they thought they were doing. This research strategy may elicit *"insiders' perceptions"* about their conversational goals, perceptions of self and other, development of meaning through the exchange, and the element of reversal humor at the end. Ideally, ethnographers should attempt to collect both outsider and insider information.

The following list of questions and issues can be helpful:

What Is the Frame/Context?

■ *Where does the action take place?* What are the physical, economic, social, hierarchical, and political contexts involved?
■ What kind of *speech act* is it?
■ What is the nature of the *episode?*
■ What is the nature of the *relationship?*

What Is Being Said?

■ What is the "work" that the words are doing?
■ What are the symbols that must be read as signs?
■ What are the "power" terms?
■ What "indexes" are available?
■ What is the role of silence/the unsaid in this episode?
■ What are the influences of *fixed positionings*:
Gender?
Race/ethnicity?
Social class?
Region of the country?
Other?

- What is the *"story"* being constructed here? What is its rhetorical form? Its narrative form? Are there available cultural, social, or relational frames for interpreting its meaning(s)?

How Is It Being Spoken?

- What are the *rhythms, the vocal tones, the silences* contributing to the overall meanings?
- Where does the *storyline* come from? From personal history? From cultural myth? How is it gendered?
- What are the *life scripts* being invoked?
- What does it all add up to? What does it *mean?*

Where Are You in This Scene?

- What attracts you to it?
- How did you participate in it?
- What do you see happening in it that references past experiences you've had?
- What strikes you as "novel"? Why?
- What frames your reading of this episode/event?

Finally, I ask students to write out responses—in their personal journals or professional notebooks—to two interrelated issues:

- What constitutes "communication" for you?
- What constitutes "communication" for those whom you observe and analyze?

These last two questions are often the most difficult for students to answer. But I figure that if we are going to be engaged in critical and cultural analysis of *communication* between persons, we ought to have some understanding of what "communication" consists of *for them,* as well as *for us.*

WHILE I AM ABOUT the business of being a (relative) pedagogical modernist in terms of categorizing and coding fieldnotes, allow me to share with you an additional level of detail I typically provide about writing fieldnotes and coding types of exchanges in conversations.

The basic typology offered in the previous section allows students to sort out *basic forms of social exchange* for the purpose of setting up a *second* level of categorization and analysis. This second level is aimed at getting closer to the *personal meanings* of the exchanges, which is a formal way of suggesting that *you* are isolating key moments in the exchange and attributing special meaning to them. There are many ways of doing this, depending on the purpose of the study, the issues being addressed, and the methods being used, but I typically begin with the following categories:

- "Rich points" (Agar, 1994) are those episodes or speech acts within conversations that contain cultural knowledge; these are sources of critical deconstruction of how cultures are understood from the inside. Typically these occur as verbal exciters or clear punctuations *within basic informational exchanges or routine discussions.* Examples include:
  - Slang or non-normative terms
  - Jargon or in-group speech (including the use of assumed voices or persona)
  - Turns of phrase that do not refer to their literal linguistic referents but are commonly used and understood among members of a culture or subculture
  - Purposeful misrepresentations of others used to conversationally devalue them

- "Turning points" (Bullis and Bach, 1989) are those times when talk produces critical life decisions or ultimate interpretations of the meaning of persons, relationships, organizations, and institutions. Typically these accounts occur within *personal and organizational narratives.*
- Habits of speech, mannerisms, gestures, facial expressions, and the like, that "come with" conversation and should be included as part of how the social text gets culturally constructed (Goffman, 1959, 1967, 1974, 1980).

Students can learn to focus on these conversational resources as basic communication data that shape and inform an interpretation of a culture or subculture. The typology is useful as a teaching device because it lessens the initial ambiguity of going into the field by providing something *specific and concrete to observe and write down* as fieldnotes.

I AM ALWAYS CAREFUL to add what I consider to be a vital caveat to problematize the categories.

Kenneth Burke (1989) wisely instructs us to understand that "trained incapacities" to (rhetorically) see occur as a result of "occupational psychosis," a condition he attributes largely to the ways in which received forms of knowing operate (rhetorically) on the perceptions and understandings of its users. The basic distinction is the difference, always present, between categories that make life sensible, and sentence-able, for the *observer,* and those that the *interactants* use for *their own* sensibilities and utterances. I stress the value of asking whether or not the categories brought into the field actually represent what is going on, or whether they are *impositions of order* of a privileged (read: academic) kind on the otherwise perfectly understood cultural meanings held for talk by the local participants.

If you can't answer this question satisfactorily, you might consider writing about the fact that you can't. Writing is a form of inquiry, and in this case it may help you figure it out. But either way, it is vital to let your readers see the processes you bring to the interpretation, even when some part of that interpretation is left unresolved.

QUESTION, PROFESSOR: How do you ever know?

The easy (and often, wrong) answer is to simply ask the people you were observing what they thought they were doing, or at least to check out with them your observational and representational categories. While this is, at some times and in some places, a good idea, it doesn't always work. Informants may strategically lie, conceal the truth, or omit information they are embarrassed by (see Shulman, 1994, for a review). The question may also elicit from them a kind of *false collaboration* based on their desire to appear either as smart or as informed as you. Or it can gain from them a quick agreement for the purpose of getting rid of you.

Your question may also inspire anger. Remember, not everyone assumes academics have automatic licenses to observe and analyze *them.* Turn it around for a moment and see whether *you* would be comfortable with someone else—an unknown and differently educated person—watching and categorizing what *you* say and do, using that data to draw inferences about you and your culture. Chances are pretty good that this idea makes you a little nervous, if not angry. Probably on reflection it also makes you dubious about the validity of what this other person would actually learn.

I want you to remember what you are feeling at this moment. Inscribe it on your soul.

If you do, you will have a helpful referent for the tentativeness and vulnerability of all fieldnotes, of all fieldwork, and certainly of all conclusions about culture drawn from them.

BEYOND WHAT THE CULTURAL PARTICIPANTS believe about your fieldwork, you should also consider the relationship of your fieldnotes to the intended *audience* for them. Namely, other academics and interested laypersons.

My point here is that your informants may not give a tinker's damn about how you "code" their "performances," but your academic colleagues will give a very large damn about it. Words like "ritual" or categories such as "race, class, and gender" have distinct meanings and theoretical (as well as political) framings in our discourse community. However, it may well be the case that these meanings are counter to, or even offensive to, your informants. So don't be disappointed if, when you ask an informant to read your account, the response you get is "Huh?" Or "Huh?" accompanied by "What, are you *serious?*"

One of the ethical issues raised about ethnography has to do with the appropriation of others' cultures, performances, life histories, and so on, for the purpose of advancing an academic career. Viewed this way, to observe others is to *colonize* them. To write their experiences in your book or article is to *use* them. It is to place yourself, as author, in a *superior relationship* to the persons you are observing, hearing-in, and analyzing.

One result of this ethical challenge has been to advise students to be more courteous about asking permission of others prior to doing fieldwork. Another response is to "give something back" to those who have helped you fashion your text and build your career. Still another outcome has been to turn the ethnographic lens back on the ethnographer *entirely*. If we are willing to study others, we ought to be equally willing to place ourselves, our lives, our families, under the same critical scrutiny. This is one of the reasons often cited for autoethnography (see Ellis and Bochner, 1996, for examples), in which the self or one's own experiences are constructed as an "other."

Ethics and politics aside for the moment (see Chapter 4 for a lengthier discussion), *narrative and rhetorical* implications also come into play. Writing about another's culture for the edification and pleasure of your own fully brings into the open questions of "who owns [the literary rights to] this experience?"

I can't resolve those questions for you. Nobody can. There aren't any easy answers.

What you must learn to do is recognize that the *"crisis of legitimacy"* (Denzin, 1996) for ethnography is constituted precisely because of these representational and political questions. Diverse audiences make diverse—and often *contradictory*—demands on a text's construction and uses. What sounds great when read aloud in a classroom can be morally or personally offensive to those who contributed their voices to it, and vice versa. (If you doubt the vice versa part of my claim, consider that it wasn't that long ago that ethnographers were prevented by the conventions of journal authorship from including profanity in an article—even though we encountered it, factually, in the field.

Our collective challenge has always been one of adapting a message to a particular, intended audience. Remember that. And live with the difficult questions of legitimacy and representation.

Practices

What members of a culture say and do routinely, or what academics call "practices," offer excellent examples of what can be observed or experienced in the field. No ethnography that I know of can do without them. As a source for fieldnotes, they offer interesting opportunities and challenges.

Michel deCerteau (1984, 1996) is my favorite "everyday practices" theorist and ethnographic guide. For example, he influenced a generation of organizational and community ethnographers to see the relationship between social class differences and power in everyday practices. One of his most widely cited and useful distinctions is between *strategies* and *tactics*. For deCerteau, strategies are deployed by dominant cultural elites to protect the *status quo;* tactics are what less powerful, or sometimes just culturally radical citizens use to deflect, overturn, or just cope with those strategies. He combines these terms with the idea of power in "cultural space." Because cultural elites own or control most cultural spaces—thus reducing the available space to those who can't work for the elites or those who might organize rebellions against them—one common practice of the homeless, and of radical organizers as well, is to "appropriate" or "poach" living or protesting space from public parks.

deCerteau's notion of everyday "practices" provides insights into how ordinary people perform the business of cultural knowledge. As such, it has wide cultural and ethnographic utility. For example, in the second volume of his series on *The Practices of Everyday Life* (1996) he examines how French citizens "do" the everyday business of shopping, cooking, talking, and eating. He locates within these practices intriguing indices of French cultural knowledge, social relations, and power.

In North America, the idea of "practices" of everyday life has also enjoyed considerable ethnographic play. Studies have investigated the everyday practices of rock 'n' roll and jazz musicians, mid-level managers, recovering alcoholics, surfers, bulimics, consultants, weekend gamblers in Las Vegas, and tourists at the Grand Canyon, just to mention a few. One intriguing study asked how white women "do" the practices of being white women together. In another application, an on-line ethnography interest group was organized by members of the National Communication Association to study the local, regional, and national practices of consumers engaged in shopping.

The idea of observing and participating in cultural practices is central to the development of fieldnotes. To illustrate, I will provide two examples of how practices were written *as fieldnotes,* as well as how they were coded, reflected on, and eventually storied.

The following entry is drawn from my fieldnotes for *Living in the Rock n Roll Mystery* (1991). The practices I am noting are those of real estate agents on "caravan" in Huntsville, Alabama. What this entry captures is what I perceived to be a difference between the cultural rules (read: organizational myths) for showing a house on caravan, and the actual practices the agents displayed.

Here are the unpublished but often clearly articulated rules for showing dreams on caravan:[3]

1 All agents exit their respective vehicles and admire the property, issuing appropriate oohs and aahs, gesturing toward the specific features that can be useful in making a sale.

---

3 In the lingo of the real estate agents, they only show "dreams"—meaning, as I learned, that the rhetoric of purveying real estate is largely based on selling potential customers on the dream of a life that could be lived within the place. The term "caravan" refers to the once-a-week practice of touring all of the new homes listed the previous week.

2 The listing agent walks up to the front door and either enters it (if the door has been left unlocked) or rings the doorbell or knocks. Said listing agent then greets each Realtor as they march up and into the house in single file, look around, note all the bedrooms, baths, etc., that may be used to advantage when making the sale.

3 Rhetoric is constituted about the property, catchphrases are tried out in small groups, notes are taken. If the property is "just right" for a particular current client, a phone is used by an enthusiastic TMT agent to make the appropriate call right there and then.

4 This tactic also has clear public relations value, particularly if the owner is present.

5 Agents exit the premises in single file, pausing once again to admire the property before reentering their respective vehicles and driving away slowly.

Here is what actually happens:

Cars line up in front of the house, and agents, in various states of health and with varying degrees of enthusiasm, stretch and complain about the ride, the music, and each other.

The listing agent knocks on the front door, opens it with a key, and yells "HELLLLLLLOOOOOOOOO" into the general interior of the place, just in case they have caught someone inside half-naked or engaging in illegal or immoral activities, which occurs, according to the agents, more often than you might suppose.

The agents enter the house, look around, comment on the owners' taste or lack thereof, compare it unfavorably with their own listings, make small jokes about the conditions of sale, and leave as soon as possible.

Agents file back into their respective vehicles and check their respective watches, wondering how much time has passed since their last interesting life experience or perhaps just anticipating lunch break. When the cars are fully reoccupied, they leave (Goodall, 1991; p. 184).

Coding: The first entry in this fieldnote represents and evokes a whole class of organizational practices known as myths. Myths are narratives that circulate within organizations about cultural ideals, ideal performances and performers, and the like. They are often contrasted with "organizational realities," a term used to represent what I am referring to here as actual practices, captured in the second list.

Reflection: I used the myth-versus-actual practices entry as a setup to introduce a longer account that depicts real estate agents in this company doing the business of caravan touring (see Goodall, 1991;

pp. 170–202). The emphasis in this study is on how agents create interpretive accounts of the lives of clients and customers based on their informed (or misinformed) readings of houses and locales. In many ways, their interpretive accounts offer a view of social life as constructed out of the language of real estate agentry and show us how a distinctive culture of trained observers make use of their personal and organizational narratives in everyday life.

My second example of writing actual practices is drawn from a personal ethnography about living with bulimia (Tillmann-Healy, 1996). This account may be painful for some readers, as it presents a powerful, first-person account:

THE FIRST TIME

I kneel in front of the toilet bowl, afraid yet strangely fascinated. As I stare at my rippling reflection in the pool of Saniflush-blue water, my thoughts turn to an article in the latest *Teen* magazine about a young woman who induced vomiting to control her weight. It sounds repulsive in light of my experiences with the flu and hangovers. Still, I want to try it, to see if I can do it.

I place the shaking index finger of my right hand to the back of my throat. I hold it there for five or six seconds, but nothing happens. I push it down further. Still nothing. Further. Nothing. Frustrated, I move it around in circular motions. At last, I feel my stomach contract, and this encourages me to continue. Just then, I gag loudly.

Shhh.

Footsteps clonk on the linoleum outside the bathroom door, and I immediately pull my finger out of my mouth.

"Lis?" my father calls. "You OK?"

"I'm fine, Dad," I answer. "Playing basketball tonight?"

"Yeah, and I'm late."

I hear him pass through the dining room and ascend the stairs.

Listening closely for other intruders, I gaze into the commode, determined to see this through. The front door slams as my father exits, and I return to my crude technique. Again my stomach contracts. When I feel my body rejecting the food, I move my hand aside to allow the smooth, still-cold liquid to pour out of me—a once perfect Dairy Queen turtle sundae emerges as a brown swirl of soft-serve ice cream, hot fudge and butterscotch, and minute fragments of chopped pecans.

Again and again, 20 times or more, I repeat this until I know by push-ing on my stomach that it is satisfactorily empty. My pulse races.

I am 15 years old.

Coding: Although Lisa Tillmann-Healy provides no specific referent for coding this data, it is clear from the entry, and what follows from it later in her finished story, that the practice is both actual and emblem-atic. This account works rhetorically on three levels. First, the practice of eating and vomiting is routinized. The mental, emotional, and phys-ical experience of it is fully rendered in sequential detail. Second, the narrative implication of her father as an unwilling yet strangely com-plicit participant in the scene mirrors later entries about the relation of men to this practice in her life. Third, the autoerotic analogy in the description of the practice is unmistakable.

Reflection: This episode occurs within a longer chronological essay built methodically out of fragments of remembered/constructed experi-ences, in which the author juxtaposes actual practices and verbal exchanges with poems, memories, and cultural messages about the need for women to maintain "thinness." One of the entries contains the following piece of self-reflection:

A SYMBOLIC PURGE

I read these stories aloud and feel conflicted. As a feminist, I'm embar-rassed by the amount of attention I've paid to my body. As a daughter, I worry that these revelations will hurt my parents. As a scholar, I am con-cerned that my fellow academics will dismiss my work as self-absorbed.

One after the other, over and over, I take these in. I swallow the words and feel them waddle down my throat. More voices, new doubts, I ingest them all.

At last, my stomach tumbles and churns, twisting, sloshing. In a mass eruption, the words rush out of my mouth—a symbolic purge. On the page, my insides lay bare for everyone to read. Perhaps I should be ashamed, but somehow, I feel only relief (Tillmann-Healy, 1996, p. 86).

Both of these examples, diverse as they are, reveal a *common pattern* about writing fieldnotes dealing with cultural practices. In each case the authors follow a fairly *strict chronology* of events, and the focus is on the *micro-level episodes* that structure the overall events. The uses of *descriptive and emotional details* are built into the accounts at the moment of their occurrence within the overall stream of activities. There is an interplay—

at least in these published accounts—of *personal reflection and actual practice,* which operates rhetorically to induce the reader's involvement and (possibly) identification with the observations or practices.

Now that we have examined two varieties of fieldnotes about *practices,* let's see what can be done with them. By "done with them" I mean our academic/cultural practice of linking them to theoretical frameworks that are capable of inspiring and guiding interpretations of meaning.

▢   ▢

I construct ethnographic practices as "performances" of everyday life because my basic interpretive schema is organized *dramatistically* (see Burke, 1989; Goffman, 1959, 1967, 1980; Turner, 1969). I view the social construction of realities through the *organizing metaphor of dramatic action.*[4]

Like Burke, but unlike Goffman or Turner, I do *not* think that the Shakespearean phrase "life is a stage, and we are merely players" is an elaborate metaphor for social life. I believe that dramatic action is the *baseline* for interpreting what people say and do. People *act on* the world, we don't just move along with it. People *create* meanings, we don't just receive them. We actively, sometimes mythically, *imagine* our lifeworlds. Then we walk, purposefully, and dramatically, into them (see Goodall, 1996, for elaboration). Here are my assumptions:

1 We *symbolically act in, and on, the world* through forms of communication. Primary among these are verbal exchanges and routine practices.

2 These symbolic actions are *representations* of our interpretations of the social world.

3 Patterns of symbolic actions can be organized, understood, and represented as *cultural performances* of everyday life.

Patterns of everyday *performances* may be coded and analyzed as:

■ *Routines:* What we "do" every day. If you ask an informant to describe what she or he "does" everyday, chances are the practices, events, and episodes that you will hear about, or read about, are routine performances. Routines help us structure the day; if they

---

4 As explained in the Preface, I also view writing as a "performance." As such, writing ethnography is a form of representing, evoking, and using dramatic action to build a relational dialogue with readers.

are interrupted, we notice and respond to them as interruptions. Observations of what informants do—writing down the movements, the activities, the context for those actions—provide a written record of how everyday practices "achieve routine" (Eisenberg and Goodall, 1997). For the real estate agents, routines were captured in the second set of entries. For Tillmann-Healy, the routines were captured in her physical description of her own induced vomiting.

■ *Rituals:* What we "do" every day that counts for us (and usually for others) as particularly and symbolically meaningful. Ritual practices may be personal, familial, social, organizational, and institutional, or combinations of them (Rothenbuhler, 1998). Rituals tend to be anticipated, experienced, and interpreted by participants as important organizing events or episodes, and in some cases as *sacred* activities. Rituals constitute meaningful episodes that, if missed or interrupted, create a *profane violation* of a person's (or group's) sense of *entitled* experiences.

For the real estate agents, the experience of "caravaning" the "dreams" was elevated to the status of ritual, in which each of the routines were constituent elements. For Lisa Tillmann-Healy, the practice of purging became a ritual, complete with an established set of physical and mental preparations and practices.

■ *Rites of passage:* What we "do" that *significantly* alters or changes our personal sense of self or our social or professional status or identity. In many cultures, young men and young women attain adulthood through elaborate ceremonies, some of which include practices such as body mutilation, drug-induced ecstatic experience, public sacrifice, or the exchange of marriage vows and rings. Other rites of passage practices are less severe, but are equally meaningful. Organizational employees often describe the day when they knew they were accepted as a member of a team after undergoing a "rite of passage." Many companies hold ceremonies marking the end of an employee's career. Families mark the end of a life with funeral ceremonies and burial.

Neither of the fieldnote examples used above reveal "rites of passage"; however, the longer essays from which these excerpts were drawn do. For real estate agents, the rites of passage are primarily organizational (including admission to the certified body of brokers known as Realtors). For example, one significant rite of passage includes a (rude) symbolic act that bestows full membership on an initiate. For Lisa Tillmann-Healy, her symbolic passage from a person who experimented with vomiting as a means of weight control to admitting that she was, in fact, living with bulimia, constitutes a personal rite of passage.

Routines, rituals, and rites all contribute to our appreciation and understanding of how a culture organizes the actual practices in every-day life. As such, these symbolic activities frame bodily actions and exchanges of words and symbols as being "one kind of thing" instead of "something else."

Ethnographers also make interpretive use of isolated practices that mark important cultural terrain outside of the broader boundaries of routines, rituals, and rites. They are:

- *Surprise-and-sense making episodes* (Louis, 1980, Weick; 1995): Any newcomer to a culture must learn how to make sense out of the actual practices and verbal exchanges of its members. In many cases these practices surprise us because they represent the new, the unanticipated, and the unexpected. Novice ethnographers, for example, often find that they gather more fieldnotes in the first week than in the rest of the time spent at a particular site. The reason? *Everything* is new.

- *Risk-taking episodes* (Rawlins, 1992): Ethnographers often encounter episodes of actual practice or verbal exchange in which "something risky happens" and the interactants must account for or otherwise deal with it. One example is when one partner in a friendship tries to move the relationship to a romantic level. Another example is when an employee confronts an organizational superior without the usual deference, or behaves in a way that risks her or his job.

- *Face-saving episodes* (Goffman, 1959): At the levels of verbal exchange and actual practice, the performance of face-saving pro-vides intriguing and potentially rich ethnographic data.

- *Crises* (Adelman and Frey, 1997; Conquergood, 1991, 1993): Communication ethnographers are interested in how, through practices, people come to grips with AIDS, cancer, poverty, the expe-rience of a loved one's death or disease, or other intense forms of personal, familial, interpersonal, organizational, and communal cri-ses. Crisis can be located in a specific event or episode, or as an overarching pattern that marks lived experience in a definitive way. Practices that constitute awareness of, and responses to, these deeply powerful occurrences often redefine what is meant by collecting "hard" data (Pacanowsky, 1988).

QUESTION, PROFESSOR: What should fieldnotes look like?

This question always makes me smile.

If I can anticipate its occurrence in a class, I try to bring in samples of my own fieldnotes. I show the scrawl on unnumbered pages of discolored notebook paper. A phrase I overheard at a restaurant and scribbled on a napkin. Various artifacts gathered from ordinary and exotic places, each one carrying the symbolic weight of its own precious memory. Finally, I show them the thick manuscript-looking continuous-feeding roll of computer paper that was my attempt, Jack Kerouac-style, to record all the events that happened to me while I was on the road with my band, Whitedog.

My point is that where you write fieldnotes, or what you compose them on, doesn't have to follow a prescribed format. You write what you need to write, to record what you need to record, whenever, wherever, and however you can.

Editing and reflecting on them, however, is a very different activity (see Chapter 5).

LAST QUESTION, PROFESSOR: When, or how, do you "make an academic something" out of all those fieldnotes?

This question gets at the heart of a beginning ethnographer's concerns about the relationship of experience to intelligent analysis and self-reflection. As I stated previously, in one sense it is a question of *balance*. But it is also a question about very practical *writing* matters.

Such as: *How* do you translate fieldnotes into an interesting academic tale?

The hard answer is that there is no one answer, at least none that I know. The easy answer is that you do it the best way you know how. Between these two pieces of relatively useless advice lies the whole human territory of writing experience. How anyone makes a text out of fieldnotes, professional notebooks, or diaries is largely learned from trial and error, productive mistake-making, unproductive mistake-making, frustration, anxiety, moments of true insight that are found to be false, moments of true insight that are found to be just moments, and, once in a while, a found groove in the writing experience that works so well you never want to leave it.

All I can say is: You have to *write* to *find* that groove.

Here's what I do:

I begin by *transcribing* and *working with the patterns* that emerge from my fieldnotes. During that process of keying in what has been sloppily written down and noticing how *this* relates to *that*, I add in personal reflections and references to the professional literature where they seem appropriate. Because I write every day, I always begin a transcription session by reading over and editing the material I wrote the day before. This practice helps me in two ways. First, it helps me recall what I've thought about and written, so that when I continue the transcription and analysis I don't repeat myself. Second, it provides me with a good opportunity to edit and refine my previous work.

While I am doing this, I begin to see patterns in the fieldwork that correspond to personal experiences and pieces I've read. When I begin to see those patterns emerge, I follow them. I try to connect those clues, those dots. I ask questions of the lines of reasoning and intuition that connect them in my head. Then I try to analyze and understand the making of those lines of reasoning.

I am, of course, piecing together clues. I am connecting fieldnotes to an emerging story.

From Coding, Analysis, and Making Connections to Writing Stories

Thus far our discussion of fieldnotes focused on the qualitative social science notions of "coding" and "analysis" to describe how ethnographers make sense out of everyday practices. While I believe these terms refer to basic skill sets that are important intellectual equipment for any ethnographer, the point of this analytical work for a *new ethnographer* is to get from writing and interpreting fieldnotes to constructing a *story*.

Elizabeth Chiseri-Strater and Bonnie Stone Sunstein put it this way:

> Every field study has two stories to tell. One is about the culture itself, what it means through the perspective of the informants. The other story is the one about you as a researcher and how you did the research. The story about your research process is what compositionist Ken Macrorie calls the "I-search paper." While the story about the culture you're investigating is the critical one, the subplot of how you negotiated your entry, conducted your interviews, and collected other data should also be part of your study.... There is

no formula for the balance between these twin narratives; they form and inform a dialogue between self and other (1997, p. 291).

What I have described so far is the acquisition of information leading to the writing of a *story of culture*. Viewed this way, analysis and coding of conversations and practices—as well as interpretive reflections on the meaning of them—are really parts of the overall process of finding patterns that are capable of suggesting a story, an emerging story of your interpretation of a culture. I say "emerging" because that is the role and function of fieldnotes in this process: writing them helps shape your inquiry, helps answer some questions and not answer others, helps you come up with ways of connecting what needs connecting to make sense of what you are studying.

But another story is emerging from your fieldwork—indeed, from your life—that has yet to be composed. And that is the story of *you*, as a *researcher*, as a *person*, within the context of this emerging cultural construction. In the above quoted passage, it's called the story of the "I-search," a journey of self-discovery, a way of using the writing of fieldnotes to connect the story of culture to the story of *yourself* within the culture.

Every ethnographic account tells these two stories. For writers of traditional ethnographies, the balance is tipped toward a representation of the fieldwork experience as one of the researcher's straightforward entry into a culture and systematic analysis of it. The episodes in the story reveal an omniscient narrator who is armed with preconceived questions and theoretical framing, and who proceeds to create knowledge by coding and analyzing data. The ending of a traditional ethnography is derived from the conclusions of the study, with a final nod to the heuristic implications of the research. Embedded with this form of storytelling is a journey of discovery, though one created less out of the stuff of a story of an emerging self than out of the "objective" and systematic answering of scholarly questions.

For interpretivists, the balance tips toward *an evocative representation* of the fieldwork experience. The journey of the writer is often foregrounded, and the research questions, the theoretical framing, the coding and analysis of data, as well as the heuristic implications, unfold not by the dictates of textual formula but by the narrative weave of the tale. The journey of discovery, for the writer, becomes part and parcel of the story itself. In this way, interpretive tales of the fieldwork tend more often to read like good short stories or novels than like standard research reports. And, as is the case in good novels, embedded within the telling is a *moral.*

By analogy, a moral is, for the story, *its procedural method of analysis.* The values, beliefs, ideals, attitudes, and ethical commitments that create the moral core of the story are the continuous measure of all things that happen within it. For this reason, as is the case with good short stories and novels, the events and actions that unfold to make the story into a story provide moral lessons without pronouncing the lesson *as* a moral lesson per se. Instead, the moral is *in* the thoughts, passions, and actions (or absence of them) of the characters.

When I wrote "On Becoming an Organizational Detective" (1989a) I was working from a set of fieldnotes that gradually emerged into a story. The form of the story I chose was the classic detective mystery. I chose this genre because, from my experience, the consultant-as-detective is called into a case, supposedly to investigate one thing—in this case, a "communication problem"—but that one thing usually turns into something else altogether. For me, this is an archetypal account of every consulting job I've ever had. So I decided to write the ethnographic account as a detective story—no formal introduction, theoretical framing, research questions, or anything like that—just as my fieldnotes represented it. Here is the opening, from the finished product:

His name is Edward R. Seeman.

"Call me Ed," he commands as we shake hands. We are doing the usual male thing with the squeeze, each one of us applying a little more pressure until it becomes just uncomfortable enough for one of us to release. Because he's paying the tab, I release, although I don't want to. *Call me Ed,* you muse. Call me Ishmael, and his name is Seeman. Where's the whale?

Equity thus restored I follow him to a table, each of us eyebrow admiring for the benefit of the other the significant nonverbal aspects of the hostess's rearward appearance. In the background is Muzak. It is going to be one of *those* lunches. I knew there were reasons why I got out of this business (1989; pp. 42–43).

Detective stories typically begin this way. The private eye, always a bit of a cultural maverick and usually a loner, meets someone who has a problem. The problem is explained, a fee is worked out, the private eye takes the case. The game is afoot.

In my fieldnotes, I recorded this series of events:

Lunch with Seeman. Decked out in *Esquire* clothes, wears a gold Rolex submariner. Have the feeling that he is not on the level. He mentions the work I did for Phil Davis as if this is an analogous situation. This means he's talked to Davis, which could be good or bad for me. Davis thought I was going to write a different report than the one he received. Turned out okay though. Or maybe Davis recommended me to get even. Hard to say.

Here is how I wrote this episode into the published story:

Ed leans forward, his Rolex catches the light and sparkles. "I saw Phil Davis at the Heritage Club last week," he grins, "and when I told him about my little problem he recommended you."

Thanks, Phil. I try to restrain myself from saying something like "Phil's an ass, which verifies my initial opinion of you," but instead settle for a milder form of insult. "The Heritage Club, huh? Well, my fee just went up."...

About Phil's recommendation I am less certain. Phil Davis hired me a couple of years ago to look into a "communication" problem in an aerospace manufacturing firm that ended up being a cleverly masked excuse for a consultant's report that would blame a particular department for something that wasn't its fault. Phil didn't know this, but he played along as if he knew something, which in a way is worse. I didn't play along, ended up going undercover in the organization to discover the truth, and wrote a very different sort of report. In the end, nobody got hurt, I got paid, and everyone, including Phil, looked good.

But Phil also knew I had done more, and less, than I was asked to do. So this could mean that Phil thinks I will do the same for Ed, or something else entirely. He could be getting even (1989; pp. 43–44).

Notice that in the above excerpt I include a conversation I had with Ed Seeman. I didn't record the details of that conversation in my fieldnotes. Although I recommend that beginning ethnographers write down everything, for some of us who have been at this sort of investigating longer, memory suffices. I *reconstructed* the conversation. Did I leave anything out? Probably. Did I make anything up? Unlikely. One of the rules I use for writing interpretive ethnography is that in the interests of telling a good story it is permissible to omit details that have no bearing on the tale, but it is *not* permissible to make things up.

Sounds good, doesn't it? But what about applying that rule to the line about light catching his Rolex? Did that *actually* happen? Given that there was light in the room and he was wearing the Rolex, it's plausible. But in truth, I thought the line had a certain literary quality to it. I wrote it to make the story *better*.

Now that I've shown that I have rules, but that I also break them, where *do* I draw the ethical line? My answer, which may not be your answer, is admittedly a kind of hedge. All of the good writers I know make productive use of what is commonly referred to as "literary license." I do too. We are *story*tellers. We are creating contexts for interpretation. We write *rhetorically,* which is to say, we try to persuasively adapt our message to our reader's expectations, which means that in the interests of writing a good story, we make use of invention from time to time.

The next entry in my fieldnotes reads:

Followed Seeman back to his office. In the parking lot, I watched him exit his RED Corvette, laughed to myself when I saw him carefully comb his hair before leaving the vehicle. Used some breath spray, too. Then slammed the door. No other car in this lot even comes close to his. He and his vehicle stand out. I snap some photos for the record.

Here is how that fieldnote was translated into the story:

I park my car in the visitor's space and spend a few minutes observing the parking lot. I am big on parking lots as evidence of organizational dramas because in this culture of hypercapitalism and commodity values you are what you drive at least as much as you are what you wear, eat, listen to, or talk about.

This parking lot tells a mundane tale. All the colors are muted and virtually everything has four plain doors and standard-issue tires and wheels. Nothing exotic, no flashy colors, no obvious displays of sensuality or mystique. I am at this point in my musing when Ed pulls in. His vehicle is the clear exception to the rule, a RED, current-generation Corvette.

Very interesting.

He combs his hair before exiting the car, and I get the feeling by the way he slams the door that this is the sort of guy who probably doesn't change his oil regularly or even check its level. A very bad sign. If the guy in charge doesn't pay attention to details, particularly those of a maintenance standard, he is probably the sort of guy who makes up his mind without gathering enough information and then expects others to carry out the work without any new resources (1989, pp. 49–50).

As you can plainly read, much of what was in my fieldnotes was directly transferred to the eventual story. But what is *different* in the story from the account in the fieldnotes? First, I explain my cultural reasoning, actually an enthymeme (that is, a deductive syllogism), about the relationship of parking lots to organizational dramas. Clearly that analysis is not in the fieldnotes. It is, however, part of the self-reflection I did while writing the story. Ditto for the association of Ed's door-slamming with his probable managerial style. In both cases, the fieldnotes provided me with the raw materials for my musings. I included the musings in the story because they help readers see things as I do, which, in the conversation we are developing, offers them opportunities to agree or disagree with me. I also included them because they are important to the development of the story. They provide substance within the overall shape of the tale.

For those of you who have read the whole story, you know what happens next. I call a friend of mine who works in Ed's company to see what his account of the issues might be. During the phone call my friend abruptly changes the subject and pretends to be talking to someone else. We agree to speak later. During that conversation I find out that part of the reason Seeman hired me was to help him find a reason to fire my friend. I write, in the story, these lines:

> I decide, at that moment, to take the case. Sometimes you take the case for money, and sometimes you take the case because you think you can do some good in the world, and sometimes you take the case because you don't know any better. This time it was all three, although at the time I didn't know that (1989; p. 51).

Clearly this is a bit of invention on my part. It is also designed to evoke from readers a sense of the kind of attitude and style found in Raymond Chandler detective mysteries. In truth, at this point in my fieldwork, I don't recall having any such thoughts. I decided to take the consulting gig because it seemed interesting and the money was good. It was only later, toward the end of the gig, when I realized that my motives for getting involved became part of the problem I would eventually have to face. I thought I was in control of a situation that was far more complex than I realized at the time. So I wrote that paragraph after the fact, not during the fieldwork. Again, it seemed to me that the storyline allowed it.

The rest of the story includes a lot of the ordinary practices that comprise the activities I perform as a communication consultant: phone calls, interviews with employees, collaboration with a partner on the meaning of the data we were collecting in the company. Most of the material in these scenes is drawn directly from my fieldnotes. Then, in the story, a climactic meeting takes place with Seeman. During this pivotal encounter, he informs my partner and me that we have been duped. He couldn't care less about what we "find" with our "data"; the point of hiring us was to appease his employees. He doesn't even believe there *is* a "communication problem." Furthermore, if we don't write the report in a way that is favorable to him, he'll just hire another consultant who will write the report he wants.

These events happened pretty much as they are given in the story. At the time it was hard news to receive, and the implications were personally and professionally devastating. But the larger meaning of this scene came in the writing of the story. Up until this moment all of the scenes, the episodes of phone calls, interviews, and the like, were staged as components in the "rising action" of the overall drama. This pivotal scene was positioned as the dramatic climax: the place in a drama, or in a detective story, where the original conflict is revealed and ultimately resolved.

As it turned out, this was *not* the end of the case *nor* of the story. A mysterious woman, who had played a supporting role to the character of the detective earlier in the tale, reemerges as the power figure behind Ed Seeman. Her motives for having him hire me, and for requiring me to write a consultant's report that made Seeman out to be a scapegoat instead of the cause of the company's problems, reveal several lessons— *moral* lessons—in the story First, no matter how much we may believe we are in charge of a situation, and think that we are using free will to make informed choices, chances are good that our part is but a small one in a much larger, more complex, human drama. Second, finding the truth does not always equal acquiring power, nor does knowing the truth necessarily change things for the better. The relationship between communication and truth, for consultants and for researchers alike, is complex and problematic. In real life, as in detective stories, the virtuous are not always rewarded and the wicked are not always punished, or even found guilty. Third, the telling of the story in a detective genre shows how we, as researchers but like detectives, become part of what we are studying by assigning meanings to clues and by interjecting into our accounts our views on the nature of persons and things. We are never detached, neutral observers any more than we are detached, neutral consultants, or detached, neutral writers. Along those same lines, we—researchers and consultants—must be held accountable for whatever it is we help bring about: for ideas, like actions and consulting reports, have consequences.

At the end of "The Consultant as Organizational Detective" I am confronted with these moral lessons, and learn from them. The detective/consultant believes he has done some good in the world and has gotten paid for it; he certainly has discovered some powerful truths and gained some moral lessons. But all of these events have come to him at a precious cost to his worldview, with additional damage done to his professional ethics. Seeman gets a better job in another state, and Stella Mims, the mysterious and powerful woman behind the action, remains as mysterious and powerful as ever. The story ends, rounded off by the hard moral and rhetorical dictates of the genre.

At the end of my fieldnotes about this episode in my consulting life, there was less closure, not more. All of the lessons I learned took longer to understand and to deal with than they did in the story. When I wrote the story, over a year after it happened, I was still smarting from it. I wrote it, in part, to heal myself, to gain narrative control over an experience that would otherwise remain underexamined. Through the writing I created two stories—one about the culture of consulting, another about a journey of self-discovery—that were intricately and experientially intertwined.

In writing, as in speaking, we sometimes come *to know*.

☐   ☐

I began this chapter with the idea that fieldnotes are the *grammar* of ethnography, which is to say the grammar of the ethnographer's *story*.

I want to return to that theme now.

Ethnography is, for me and for others, a way of writing the personal experience of the researcher into meaning in ways that serve as analyses of cultures. As such, ethnographic inquiry and storytelling is analogous to being involved in a *mystery* (see Denzin, 1996; Goodall, 1989b, 1991). Put simply, when caught up in it or even long after, you don't know how things are going to turn out. Nor do you know exactly what you are supposed to do about it. What you *do* know is that you are being pulled into something larger than yourself, and the pull of it against your soul is undeniable.

The grammar of that pull is how you begin to write it down.

The rhetoric that comes afterward is all about editing, connecting, self-reflecting, and piecing together what Kenneth Burke (1989) described as "the thisness of that, and the thatness of this." In other words, as the ethnographic author, you live and write at a nexus of influences—all of them rhetorical—and your job is to investigate that mystery back through the grammars that constructed it. Your task is to find out *why* by figuring out *how*.

That is the "this" that you write.

Writing Experiments

Begin a professional journal by taking fieldnotes on conversations you observe (and participate in) for a week. Practice coding them using the schema presented in this chapter. Compare your writing of the field-notes and your coding with other members of your class. Can you see why different people record fieldnotes in differing ways? What do these sources of difference teach you about the relationship of fieldnotes to "realities"?

If you don't already have one, begin keeping a personal diary. Record your impressions of the day and its events and persons. Personalize the entries with your own observations, insights, questions, and musings. Compare the writing style that you use to develop your diary with the style you use to write your professional journal. What are the similarities? The differences? What does this experiment teach you about the boundaries of "the personal" and "the professional"?

When you compare your writing style in these documents to others in class (although you probably won't want to share the intimate details from your personal diary), what does this tell you about varieties of openness, disclosure, and evaluations of persons, places, and things? With these lessons in mind, think about the role of the ethnographer as a *translator* of culture. Are there issues that go beyond the accuracy of the "representation" involved in the intersections of the personal and the professional?

Continue your research project by taking your research questions into the field. Write fieldnotes and personal diary entries to reflect your experiences there. At the end of a suitable period of time in the field (which depends on how much time you have available as well as your instructor's requirements), move from the literature review into framing and analyzing the scenes, talk, behavior, and dress, and other factors, that further develop your study. Experiment with rhetorical techniques for combining what you have recorded in your fieldnotes with your reflections about these experiences in your personal diary. You may want to tell the story as discrete episodes. Or, you may want to state an overarching theme for the observations and then organize your "data" to support it. You may want to continue with a purely narrative format that embodies the field experiences and reflections in less traditional ways. For details about forms through which stories can be told, see Kenneth Burke, *The Philosophy of Literary Form* (1957).

For Further Reading

The readings listed below will help you extend and apply the material in this chapter. I've included a "group ethnography" (Communication Studies 298) as an example of new ethnographic writing derived from a unique, *team-based* collaboration on fieldnotes, personal narratives, and analyses of observations, conversations, and practices.

Agar, M. 1994. *Language shock: Understanding the culture of conversation.* New York: Morrow.

Bochner, A. 1994. Perspectives on inquiry II: Theories and stories. In *Handbook of interpersonal communication,* edited by M. Knapp and G. R. Miller. Newbury Park, CA: Sage.

Communication Studies 298, California State University, Sacramento, 1997. Fragments of self at the postmodern bar. *Journal of Contemporary Ethnography* 26: 251–292.

deCerteau, M. 1984. *The practice of everyday life.* Berkeley: University of California Press.

Sanjek, R. 1990. *Fieldnotes: The makings of anthropology.* Ithaca, NY: Cornell University Press.

Tedlock, B. 1991. From participant observation to the observation of participation: The emergence of narrative ethnography. *Journal of Anthropological Research* 47: 69–94.

4 | Voice, Reflexivity, and Character: The Construction of Identities in Texts

> *A writer may interrupt his narration not only with his voice but also with his disconcerting presence. Borges appears in his own work as a mythical intelligence. Nabokov graces his own novels as a figure—a figure at once majestic and ironic, the way Alfred Hitchcock appears in his own films. All of these interruptions and cameo appearances celebrate the art of it all: they remind us that we are as it were in a theater, and that the narrative itself is a conscious and willed artifice.*
>
> ANNIE DILLARD
> *Living by Fiction*

Who *are* you?

Who are you when you *write?*

Who are you *in your writing?* What are the differences, if any? If there are differences, are they ones that *matter?* To the work? To your audience? To those whom you've studied? To you?

This chapter is dedicated to the proposition that the persona you create to represent your ethnographic self, and the voice that carries it through the narrative, is the source of your *authorial* character, your rhetorical *ethos.* Akin to the function of self-disclosure in friendships, authorial character is derived from how your persona narrates the story, treats people in it, reflects on experiences in the field, and explains things. Your persona also creates perceptions of the kind of person *you* are. Personal history passages, choices of theoretical framing and explanatory metaphors, displays of human vulnerability and emotions, the questions you ask, the way in which you arrive at answers—all of these narrative and rhetorical devices reveal your motives, goals, habits of mind, and behavior. Together, a reader's evaluation of your narrator's "character"—her or his rhetorical *ethos* and narrative *personhood*—has a lot to do with the success of your writing.

And the construction of your narrator's character, on the page as in life, is all about *rhetorical and narrative choices.*

"CHARACTER" IS THE CLOSEST SUMMARY WORD we have for textually answering the question "Who are you?" *Character* attains meaning in at least two interrelated senses: as *writerly* and *readerly* constructions.

First, *character is a writerly construct.* This construct refers to the rhetorical figure of your self as it is prosaically carved into the fieldwork story. It is the public "I" and the "eyes," as well as the private "me"; it is the applied intelligence, the manifest consciousness, and the signature expression of how you "do" the prose performance of being-in-the-world. Character, in this sense, is the *person a writer reveals and constructs her- or himself to be* in the narrative. It is the narrative equivalent of a storyteller's steady eye contact, the rhetorical manifestation of facial expressions, body posture, and gestures. Character, like an accumulation of nonverbal clues accompanying a series of small self-disclosures, adds up. Interpreted within an overall narrative context, a writer's choice of words in questions, resources used to arrive at explanations, consideration of available actions, moments of self-examination and discovery, all work together in the story to construct the public expression of your personal identity.

How is it accomplished? How do you *write* who you are? How do you build confidence among readers about the choices that you have made in the field? Or in your personal and professional interpretations of events, episodes, contexts, and others?

Let's begin answering this question by examining character *as a narrative and rhetorical construction,* as a *writerly* construction. Viewed this way, character emerges from the prose intersection of three "positionings" (Chiseri-Strater and Sunstein, 1997, pp. 57–58) or ways of discovering—and revealing—the influences that shape who you are and what you think about, value, and are prone to believe and do. The three positionings are *fixed, subjective,* and *textual.*

Fixed positions refer to "personal facts that might influence how you see your data—your age, gender, class, nationality, race—factors that will not change during the course of the study but are often taken for

132

granted and unexamined in the research process" (p. 57). In this way, your character on the page is partially shaped by the same fixed characteristics of your life that you carry into the field and into everyday life. For example, does being female (or male) affect your perceptions and feelings about lived experiences? Of course it does, but not always predictably. The same can be said of other sources of "fixed positionings":[1] your age, class, race, and nationality. The hard part is analyzing yourself closely enough to be able to "read" these features of your makeup in a way that allows a critical and cultural perspective on them. Fortunately, the expanding literature on how differences in age, race, class, and gender influence communication teach us valuable lessons we can apply to such self-analyses (see, for example, Wood, 1996).

Subjective positions refer to "life history and personal experiences" that also affect our research (Chiseri-Strater and Sunstein, p. 58). For example, Ruth Behar created a gripping account of growing up as a Cuban-Jewish immigrant in *The Vulnerable Observer: Anthropology That Breaks Your Heart* (1996). In it, her personal need to deal emotionally and narratively with the death of her grandfather sheds professional light on why she believes ethnographic research ought to include a search for personal and subjective experience in fieldwork. Subjective positionings are usually derived from *deeply felt lived experiences* because they recall a life's self-defining moments, decisions, or turning points. Examples include instances of birth, death, divorce, separation, natural disasters, war, violence, love, or illness. But subjective positions need not be derived solely from dramatic circumstances. As an only child born in West Virginia but reared in Europe prior to coming to "my native home" in the United States, I constantly find new ways in which my nature was nurtured. For example, subjective experiences have shaped my habits (and assumptions about) dress and deportment, certain food preferences, beliefs about family size, insensitivity to humor directed at Appalachians, my appropriation of a British dialect to make points about culture, and so forth. Part of my quest as a self-reflexive ethnographer is to take account of my subjective positioning based on these, as well as other, influences.

---

1 The term "fixed" is problematic for me, as it was in the original construction for Chiseri-Strater and Sunstein. Age obviously changes, and for some of us, so does social class. Views on the meaning and relevance of race and ethnic or national origin may be altered as a society grows and matures. Nevertheless, these "fixed positions" tend to define for us a way of seeing and being in the world, and as such form the experiential and rhetorical foundations we carry into our work.

Textual positions refer to "language choices you make to represent what you see" (Chiseri-Strater and Sunstein, 1997, p. 58). Language choices—by which I mean the selection and arrangement of nouns, verbs, adjectives, adverbs, and so forth to represent experiences and evoke responses in readers—are *rhetorical* issues that reveal character in the text. For example, the choice of using first person, second person, or third person pronouns and perspectives reveals how you choose to represent your closeness to or distance from others in the field. Uses (or not) of humor, sarcasm, irony, and inventive analogies/metaphors provide clues to the way in which you "see" the world, as well as how you act in it. Word choices constitute the tones and shadings of "voice" used to create impressions of your fieldwork and investigative methods. The amount and level of emotional intensity is rhetorically within the province of personal narrative disclosures as well as the selective deployment of adverbs and adjectives throughout the story. All of these narrative and rhetorical devices are "telltale signs" of character acquired through lived experiences, and they help position "who you are" in relation to contexts and others.

So far in our account, it would seem that a writer has control over evaluations of her or his character, right? Select the right words, organize them in some "proper sequence," disclose something personal designed to elicit identification and sympathy along the way, and *ta-dah!*—you have the formula for a reliable, likable ethnographic character. But of course it isn't this simple.

The reason that character is not simply a matter of vocabulary choices and rhetorical flourish is that *texts don't belong to writers,* they belong to *readers.* The meanings associated with the telling of a story are located in the lives of those who read or hear them. By comparison, this is akin to saying that no matter what a speaker intends, the listener is free to interpret a message according to his or her own preferences. Ideally, we think of the "work" of a story, the "work" of conversation or dialogue, as a *collaboration,* or joint activity. The meanings of texts are arrived at through ongoing interpretations, conversations, negotiations, co-constructions. The writer does whatever she or he can to tell the story; the reader brings to the reading all of the available means of interpreting it. They meet on the page, warm up gradually, and do a workout together. This collaborative text-production principle— because it guides all reading—also guides our understanding of how interpretations of character are *co*-created.

How does a reader interpret character? What is the "work" of such interpretations? Viewed from the perspective afforded by these questions, *character is a readerly evaluation* of the personal and professional worth of that writerly identity *within the relationship* we have established on the page. Such character assessments are intensely *personal* and deeply *processual.* In part, they have to do with whether a reader *personally likes and approves* of the narrator as the persona as it is understood and interpreted on the page. Similar to the concept of "fidelity" in narrative theory (Fisher, 1987), wherein the events of a story are measured against the reader's experiences to see if they "ring true," in our case a reader also examines a story to see whether the *character of the narrator* rings true. The relevant questions include: Is this person believable? Is the person telling this story someone I would trust? Is it someone I would like to spend time with? Is it someone with whom I can emotionally and intellectually identify?

Additionally, evaluations of character are derived from the story's *processual* development. By "processual," I mean the paragraph-by-paragraph displays of professional identity and judgment as they are measured against *what the reader ultimately learns* from the reading experience. Like the concept of "coherence" in narrative theory (Fisher, 1987), wherein a reader examines a text to see whether the story "hangs together" as a story, a reader also evaluates whether the thoughts, passions, observations, and actions of the narrator in the story lead up to warranted and interesting conclusions. Thus, part of the assessment of character is derived from an old-fashioned equity principle: Are this narrator and this story worth my reading time and effort? As you can see, the assessment of character in prose is, in some ways, very much like the assessment of character in the flesh.

In summary, character is, from a *reader's* point of view, about how similarly life-positioned, experienced, trustworthy, intellectually and emotionally evolved the persona, or narrator, is. Character is how a reader constructs the personal, moral, professional, and ethical dimensions of your narrator's active presence and actions in the world. These dimensions include your character's relationship to—and with—the reader, the credibility of the story you are telling, and your personal and professional contributions to the reader's learning.

Considered textually, revealing and constructing a narrator's persona is a major writing challenge. It is the word-by-word, sentence-by-sentence joining of complex experiential, narrative, and rhetorical activities. Your character on the page acts as a rhetorical figure "responsible" for the narrative and "accountable" to readers for what the narrative says and does to them. Delicately—tenuously—balanced between personal and professional dimensions, character is the warrant that systematically links all the evidence given to all the claims that are made (Clifford, 1983). Dialogically and dialectically, these engagements between writer and reader drive the work of a reading.

FOR ALL OF THESE REASONS, I maintain that learning to write "who you are"—the character of your narrator or persona—is the *soul* of good writing. Good *ethnographic* writing.

By "soul" I mean two things. First, along with James Hillman (1991), I mean how language creates deep, intimate relationships between and among people:

> [Soul is] a perspective rather than a substance, a viewpoint toward things rather than a thing itself. This perspective is reflective; it mediates events and makes differences between ourselves and everything that happens....
> We need to recall the angel aspect of the word, recognizing words as independent carriers of soul between people (1991; p. xx).

But I also use the term "soul" to mean a way of opening up a deeply personal space in your life from which to create understanding. As the novelist Will Blythe (1998) writes:

> By soul, I mean a certain depth, an inwardness, a watchfulness. Detachment, solitude, stillness.
>
> You might find it in a man sitting in his backyard on a summer night, clinking the ice in his gin and tonic. Staring into the window of his own house, watching his wife watch the Atlanta Braves on the Superstation. He's trying to remember exactly what passionate love feels like, the difference between eternity and boredom.
>
> You might encounter it in a securities lawyer. She is supposed to be working this weekend but instead stares moonily out the window at the Woolworth Building, thinking to herself how peculiar it is to be alive at four o'clock on a Saturday afternoon. Just strange. She can't quite get over the oddness of it all.
>
> You'd also be likely to discover soul in someone quietly reading. I can almost guarantee it. And indeed, the corollary to the question of why one writes is the question of why one reads (p. xxi).

In both of these usages, the "soul" of good writing is *the deployment of a writer's "coming to know" perspective* on selves, contexts, and others (Goodall, 1996). It is the substance—both argumentative and poetic— of *understanding* "lived experience" (Jackson, 1989). It is the vital stuff out of which we create, constitute, and live *meaningfully* within the stories of our lives (Bochner, 1994; Ellis, 1993).

❑   ❑

Among ethnographers, the theoretical concepts associated with persona are "reflexivity" or "voice" or both (see Hertz, 1997, for an overview).

Properly speaking, reflexivity refers *to the process of personally and academically reflecting on lived experiences in ways that reveal the deep connections between the writer and her or his subject* (see Behar, 1993, 1996; Ellis and Flaherty, 1993; Goodall, 1989a, 1991; Krieger, 1991; Mykhalovskiy, 1997; Richardson, 1997; Rosaldo, 1989; Rose, 1990). To be "reflexive" means to turn back on our self the lens through which we are interpreting the world. It "implies a shift in our understanding of data and its collection—something that is accomplished through detachment, internal dialogue, and constant (and intensive) scrutiny of 'what I know' and 'how I know it'" (Hertz, 1997; pp. vii–viii).

Below is one example of how this kind of writing may be done—in this case, drawn from fieldnotes I wrote when it occurred to me that I needed to take a much fuller account of my feelings and my thoughts about citizens who inhabit the rural regions of northern Alabama:

> We are in rural Dixie when we are in the regions of this North Birmingham, which is not really North Birmingham but is called that just the same. We are in the rural Dixie of my imagination, or at least the parts of my imagination that have been informed by a particular, privileged reading of history, novels, hearsay, and films. This is a mythical, substandard land where Confederate flags still blazon the rear windows of dangerous pickups, pickups that proudly display gun racks upon which are mounted real guns, driven by thin, angry women who say to hell with the Surgeon General and who bear military children for larger, less articulate, unkempt and hated men who say to hell with everything except you and me, and I ain't so sure about you. In my imagination those guns of theirs are always loaded, those women are always sucking the death out of red-box hard-pack Marlboros, and those men are always laid up half-drunk or just plain mean. Every one of them is in real and constant need. They live in houses

that need paint, that need furniture, they have children who need clothing and education, wives who need consciousness and better hygiene, husbands who need understanding and a more liberal God.

There is just no way that any of these needs will be met, so in my mind they just hate everybody and everything that cannot be generically reduced to their own rotten sameness or is not genetically related to them. In my mind all they do is drink, fuck, shoot, and hate, and in my mind they hate, most of all, just me. They hate me for what I am, and for what I'm not. I can feel their hatred in convenience stores, liquor stores, in the heat of their stares that dare me to cross over some unknown line in various American parking lots. I might as well be black, this might as well be fifty years ago.

But this is all in my mind.

The truth is much harder, and far more complex. My sense of hatred is partly projection derived from the nervous edges of fear, and partly from the guilt I feel, as Kenneth Burke puts it, from being "up" when others are "down." I am the one interpreting those houses, those women and children, and those stares. I am the one attributing significance and meaning to the unknown within of the Other, seeing myself as someone meaningful in the stuff of their lives, someone worthy of the deep hate that, in truth, is part of what I hope for. As if their hatred justifies me, my choices, my place in the commonweal, my mind. And in this privileged mental territory of my own cultural construction I grant no room for individuality, much less bricolage, to the Other; I fear the mere possibility of human connections between me and them based on the joke of a life that rushes us all too quickly to nowhere, regardless of our birth, looks, language, or money, and that requires us all to pay taxes along the way, taxes that are taken from wages that are never enough, wages that take time away from a life that is never enough, when what waits for us is the great trapdoor at the bottom end of the twentieth century that should mark our common tombstones thusly:

This citizen was born, reared, and educated,

Got a job in order to consume,

Consumed like hell,

Was famous, locally, for it,

Realized that no matter how much was consumed it was

Never Enough,

Then retired,

Then died.

These are my thoughts as I pull off the main highway onto a two-lane blacktop that degenerates into a poor dirt road riddled with potholes, both real and imagined. We pass an old Ford that crashed into an oak tree and burned long before I was born and whose charred skeleton lives still by the side of the road. The air is dense and still. An old blue-tick hound ignores our passing, or maybe just ignores me, or maybe is just blind (Goodall, 1991, pp. 179–180).

The above passage reflected my thoughts and feelings about a class of Southerners colloquially referred to as "rednecks." By turning back on myself the critical lens I normally use to describe and evaluate others, I take into account the role that my imagination, my reading of history, and many other factors play in framing my experiences with this stereotype of lower-class Southern others.

In so doing, I expose some fairly ugly truths—to myself, and to my readers—about my character. My biases. My prejudices. My fears. My fixed positionings. But I also try to come to grips with them. By the end of this passage, I have found a simple, yet powerful human connection. Within a consumer-capitalist culture we are all, in our own ways, burdened by the heavy imprint on evaluations of character and worth based on abilities to produce and consume according to middle-class standards. As long as I rely on such stereotyped hierarchical distinctions, I am bound to endure such distinctions and resultant anxieties and unhappiness. Ironically, one cultural byproduct of our material wariness is that each one of us is convinced we have some imaginary upper hand, when in fact we are bound by the same system of class-based social and economic constraints.

I'd like to say that these insights have significantly altered my perceptions of members of this social and economic class. Probably the truth is that writing through my perceptions has made me more aware of them, and at least a bit more sensitive to how I use them in my work. But I still find myself wary in convenience stores. No need to *romanticize* all members of this class of others because of one true moment of self-examination, right?

Which is why I am not always such a hero.

And my soul is not so pure.

"VOICE" IS *the personal rhetorical imprint of who we are in and on what we write* (Ellis and Bochner, 1996; Charmaz and Mitchell, 1996; Ellis,

Kiesinger, and Tillmann-Healy, 1997; Goodall, 1994b). Singularly and multiply, voice is the *sound* of a character *speaking*.

Voice sums the way in which prose communicates a writer's vocal range and tone, her or his sensitivities to the nuances and passions of spoken language, and the essential *phenomenological essence* of what is being said. Voice is the sound of the ethnographic world being *called* into being. It is a pattern of heard recognitions, and of differences, that convey to readers the self that is textually constructing others and contexts.

Reflexivity and voice produce the rhetorical character of the self as revealed in and through the ongoing conversation with the world. Done well, the manifestation of reflexivity and construction of voice transform a reading of the narrative from a routine, boring monologue to inspired dialogue.

Done *well*, that is.

HERE'S SOMETHING IMPORTANT, and annoying, to think about: Voice, like consciousness, is derivative.

At its most fundamental level, voice is derived from the confluence of the many voices and personal stories that have constructed you. Consciousness follows a parallel pattern, as the literary theorist Mikhail Bakhtin expresses it:

> Everything that pertains to me enters my consciousness, beginning with my name, from the external world through the mouths of others (my mother, and so forth), with their intonation, in their emotional and value-assigning tonality. I realize myself initially through others: from them I receive words, forms, and tonalities for the formation of my initial idea of myself.... Just as the body is formed initially in the mother's womb, a person's consciousness awakens wrapped in another's consciousness (1984, p. xx).

Additionally, voice is derived from the many writers who have taught us how to read and identify with their characters, actions, and stories. For example, I can examine my own work and find easy evidence of borrowing from other writer's stories, from their voices, and indeed from their consciousness. In this way, all my writing is coproduced, and multivocal. Many people and many influences are more or less represented in this text. Stylistically, I make use of lessons I've learned from Barry Hannah about paragraphing, about separating sections with graphic symbols, and about phrasing—particularly phrasing that strives to be somehow poetic and yet rude. From Walker Percy, I've acquired a deep appreciation for the strangeness of everyday life, when viewed from the center of its own seeming normalcy. From my father, I've learned how to ask questions for which there are no answers, and how to induce readers to live, as I have, with the irresolvability of them. Each chapter in this book begins with a quotation I've lifted from someone else, and all of them represent sentences that speak directly to me as well as, I hope, to you. And on and on and on…the known influences are enough to make even an immodest writer humble in his or her own derivativeness. And that doesn't even get close to the influence that *you*, the reader, have on what is happening between us, on this page, *now*.

For these reasons—and here is the annoying part—there are no truly original voices, any more than there are any new stories. But we hear the term "original" so often—what on earth can the expression "original voice" actually refer to?

When someone says "hers is an *original* voice," what they usually mean is "here is someone who is writing in—filling in—a vital gap between all that I have read and lived through, and the result is something that speaks to me in a way that no other voice ever has." In many ways, this sentiment is very much like meeting someone you are suddenly and strongly attracted to, in whose shared conversation you find new meaning, in whose voice, in whose questions, you find a path to answers you are searching for. The voice of the other in this relationship is "original" because it speaks to your heart, because you haven't heard it before, and because you closely identify with it.

Originality in writing, as in all relationships, is never a solo act. It requires a reader's—a friend's, a lover's, a teacher's—participation, creativity, and judgment. Many beginning writers believe that *the only* good writing is "original," and as a result, they end up aiming for the wrong thing. In a way, this is like what Aristotle meant when he said that those who aim for happiness never attain it.

THINK OF THE ROLE of self-reflexivity in voice this way: Reflexivity begins with asking yourself the same questions that guide your analysis and interpretation of others. These questions should be thought of as navigation instruments, because asking them puts you on a particular language highway wherein the route itself is defined by words that otherwise might not have ever been spoken. Where some symbols cannot be read as anything other than signs. And the signs point you in the direction of associations, of meanings, of referents, you wouldn't otherwise have had. Your struggles to articulate those connections and their meanings separate your voice from all others, because the story you have to tell is made out of it. Too, there are those vital silences between words, the drawn ellipses between sentences. The stops that define the starts.

The ineffable "IT" between people and cultures.

The mystery that "IT" *is,* that silence that exists between you and the call of all of IT, and that without your particular words would remain unknown and unspoken.

You want to know what "voice" is?

Voice is how *you* call IT into being.

FINE THING! I've now written *myself* into a prose conundrum. My voice has gotten me into trouble. *Again.*

I've claimed that voice is a matter of writing choices, and that these choices are rhetorically situated. I've said that character, on the page, is technically constructed. And I've said and claimed these things within the context of a book that purports to be a guide to writing ethnography.

Hence, I've written myself into a place wherein providing good advice about character construction appears to be the only way out. And yet, to provide *you* with the rhetorical and narrative devices for constructing *your*self seems at best ironic, if not deeply weird.

Yikes!

Who are you?

How would I know?

Here's what we'll do….

❏   ❏

Let's try some preliminary writing experiments.

1 *Who are you?* Construct a narrative account of who you are. Begin with the oldest stories about yourself that your family tells about you (for an example, see Goodall, 1991, Chapter 5). You grew up within the webs of these spun tales, so within each one of them lie clues to your personal and relational identities. Add in remembered images, episodes, and conversations that are part of

those stories. These are symbolic moments, perhaps moments of personal transformation or change, turning points in your life story, or simply "flashes" that you can't quite get back to, or hear into, clearly. Write all of them that you remember.

Then ask: how do these tales, remembered events, and persons, *shape the words in and through which I can express who I know myself to be?* And how have they taught me to see and respond to others? How do these personally and culturally significant symbols contribute to the world as I experience and write about it? How did they rhetorically create and constitute the internal realities of "me"?

2 *Where do you come from?* Ethnographers are dedicated writers of *contexts.*[2] But we approach our interpretations of contexts from "fixed positionings," which means we see and respond to our environments from those "fixed places" where we perceptually "come from"—our age, gender, race, nationality, and on and on. So it is that your perceptual and experiential sense of *place* matters to what you write about. To get in touch with how these influences might work in your life, ask yourself how you "naturally" talk about, discuss with others, or construct tales of landscape, of architecture, of nature, of urban locations, of the suburbs. What kinds of places do you regularly, perhaps longingly, imagine? What makes these tales and imaginings seem "natural" to you? What are the narrative details you "effortlessly" produce? How have they been shaped and informed by where you grew up and were educated? How do they encourage you to mark cultural terrain, boundaries, differences? What have they taught you to know? What have these lessons taught you to ignore, discount, or fear?

Now consider your life as a *historical* artifact. What are the historical events that hold special meanings for you? Which ones have shaped your worldview? What does this examination teach you about your perspective on others? On other's historical consciousness?

This same pattern of questioning should also be applied to the influences in your perceptual and conceptual framework constructed from gender, class, sexual orientation, and race. Yes, these

---

2 A "context" for social research must be considered as a verb rather than a noun. Historically this was the case until the rise of the Industrial Revolution and the concurrent influence of a scientific need to reify categories; for details, see my "A Theatre of Motives and the Meaningful Orders of Persons and Things," in *Communication Yearbook* 13 (1990).

are difficult questions and you may not be pleased with some of the responses you have. But, in an ethnographic interpretation of one of Henry David Thoreau's best lines, the unexamined life is not worth textually constructing.

Finally, write out responses to all of the above-listed issues in your personal journal.

3 *What makes you tick?* Or put differently, what is it that you live for? Whom do you live for? How do your fantasies, your imaginings, your longings, shape what you render (and respond to) as significant or meaningful in experience? In the tales of others? In your own prose?

Again, write out the responses to these questions in your personal journal.

All self-knowing, all formations of character, begin with these three questions. I also believe the responses you make to them form the rhetorical and narrative bases for constructing your ethnographic voice.

These three questions are, of course, only symbolic beginnings. There are many other questions, and answers, that will shape your character and voice. Writing them out narratively provides you with a self-reflexive text of your life experiences. Kept in a diary or personal journal, this is a rich resource for you to return to, time and again, to trace the relevant symbolic themes and motifs that are revealed, hidden, suggested, to be teased out of, or openly displayed in these narratives. Every time you do so, you will be uncovering the connections between who you are as a character in your own life, and what you have learned to experience as meaningful in the field. As an ethnographer, these themes, these moments, should alert you to strengths and potential weaknesses in your analyses of self, others, and contexts.

OUR NEXT EXERCISE asks you to consider your "self" *as* an "other."

The American novelist Norman Mailer, when asked to define himself as others see him, replied: "I am a man of below average height and above average weight with an enormous dragon's tail" (*Esquire*, December 1997, p. 122). In that sentence, he captures the symbolic nature of how others—particularly those in the literary community—perceive him. Or perhaps, how he *wants* them to perceive him.

The sentence also carries with it a symbolic construction of his "dragon's tail" self that doesn't require any assistance from me to help you attribute meaning to. What his otherness is made of—captured symbolically within and through those two words "dragon's tail"—is a sense of himself, his character, his position in the world, as an *individual.*

Try this writing experiment:

■ Construct a narrative account of yourself as an "other." Try to write *either* from a particular other person's point of view (for instance, your mother or father, a sibling, a friend, a boss or coworker, and so on) or from a generalized other's perspective (for instance, the "omniscient narrator" who sees all and tells all).

In your personal journal, record your feelings and thoughts about this exercise.

A THIRD EXERCISE ASKS YOU to make yourself—your personhood—the *subject of someone else's biographical/ethnographic project* (see Maines, 1997). Try this:

■ Become the subject of someone else's biography: In a classroom or seminar setting you can accomplish this task by dividing the participants into pairs and asking each member to do the same sort of research on her or his partner as she or he would do to complete an ethnographic project. For example:

1 Interview the subject.

2 Interview other people—friends, roommates, family members—who are familiar with the subject.

3 Time permitting, place an ad in the hometown newspaper of the subject asking for any information from persons who knew her or him. For a model of how to write such an ad, see any edition of the *New York Times Book Review,* the classified section.

4 Read the subject's written work, including papers for other classes, poems, letters (where feasible), and so forth.

5 Observe the subject going about the routine business—the everyday practices—of his or her daily life.

6 Analyze conversational episodes in which the subject is a participant.

7 Try to account for the motives and actions of the subject by viewing them as a member of an ethnic, racial, gendered, social, or political group or class.

8 Construct a biographical sketch of your subject and share it with him or her.

What do you think, now that you have been thoroughly (or not so thoroughly) researched, your motives and actions analyzed, your life read and interpreted through the rhetorical lens of various theoretical constructions? Did your biographers get it right? What is missing? How could what is missing be accounted for? What have you learned about the use of ethnographic and biographical data to construct the meanings, motives, and measure of a human life?

Then ask: What should this experience teach me about doing research on other's lives? In what ways can I improve how I write my fieldnotes and perform my analyses? How did it feel to be "vulnerable" to another's intrusions into my routines, subjected to her or his interpretive skills? How can I use that vulnerability to develop empathy with my subjects' lives? What have I learned about constructing the meaning of circumstances, the motives behind perceived behaviors and actions? About the writing choices involved in representing lived experiences? Finally: What does this account teach me about the *character* that others see "me" as, and respond to?

The point of this exercise is to see how it feels to have your own life examined and interpreted in some of the same ways you plan to examine and interpret the lives of others. Probably, this will teach you to have greater respect for the rhetorical complexities involved in writing lives, interpreting causes from behaviors, reconstructing a past, and making sense out of the present.

THESE EXERCISES SHOULD HELP YOU to understand more about the influences on who you are, as well as to appreciate the rhetorical challenges of constructing the persona that will narrate your ethnographic writing. What they *won't* do is answer specific questions about the narrative application of rhetorical character to a particular piece of work.

This is because some aspects of voice are *acquired through the writing process*. By analogy, in every sport it is important to practice, but no amount of practice can prepare you for the unexpected exigencies and emergent, evolving, interdependent nature of what needs to be done during the game. So, too, is it with writing. Your character, your voice, *will* emerge in the context of your work. It will emerge in response to *textual* exigencies.

Allow me another personal example. In an essay for *Communication Theory*, I composed an ethnographic account of my search for academic community (Goodall, 1999). In one section, I discuss a time when I was teaching at the University of Alabama in Huntsville (UAH) and I offered this observation:

> For awhile, we had an interesting group of intellectually dedicated, fun, and hard-working people who formed a diverse, but supportive, community. We talked regularly about ideas, went out for lunch together, got together on weekends, and had majors who went off to fine graduate schools. Collectively and individually, our star rose.
> We had community. Locally (p. 19).

One of the better things that can happen to an interpretive ethnographer is to place your work in the hands of a good editor. The guest editor for the special issue this piece appears in, Patricia Geist, is such an editor. She read this passage, worried over it, and suggested to me that I needed to make it *more* self-reflexive. She asked me to think about the implications of attributing to a group of diverse people the same evaluation—in this case, the same sense of "community"—that I had. Immediately, I saw the importance of her comments and revised the section by adding to the above sentences the following passage:

> Or at least *I* thought we did. These days, looking back on those few years, I wonder. Did we *really* have "it"? Was there an "it" to "have"? Or is this crude representation more a narcissistic reflection of my own imagination, or even worse: a coded masculine interpretation that mistakenly equates ownership (and therefore, control) with what is probably more pluralistically understood as shared, but disparately interpreted, gendered experiences? I mean, really, would the women and men of the Department of Communication Arts at UAH all view what we did have in similar ways? I doubt it. So what is it that we did, that we performed, everyday, which made whatever it was we did have *feel* like "community" to me? What *were* the significant conversations, the rituals, the turning points? These days I can ask such questions and live comfortably with them, but then I needed, and could only be comforted by, answers (p. 376).

I include the above passage to illustrate two points. First, self-reflexivity is not necessarily about using self-examinations to come to final judgments about persons, places, or things. Or, even about yourself. Sometimes, it is reflexive enough just to raise relevant questions. Why? Because the questions you raise reveal how you think, what you are considering relevant to the task of interpreting an event, and what values and attitudes you carry into that activity. *The questions you ask reveal character, too.*

My second point is that self-reflexive writing can improve the quality of an ethnographic passage. If you compare my initial paragraph with the edited self-reflexive one, I think you will agree that the second, revised effort is superior. Why? First, because the prose additions are *more fairly representative* of the diversity and complexity involved in the situation I describe. Second, because the additional questions and concerns *reveal the thoughts I have* about how I construct community. Therefore, the self-reflexive additions add to the information level and accuracy of the passage.

As you can see from this example, self-reflexive does *not* mean self-indulgent. It does mean to examine your prose for those places in your writing that may be improved by turning the interpretive voice you use to examine others and contexts back on your self. In so doing, this process of self-inquiry should unmask a deeper level of understanding.

◻   ◻

So far, our discussion of self-reflexive writing has been about coming to terms with your positioning, and adding information value to an interpretive piece. But there is another use for self-reflexive writing, a use that also bears directly on the narrative construction of voice and character. Specifically, there are times when *you should account for your own complicity* in the evolution of events and the construction of meaning in, or about, an experience in the field.

In the same essay where I was asked to be more self-reflexive— "Casing the Academy for Community" (Goodall, 1999)—I also discuss my time on the faculty at the University of Utah. Although there was much to enjoy and learn from in the Department of Communication at Utah, I also found a pattern of silence reinforced by a culture of constant work that impeded "community." Yet, like an ethnographer in the field, I was there not as a neutral observer but as an *active* member of the faculty. I was involved *directly* in the situations I critiqued. I both *contributed to* and *was complicit in* the aspects of community I found lacking there.

As an ethnographer, I wanted—and needed—to discuss my role in the department. I was morally obligated to. As a writer, however, constructing sentences that provide insight into one's own shortcomings are never easy ones to compose. Additionally, I could envision this section deteriorating into the ethnographic equivalent of "whining and complaining." I didn't want that. So, my prose challenge was to reveal my role in the failure to achieve the kind of community I thought could have been achieved there, but without making the role I played sound overly sentimental, critical, or condescending. Here is what I wrote:

> Throughout all of this time, there was an overarching social friendliness and an underlying culture of hard work to compensate for the loss of community....
>
> In retrospect, I've learned that anytime I feel I am in a place that feels like it lacks community, I should learn to look at *myself*, my contributions to the problem. The same is true when I perceive that there is something *lacking in* a community. Like a hologram, a community is where the parts stand for the whole and the whole can be read within the parts. Thus, while it was easy for me to find the sources of unspoken tension in the department, the necessary truth is also that I wasn't doing much speaking *myself*. I was mostly content to let the discontent ride, *not* to name what I perceived as the cause.
>
> These days I look back on that rude fact and wonder why I *speak* out, why I *didn't* try to repair the hole I perceived with some rhetorical needle and team-based thread. One truth is, I think, that my focus was not really on the community, but, instead, on my own writing. I was self-absorbed, lost in scholarly space, and selfish about what I chose to spend my time doing and saying.... I, too, had another book to write, a panel to prepare for, students to teach, papers to grade, a committee to serve on. I had to earn tenure again. I was more into "me" than I was into "community" (pp. 384–385).

You can decide how closely I achieved my writing goals. But I think I was able to reveal my complicity in a situation without making that self-examination the point of the passage. I was *part* of the department, and therefore implicated in the problem I describe. But, I was only one part of it, and not the main part. The drama was much larger than my role. Therefore, this self-reflexive passage was necessary to the telling of the story, but the writing needed not to deflect too much attention away from the larger theme.

EARLIER I USED A SPORTS ANALOGY to indicate how no amount of writing practice can prepare you for unexpected exigencies in the field. It's a good analogy for making that point, but it also has limitations when applied to writing. In any sport, you only get one shot at a particular play or episode, but in writing you have a second chance.

A third chance.

Sometimes, even a fourth or fifth chance.

This is to say that whatever your character is revealed to be in the context of your initial draft, it will require *editing*.

Which is the subject of our next chapter.

(More) Writing Experiments

1. Continue your fieldwork and writing project by examining where, in your account, you should insert material about *who you* are and *what you value*. Ask: When and where it is appropriate for me to tell about myself to a scholarly audience? And what, exactly, should your telling *help the story accomplish?*

2. Locate three examples of writing that have distinct "voices." What are the *rhetorical devices* used by the author that evoke this readerly evaluation? Does your evaluation emerge from clearly identifiable "fixed positionings"? Particular uses of language? From "original" metaphors? From humor or double entendre? From the layout of the work on the page? From stylized forms of expression? From unusual characterizations of self, others, or contexts? Are there patterns of distinctive language usage—identifying one sort of sensory experience with another (for example, seeing events as colors, or sounds, or smells, and so on). What is it, rhetorically, that constructs this voice as *distinctive?*

Select one of the passages you have identified. Now try to write two or three pages in imitation of it. What choices are you consciously making? Can you begin to "feel" how this voice is constructed?

3. One of the best ways to develop self-reflexive skills is to isolate passages in your work where you attribute motives, feelings, or understandings to others. Select a passage from your fieldnotes where you do this. What questions should you raise about this passage? Is it possible that you are attributing meaning to others that is more realistically a reflection of your own perspective, biases, preferences, or positioning? How would you add to your work a self-reflexive section?

For Further Reading

The readings listed below should help you extend and apply the material in this chapter. I've included a series of new ethnographies—Behar, Benson, Corey, Eisenberg, Ellis, Goodall, Jones, and Trujillo—that display unique voices and styles of reflexivity. I've also included two works by Bronislaw Malinowski; compare the writing in his personal diary with the book that emerged from those notes. What might be said about his use of voice in the book to *mask* aspects of his character in the field?

Behar, R. 1993. *Translated woman: Crossing the border with Esperanza.* Boston: Beacon.

Benson, T. 1980. Another shootout in cowtown. *The Quarterly Journal of Speech* 67: 347–406.

Corey, F., and Nakayama, T. K., 1997. Sextext. *Text and Performance Quarterly* 17: 58–68.

Eisenberg, E. 1998. From anxiety to possibility: Poems 1987–1997. In *Fiction and social research,* edited by A. Banks and S. P. Banks. Walnut Creek, CA: AltaMira Press.

Ellis, C. 1995. *Final Negotiations.* Philadelphia: Temple University Press.

Geertz, C. 1995. *After the fact.* Cambridge: Harvard University Press.

Goodall, H. L. 1999. Casing the academy for community. *Communication Theory,* 9:365–395.

Hertz, R. 1997. *Reflexivity and voice.* Thousand Oaks, CA: Sage.

Jones, S. H. 1998. *Kaleidescope notes.* Walnut Creek, CA: AltaMira Press.

Malinowski, B. 1922. *Argonauts of the Western Pacific.* New York: Dutton.
_____. 1989. *A diary in the strict sense of the term,* 2d ed. London: Athlone.

Trujillo, N., 1998. In search of Naunny's grave. *Text and Performance Quarterly* 18: 344–368.

5 | *The Ethics of Writing Ethnography*

When you write vulnerably, others respond vulnerably.
A different set of problems and predicaments arise
which would never surface in response to more
detached writing. What is the writer's responsibility to
those who are moved by her writing? Devereaux spoke
in great detail of the observer's countertransference, but
what about the reader's? Should I feel good that my
writing makes a reader break out crying? Does an
emotional response lessen or enhance intellectual
understanding?

RUTH BEHAR
The Vulnerable Observer

The application of ethical principles to fieldwork has been an inconsistent historical concern, which is why it has served as a more recent source of professional critique (see Hastrup, 1995; Said, 1983; Rosaldo, 1989; Marcus and Fischer, 1986). For example, consider the following list. The *italicized* words, all of which bring a more focused ethical conscience to fieldwork practices, arrived with the *post*modern era. Please take a few minutes to reflect on how these words problematize and complicate otherwise "ordinary" issues pertaining to fieldwork.

- How do you gain *appropriate* entry to a site?
- How do you *legitimately* gain the confidence and trust of informants?
- How do you conceal or *reveal* your identity and ethnographic purpose?

153

■ How do you deal with the everyday questions of *your own position in relation to your subjects' lives?* Your own *interference* in and with their lives?

■ How *should you handle intimacy* with informants? What kinds of relationships and levels of interpersonal contact *are appropriate?*

■ Under what conditions, if any, *should you acquire, use, or appropriate their cultural knowledge for your own career advancement?*

■ *How should ethnographers represent* what may, to an academic audience, appear to be the "inarticulateness" of cultural others *as having been fully articulate within their local context?*

■ What *should you* or *should you not do* with information about illegal, unethical, or immoral activities?

■ How do you prepare yourself *and your subjects* when you plan to leave the fieldwork site?

■ *What should you be expected to give back to those whom you lived with and studied?*

These issues point to a need for a clear, consistent, and focused *ethical stance* to inform fieldwork practice.

But what about *writing?* What are appropriate ethical standards for evaluating new ethnographic narratives?

THE ETHICS OF WRITING AND EDITING fieldwork has been less fully explored.

In part, this has resulted from the modern ethnographer's "legitimate license" as a social scientist to record impressions of those less privileged by the educational and social hierarchy. Furthermore, that license was accompanied by deeper cultural presumptions of "immaculate perception" (Van Maanen, 1988), or the idea that whatever a properly trained ethnographer experienced could be rather directly transferred to a text. Additionally, the nature of scientific inquiry guaranteed publication only to those examples of work judged by one's peers to be "genuine contributions to knowledge." Ethnographers were presumed to have told the truth in their writing because their task was to record *facts* as they *actually happened,* and analyze them within the known theoretical and methodological boundaries of professional excellence.

The primary bottom line for the ethics of modern ethnographic writing can be summed up as an adaptation of the hoary courtroom oath: "tell the truth, the whole truth, and nothing but the truth."[1]

ANOTHER MODERNIST ETHICAL BOTTOM line was always there to be dealt with. It was a secondary concern, because writing was widely considered a secondary ethnographic activity, something that was done after the harder fieldwork—the *real* research project—was completed. This ethical principle concerned the *mechanics* of scholarly *referencing,* or the textual acknowledgment of other writers' influences on the conduct and interpretation of fieldwork.

Two issues concerning referencing were, and still are, of considerable importance.

First to raise its ugly head is the issue of *plagiarism.* Plagiarism is *the unscholarly appropriation of another's words or concepts without proper attribution.* For example, plagiarism includes the *absence of quotation marks* around passages "borrowed" from other texts, and the failure to acknowledge previous work by someone else while "lifting" concepts from it to inform your study. Plagiarism operates rhetorically and pragmatically as a strong and no-nonsense authority figure in discussions of the ethics of writing.

For good reason. The basic premise of scholarly writing is that your words are your textual identity and signature, as well as your scholarly *property;* therefore, your writing *belongs* to you.[2] If someone else attempts to take credit for what you have written, it is very much like stealing someone's prized possession while making off with his or her identity.

Academic culture's sanctions against plagiarism are professionally akin to being summarily sentenced to death. The offender is usually expected (or asked, or forced) to formally apologize for the crime, leave

---

1 This seemingly sound principle of ethnographic conduct has been dramatically challenged recently with the publication of "fictional" ethnographies and cultural studies (see, for example, Banks and Banks, 1998; Corey and Nakayama, 1997). However, the creation of "composite characters" or the renaming of real people— and repositioning their locations and lives—to mask their identities has always been regarded as an acceptable, if ethically arguable, practice. Furthermore, how should we deal with "flights of the imagination" that often characterize writing about fieldwork? They may have "really happened," but are the products of imagination real? Clearly, where the line is drawn between "what really happened" and what is written about is both theoretically and pragmatically contestable.

2 Or to your publisher.

the institution that employs him or her, make an exit from the discipline, and, in some cases, abandon academic life, *forever*. As a result of being labeled a plagiarist, her or his life's work may be dismissed, or at least be considered highly suspect. His or her name is then referenced only in relation to the crime, used as an example to graduate students of what *never* to do. For these reasons, leading the list of academic commandments is the clear pronouncement: *Thou shalt not plagiarize!*

Clear enough? Yes. How could it *not* be?

However, knowing what we know now about the politics of representation and the crisis of legitimation, as well as the rhetoric of writing and the narrative construction of representations of fieldwork, is there a fair definition of—and penalty for—what we think of as "appropriating" another's work?

Until recently, we have thought so. However, our high cultural regard and scholarly expectations for the proper referencing of other scholars' work has lately been coupled with serious questions about the ethics of *appropriating* the studied *others'* lives, rituals, rites, histories, cultural stories, myths, legends, and words. What is termed the postmodern "crisis of legitimation" (see Denzin, 1996) is, in part, a crisis derived from this *newly* articulated ethical question: *Whose story is this, anyway?*

I am reminded of a literary parallel (see Goodall, 1980). During the late 1920s and early 1930s Zelda Fitzgerald tried to establish herself as an artist and a writer. She was increasingly dissatisfied with the fact that her husband, the already legendary novelist F. Scott Fitzgerald, had been largely credited with their success, while her own part in the story of their lives was obscured. She was a woman, and, she felt, she was therefore always considered little more than a glittering accessory to Scott's fame. In fact, many of his most memorable scenes and almost all of his *femme fatale* characters had been transparently drawn from— some would say, appropriated from—her life, antics, and stories. She had coedited *The Great Gatsby,* suggested some of its dominant symbolic flows, and corrected proofs on many of his short stories. As his literary light began to fade, he encouraged her to perform more dangerous and riskier public stunts in the hope that he could recapture some of his lost writing energy. When she collapsed of nervous exhaustion, he told friends that he had lost his inspiration.

Her plan for recovery and rehabilitation included writing her own novel. It was a thinly disguised account of their life, told from her perspective. She worked on this book for years. During this time, she fought about "who owns the rights to our life" with Scott, and he encouraged arguments about whether a woman should be allowed to air her side of the story with his friends and contacts in the publishing community. Finally, in 1934, her novel was published under the title *Save Me the Waltz.* The publisher didn't hype it, it wasn't reviewed widely, and so mostly it was ignored. She was devastated.

Her story—so typical of the literary plight of women and minorities— also serves as an analogue to some of the ethical pressures experienced by ethnographers when writing about "their" fieldwork. For example, I have wondered as I read work by known and respected scholars how differently the story might have been told *if their subjects had written it.* While it is true that every text is a collaboration, it is also true that rarely are the collaborators given equal credit for their participation in a study. Their names do not appear as coauthors. They are usually relegated to a brief, if heartfelt, mention on the acknowledgments page.

In my own experience, this inequality of authorship over jointly produced and performed lives has a clear example. When I wrote *Living in the Rock n Roll Mystery* (1991), I asked the band's lead guitarist, Drew Thompson, to write his account of the Whitedog experience for inclusion in the book. I felt the book would be stronger with the addition of a nonacademic's perspective on the events, the people, the experiences I had written about. He enthusiastically agreed and wrote a story called "Truly." It was a powerful account of a band living from moment to moment, hoping for the big break that never comes. His writing was clear and graceful; he was a songwriter, a craftsman, who took words seriously and knew how to tell a compelling story. He also captured aspects of the experience I hadn't witnessed or participated in, and brought to the book what I thought would be a welcome and refreshing look at what having a resident ethnographer in the band meant to a group of professional musicians. He included jokes that had been told behind my back, including the oft-repeated line, "Shit, man, is *this* going to end up being in that *fuckin'* book?" He wrote with kindness about my struggles to master rhythm guitar. And he dealt openly with issues of sex and stimulants that I had conveniently obscured, or omitted, out of concern about future legalities. All in all, I thought "Truly" would make an appropriate contribution to the book.

But it was not to be. My editor refused to include it. He agreed that it was well written and that it would be an interesting, provocative addition. But he worried about telling even more revealing details about the band's personal lives than I already had included. He was concerned about law-suits, repercussions. When I insisted, he said that I could choose between seeing the book published or not. For him, it was a deal-breaking issue. Finally, exasperated by my counter-arguments, he said, simply, "Look, nobody wants to read an ethnography an amateur has written. It will kill the book."

I told Drew what had occurred and he said, typically, "No big deal." He was still pursuing the dream of a rock 'n' roll career, and the failure of placing one story in an academic press book hardly concerned him. He was pleased to hear that my editor thought it was well written, and accepted his analysis of why it would kill the book. He told me I would be a fool not to publish the book, or to make any more out of this situation than I had already done.

I decided to go ahead with publication without his story. In my head, where often I make the worst decisions, I determined that because I had a new job and no longer had tenure, I needed the publi-cation more than I needed to stand on principle. And I believed that some of my best writing, and my best fieldwork, had been done for that book. I could go on with further rationalizations, but I'm sure you see my point. I copped out. And, in my heart, I know I was right about my evaluation of Drew's story and its place in the book, so maybe I was wrong to compromise with my editor.

Ethical choices, as my colleague Heidi Reeder puts it, are always difficult because they ask you to choose between a "right" and a "right." This case was certainly that kind of choice. And sometimes, when I try to claim that going ahead with the publication of the book was just a "means to an end," I am reminded of Gandhi's dictum: "Means are ends in the making."[3] Regardless of how our ethical dilem-mas turn out, we live with the consequences of them.

Right, or *right.*

❏   ❏

Ethical choices about "who owns the rights to this story" can make absorbing theoretical discussions. But for any fieldworker other issues, other ethical choices, are more pragmatic.

For example, how and when should you inform your subjects of *your identity as an academic researcher,* as well as *your purpose* in

---

3 Thanks to Dr. Sharon Bracci for providing this line.

studying their culture? The easy, and often romantically flawed, answer is "before you do the study." This answer is also the one that many university human-subjects boards (faculty committees assembled to approve research involving human beings) assume as well. Their history, which dates back to ethical and moral issues raised over the conduct of experiments with human subjects, tends to privilege the traditional, received view of social science. Under this model, explaining to subjects what you are doing, and who you are, prior to conducting an experiment is the only acceptable way for legitimate academic work to proceed. In many cases, the researcher is also required to obtain signed permission forms from the subjects.

So what's the problem? Seems right-minded, wouldn't you say?

If your research is conducted out in the streets instead of in a laboratory, the issue of obtaining permission to conduct your research may not be as easily resolved. What if you don't know who your subjects are likely to be until they emerge within a proposed context? What if you can't specify the exact questions you will ask them? Or, what if you don't know how their behavior may be influenced by your activities? Or, what if you haven't determined what the resulting text will be about, or how it will be written? In other words, what if the nature of the ethnographic fieldwork and writing is at odds with the traditional model for gaining approval from academic research boards? Here again, the ethical choice is often between a "right" and a "right"—an institutional right and an ethnographic one.

In many cultures and subcultures I can name, to announce your presence in a community as an ethnographer, a college professor, and an intellectual would be (and has been) the kiss of death. Dwight Conquergood (1993), for example, explains that he himself lived for months in "Big Red," the housing project he focused on in his study of street gangs in Chicago, before he ever divulged his professional identity or ethnographic purpose to anyone. Eventually he did disclose it, but only *after* he had gained the trust of members of the community. To have behaved otherwise might have seriously compromised the study, or even placed his life at risk. The issue of when to announce your identity and purpose may be significantly complicated by many circumstances. Telling someone you don't know that you are "studying them" is an unlikely way to gain their trust, or their cooperation.

And yet, it is absolutely essential that you do so. *Eventually.*

ISSUES OF AUTHORSHIP further complicate the ethical dilemmas faced by ethnographers.

Writing about others, writing about our selves with and among them, is a terribly personal way to conduct social research. That we were once able to identify ourselves as "researchers" and the others as "subjects," and that we are now not as easily able to do so, is one sign of the complexity of personal ethics in the field, as well as in our texts.

As I mentioned in the Drew Thompson example, the idea of asking subjects to collaborate with you on a writing project seems like a reasonable alternative. Yet, as I learned, even this "radical" move is not without its own ethical problems and rhetorical entanglements. Which members of the culture should we elect as "representative," or "legitimate," spokespersons? In the Whitedog case, if I had asked our drummer, or our lead singer, to write accounts, each of them would have differed from mine, from Drew's, and from each other's. Every text, every story, privileges someone's point of view. The question "who owns the truth about a culture?" is not easily resolved by simply increasing the number and diversity of voices in a text. Indeed, what you might gain in ethical display, you may lose in narrative coherence.

Another question that can arise is: "What if naming a subject as a coauthor places her or him at risk within their culture? Or in ours?" If you view Dwight Conquergood and Taggert Siegel's ethnographic film *Hearts Broken in Half* (1990), you will see that they digitally "masked" the faces of gang members. They did so because police departments could use the film to harass, or indict, individual members of the gang. In many ethnographies, people's names, professional identities, and locations are changed for similar reasons. In one case, a Clintonite pal of mine wrote a "political novel" based on his personal experience, research, and fieldwork (Wilkes, 1998). He calls it a fiction, but in truth it is pure "faction"—facts disguised as fictions to prevent investigations and potential lawsuits.

No simple solutions are on hand to resolve these broadly political and highly contextualized ethical issues. At least, there are none that I know of. Every conceptual line that we draw is ultimately problematic for someone, or privileges a particular way of telling for a particular target audience. The best advice is probably to be conscious of ethical issues and questions while in the field, *raise them within the text,* and deal with the consequences of them in the one way that affords the least opportunity for harm to be done.

ANOTHER ETHICAL ISSUE FOR WRITING the new ethnography that is derived from traditional modernist concerns involves how the rhetorical activity known as *referencing* is carried out.

It is *not* just enough to cite your sources. Any writing, including the referencing and listing of sources, is a rhetorical activity whose meaning occurs within a highly defined professional and moral context. How you cite them, in what form, and what the use of them may be within a particular research context are all aspects of ethical referencing.

For example, Charles Bazerman (1987) points out that the American Psychological Association stylesheet is, in fact, a *political* document. It privileges particular ways of referencing scholarship and obscures or marginalizes alternatives. His argument could as easily be applied to the *MLA* second edition or to the various editions of the *Chicago Manual of Style*. The point is that any rhetorical system for coding scholarly references carries with it an *ideology*. For the APA, this ideology sanctions and gives rhetorical authority to the additive nature of scientific research and theory-construction.

One example of how an ideology applies to references is the APA requirement for citing sources this way: (Goodall, 1999). At a basic information level of interpretation, the citation means that somebody named Goodall published something in 1999. The ideological assumption is that whatever Goodall published in 1999 provided a theoretical link (that is, framework, justification, or research finding) to the statement preceding the reference. One objection to this form of coding a reference is that while published research in scientific fields tends to limit authors to one "finding" per article, work in the humanities and social sciences doesn't have to. So Goodall may have authored an article about the history of ethnographic writing in 1999, but the use of this format for referencing *doesn't provide a clear account of precisely what, in his work, is being referred to.* Is it the *whole* of his argument? *Part* of it? The fact that he wrote an account of this history? Or, maybe that something was *left out* of his account?

See the problem?

It becomes more complex and confounding when a sentence ends with a "chain-link reference," such as: "(Adams, 1985; Bobo, 1992; Jones, 1997; Simmons, 1989; Zevra, 1990)."[4] In the sciences and social sciences, the whole (or at least *recent*) history of an idea, or line or

---

4 Yes, I am guilty of using these as well.

research, may be chained together with a series of names and dates, then enclosed within parentheses, and the citation conveys a highly elaborate but sensible shorthand. The individual differences between or among researchers and their studies are less important than the *additive construction of the idea,* wherein the present study is considered a new "contribution." Explanatory footnotes (which may be about those individual differences or contain important information or details about a study) are relegated to "endnotes," which are rare in APA-governed work.

For fans of the APA approach—which you will have noted is used in this book—all of this makes perfect sense. After all, research in the physical and natural sciences is *supposed to be* additive, and there are *not* supposed to be stylistic variations in the reporting of methodologically sound, theoretically current research. Even among social scientists, who have chosen to mimic the physical and natural sciences in many ideological and methodological ways, the appropriation and use of this referencing standard fits within their general cultural conventions. As long as everyone practices social science in the same ways, and writes research reports in the same style, the cultural practice of writing citations in this way works accordingly.

However, research styles and reports among the social sciences exhibit considerably more individual and disciplinary differences than the APA format was intended to handle. Consider, for example, chaining together the names Malinowski, Carbaugh, Mead, Adelman, Evans-Pritchard, Neumann, G. Bateson, Keisinger, Levi-Strauss, Katriel, Geertz, Philipsen, Van Maanen, Rose, Trujillo, and Behar. Aside from the fact that all of the names in the chain belong to ethnographers who have important lessons to offer about fieldwork, there may be *little else in common among them* or in their work. To reference them in an APA-chain enclosed by parentheses is to textually commit them to something that, if they were to meet in a common room to discuss, the authors probably would not agree to. Is it ethical, therefore, to place together in a chain-linked reference the names of persons whose views are divergent or even polar opposites? Is it a good professional practice to do so, when you know that some—perhaps most—of your readers are unfamiliar with the specific work, or theoretical position, of those scholars you link?

A related issue is *how much* of a cited author's work *you actually agree with,* or want to include, in the case you are making. For proponents of the MLA or Chicago stylesheets, the ability to use explanatory footnotes provides opportunities to deal with theoretical objections, historical developments, methodological subtleties, nuances of argument, and so forth, any or all of which complicate, deepen, and enrich the reading of the text. This is because, in the humanities, the point of an article or book is seldom limited to a particular "finding"; no argument can or should be judged on the merits of its conclusion alone. Therefore, to limit how you may cite or comment upon a reference is, in fact, in itself an ideological decision.

Beyond the ideological stance represented by choice of stylesheet, some ethical issues remain, dealing with the rhetoric of writing references that should apply to all citation formats:

- You should have read, *in their entirety*, the articles and books you cite in your list of references.
- Do not "pad" your references simply to appear more learned.
- Avoid burying the "real" citation in a chained list; if the work you relied on was drawn from a specific source, cite it and *only* it.
- Try to limit citations to published or otherwise easily accessible work.[5]
- Avoid citing obscure studies you've done, in the vain hope that someone notices them.[6] If you must use something from an obscure source, quote from it extensively in the body of the article so that a reader can gain a reasonable idea of its context and what it says.

The above recommendations are part of how we acculturate our graduate students to the ethnographic writing life. A good ethical question may be: Is this how we *really* behave? Do our ethical intentions fit our cultural practices?

THE CULTURAL INNOCENCE of the antiplagiarism and proper citation advisories became more noticeable, and problematic, as the interpretive and postmodern era gained academic presence and power.

First, as I mentioned earlier, the twin crises of representation and legitimation came to the forefront of academic discussion and began to

---

5 Avoid referencing material that a reader would have to write away for, such as convention or conference papers.

6 I am thinking here of material contained in "state" journals. In many cases these journals are not even carried by college or university libraries *within* the state of origin, making the task of actually tracking down a cited piece unnecessarily difficult.

inform the peer review process. Ethical concerns no longer were limited to what was written about, but also related to *what was being left out* of the report. New questions arose about what ethnographers had witnessed, or experienced, but marginalized in their accounts, usually because to acknowledge them either would prove professionally embarrassing or would fail to be accounted for by the theoretical and interpretive frameworks they used to draw conclusions.

Additionally, there was—and is—a more general representational concern for including in the account the perspectives, experiences, and voices of cultural minorities, women, "outsiders," and others whose lived experiences may have challenged a particular thesis being pursued. Indeed, as Stephen Tyler's (1988) critique suggested, there was a vast and underexplored rhetoric of the *unsaid*, the *unspoken*, and the *unheard*, which ethnographers had to learn how to account for.

ANOTHER ETHICAL CONCERN AROSE as *what was said* became more diversely expressed. As we have seen, "blurred genres" (Geertz, 1983) emerged. What once looked like a standard field report became as likely to be written as if it were a novel, or be represented as a drama, or given as a poem. Hence, the textual creation and editing processes became apt material for academic debate.

It was one thing to write—as modern ethnographers did—with the assurance that what counted as "truth" followed naturally from form, and to decide—as modern ethnographers did—that there was a preferred form for scholarly writing. But to suddenly encounter an ethnography written as a detective story (see Goodall, 1989b), or as a performance text (Paget, 1995), or as a poem (see Eisenberg, 1998; Richardson, 1997) presented new challenges.

One ethical challenge was how to apply recognized scholarly standards for evaluating an account of fieldwork to a text that both resisted the form of an account and problematized the standards. The ethical question was how to apply *equitably* to new ethnographies the standards applied to traditional accounts. Is it "right" to do so? Is it fair to the author, and to the work? If not, then what are the appropriate critical criteria? Is it ethical to include a scholarly journal work that hasn't been evaluated by commonly held scholarly standards? Should the scholarly standards change, or be altered, to accommodate new ethnographic representations?

A second ethical challenge brought on by new ethnographic writing centers on the "appropriate" use of—and language in—self-reflexive passages.[7] In Chapter 4, I discussed self-reflexivity as a narrative and rhetorical construction. It is not about "what happened in the field" so much as it is about "what happened *in me* or *to me*." This shift of emphasis in the text also brings with it new ethical questions. Some social scientists wonder if is it ethical to take up professional journal space with extensive self-examinations and personal musings. Other readers may be uncomfortable with knowing the personal details of colleagues' lives; they ask if it is ethical to ask them to confront material that they find personally and professionally offensive. Still others maintain that personal writing isn't scholarship, because it plays on the vulnerabilities and emotions of readers, thus raising ethical questions about the role of the emotions in scholarly writing.

These are all controversial issues. None are easily resolved. Arguments on either side tend to be divisive, as one person's ethical challenge becomes a respondent's source of textual liberation. Scholarship is, by nature, controversial. New ideas, new ways of thinking (and writing), bump into older ideas and methods with predictable results: more argument, and more controversy. These recent genre-based issues provide us with ethical challenges, but ethical challenges do not necessarily require immediate resolutions. What they do is afford us is a cultural space to consider, and to appreciate, the questions they raise and the tensions they create in our research and writing.

◻   ◻

Editing a new ethnography also brings with it new ethical considerations. To *edit* the voice—as well as what is said—is to determine how the character and communicative ability of the narrator could be, and perhaps should be, "improved." But improved *when?* And improved *how?* And improved *for whom?* It is also to ask the ethnographer to change a representation of something that supposedly occurred. Is this *ethical?*

---

7 In my account of Bill Clinton's 1992 campaign for the presidency, I problematize "where" the action is taking place by presenting fragments of personal experience alongside media representations (Goodall, 1994b). Because both forms of expression are at least one or two levels removed from reality, the question of whose experience it is and how representative it can be becomes increasingly problematic. This seemed to me to be appropriate, given the nature of political campaigning. My historical referent for this sort of account-giving is indebted to Tom Benson's "Another Shootout in Cowtown" (1980).

For a fiction writer, or a general essayist, the license to edit is a license to change any or all of the account, including the general makeup of the narrator, the scenes and action depicted, and the overall nature of the story being told. For an ethnographer, editing is supposed to be a far more *restrictive* rhetorical activity. What you *can* and *should* edit includes:

- Any *factual information* that was inaccurately reported or inadvertently omitted, but that contributes significantly to the truth value of the tale
- Any *interpretation, attribution of cause, motive, or significance* that results from editing the factual information
- Any *poorly constructed passages* that are unintentionally ambiguous, awkward, or irrelevant to the plot, or that may be simply unclear
- Overly *long sentences* (these days usually underscored in green by your user-friendly word processing program)[8]
- Grammatically *incorrect usage* (these days also usually underscored in red by your user-friendly word processing program)
- *General formatting* for consistency (for example, use of headings, typefaces, italics, footnotes, and the like)
- *Aesthetic formatting* for eye appeal (such as layout of pages, use of color, use of photos, drawings, charts, and so on; also enlarging or changing the font of a particular word for emphasis)

What an ethnographer may *add* to the existing text includes:

- *New interpretive material* that works over previously unexplored, or underexplored, implications in the symbol/cultural nature of a conversation, observational detail, general contextual surroundings, and so forth
- *New self-reflexive material* that provides useful (to the reader) contextual information or that provides thematically useful details that further the richness of the text
- *New references* that enlarge the reader's ability to connect the writing to other scholarship, or that pay just dues to an author or authors from whom you have borrowed insights, information, or particular turns of phrase

---

8 Yes, I am fully aware that I do not always follow my word processor's advice.

■ *New interpretive material written by those you wrote about in the text;* a recent development in ethnography is the multivocal text, in which the original ethnography is given to those who were studied for reading, critique, and commentary and their responses possibly used or appended in the final manuscript

Within these editing parameters you should be able to make important changes to *your writing*. What you may *not* do is change or seriously alter *the facts, the data, or the sequence of events* that unfolded to fit your conclusions.

Changing any of those representational qualities is, ethnographically speaking, cheating. As is the case with plagiarism, this form of cheating is serious business. However clear these editing rules are for keeping ethnographically pure what may appear in print, the postmodern among us have demonstrated that almost any rule can be, and usually is, problematic. For example, if we are aware of the *inability* of any prose—no matter how well written—to fully capture or represent the complexity of a human action, then isn't it true, by definition, that all attempts to render rhetorical interpretations as immutable "facts" are suspect? In other words, isn't a *factual representation* merely a *convenient fiction?*

Second, if we accept that there is no "immaculate perception" (Van Maanen, 1988) in fieldwork, how can we claim that what is obviously experienced as partial and partisan can *ever* be written as a legitimate expression of "what occurred"? Isn't our choice to write "what happened to us" simply a matter of constructing a version of reality that fits our values, our theories, our sense of perspective and judgment?

Third, and once again, *whose story is it to tell,* anyway? Would the "facts" of the case change if our subjects themselves rendered the account? Isn't the act of observing and interpreting others simply an institutionally sanctioned extension of colonialism? Or worse. As Nick Trujillo put it:

> I and my students have been studying shopping.... Now, when I follow a woman through her shopping routines, then continue to follow her out of the shopping mall all the way to her car in the parking lot ...am I an ethnographer, or am I a *stalker?* (Trujillo, 1997).

Trujillo left the question unanswered. Yet, the cultural and ethical implications for "routine" data collecting suddenly became refigured as morally ambiguous and ethically problematic.

Given these objections to fieldwork and prose comfort zones, what should a new ethnographer do?

❏   ❏

I may not have answers for all of these ethical questions, but I do have my own point of view.

I may employ both nonfiction and fictional accounts as an ethnographer, but I know when I am telling the truth and when I am not. Truth is *ungenred.* It is a quality of what you have experienced, and what conclusions you come to, that allows it, as a concept, to transcend any representational boundaries. That "truth" may be—and usually is—limited to *the truth of my experience,* but it is as close as I am likely to get to "what is" and "what was" via language. I believe the business of the new ethnography is the interpretive evocation and representation of such truths.

I think it is *vital* to edit your writing. That I am able to edit, reorganize, or otherwise enhance the evocative abilities of words for more communicative appeal and disciplinary influence may, and in fact does, alter my perception of "what is" and "what was." It does *not* alter the fact that my writing is "about" something that I have said actually occurred or that is wholly made up.

However, even within this general ethical stance lie issues, problems, and challenges for writing and editing new ethnographies. First, all writers know that there is no necessary correlation between *reporting the exact words spoken* and *placing them into the exact meaning of the context* from which they were extracted. As an ethnographer, I am ethically bound to report accurately what gets said and done, and I strive *not* to interpret it to mean something different from what was intended. I should not *decontextualize* words or practices, because this misleads readers while robbing them of details that would enhance their interpretations of meaning.

Second, as a new ethnographer, I must consider ethical questions about the role of *imagination* in ethnographic representations. What are the issues involved when writers use appeals to the imagination (such as "Think about it this way:....") or create imagined passages to persuade readers of the authenticity of an account (Atkinson, 1990)? Is it true that I may engage in flights of ethnographic imagination because such rhetorical activity is really not that different from posing alternative formal hypotheses in the social sciences? Is it so that I may "work a metaphor" through a passage because it is no more of a scholarly crime than if I "run my numbers again" with a different statistical test? These are important ethical questions that require a specific context, understanding of representational purpose, and the specific passages of prose, to evaluate. What I know would be an ethnographic crime is treating flights of my imagination, or deployment of intentional metaphors, *as if* they were naturally occurring in the field, or if I attributed them to persons *other than* myself.

Third, think about the statement Ruth Behar makes to open this chapter: "Should I feel good that my writing makes a reader break out crying?" Do displays of emotions and vulnerability lessen or deflect a reader's attentions from ordinary ethical standards? Do narrative and rhetorical devices aimed at creating pathos interfere with otherwise rational ethical judgments?

Finally, how much "artistic license" can an ethnographic writer assume when constructing a narrative? Harry Wolcott (1995) uses the analogy of the ethnographer-as-artist and the ethnographer-as-craftsperson to describe the ethical dimensions of some literary and rhetorical choices. For him, fieldwork and the interpretation of its meanings are artistic activities, while writing about fieldwork is more a craft. The difference is that an artist has more artistic license than a craftsperson does. We expect an artist to know the rules of art, but also to break or challenge them. By contrast, we expect ethnographic writers to make use of our poetic abilities, but to generally adhere to *conventions of production*. By "conventions," Wolcott means that ethnographers use:

- The *materials* of fieldwork, including observation, interviews, and personal experiences in the field, as well as the materials accepted within the scholarly community for producing publishable work—typed (or printed) single-sided on white, letter-sized, paper
- Commonly referenced *abstractions* known and cited within the scholarly literature to interpret a culture, including familiarity with academic forebears
- Recognizable *forms or genres* for expressing ethnographic experiences, including adherence to the journal's or press's approved stylesheet
- Professional standards for *regulating the relations* between writers and readers, such as a writer producing original work that is not plagiarized, is worthy of a well-informed reader's time and money,

and is capable of contributing to her or his learning as well as the field's advancement (adapted from Wolcott, pp. 55–56)

Walcott's conventions for writing ethnography conform to the cultural and ethical dictates of a craft more so than to those of an art. However, as he wisely points out, "Knowing conventions must not be confused with observing them to a T" (1995; p. 58). Scholars interested in "pushing the envelope" do so by challenging the authority and legitimacy of conventions. The difference between a craftsperson and a *master* craftsperson may well lie in how certain conventions are loosely, and locally, interpreted. Writing the new ethnographies may provide evidence of that.

DESPITE THE SEEMINGLY SHIFTING and often ambiguous standards for producing and consuming scholarly work done in ethnography, one firm ethical convention remains that, in my view, must always be applied: *authors are accountable for what they have written.*

We are accountable to readers, to disciplines, to institutions, and to each other for the quality and contribution of the stories we create. We are accountable to our subjects and to their cultures for making good on the promises we made to them in exchange for their experiences, their stories, their lessons, and their lives. We are accountable to the families and friends who support and nurture us, for not only the products of our work, but moreover for the kind of person it makes us into while we are at it, and as a consequence of it. And, finally, we must continuously be accountable to ourselves.

Here is my personal ethical test for accountability:

I have to be able to look at my own face in the mirror, professionally examine it, and not look away.

Writing Experiments

1. Reread Ruth Behar's quotation that opens this chapter. In your personal journal, write your response to it. What do *you* think the relationships might be between evaluative standards for determining the quality of an ethnographic work and an ethics for reading and writing them?
2. Construct, in your personal journal, what you consider to be the *rhetorical* differences between fictional and nonfiction representations of

fieldwork experiences. Given what you have discovered, what *ethical* principles for ethnographers are entailed?

Now go to the library and check out Anna Banks and Stephen Banks (ed.), *Fiction and Social Research: By Ice or Fire* (Walnut Creek, CA: AltaMira Press, 1998). Consider the Banks's arguments for the role of fictional writing in research. Then think about the categories they use to describe such work: "Narratives of Representation," "Narratives of Understanding," "Narratives of Suspicion," and "Narratives of Vulnerability." Which classification scheme—fiction/nonfiction or narratives of...—works best for you? Or are they necessarily mutually exclusive? Again, what are the ethical principles that should be used to guide textual, rhetorical choices? Describe the process by which you came to these conclusions in your personal journal.

3. Where and how, in your ongoing ethnographic project, should you discuss ethical challenges/problems/issues in your fieldwork and writing? Try at least two options: (1) place these discussions in the footnotes, and (2) provide internal discussions of them within the text. What message are you sending readers with each of these strategic choices? How does the inclusion/exclusion of ethical discussions in the text influence its format? Style? Rhetorical credibility? Are these issues you should write about in your project?

Now go to the library and check out Chris Anderson's *Style as Argument* (1987). Read the introductory section. Of what relevance are his arguments about stylistic choices and the writing of "New Journalism" to these issues for the new ethnography?

4. If you followed my earlier advice, in your professional notebook or journal you have been recording instances of conversations and cultural performances. Go back over some of your entries and try to apply ethical issues and questions to them. If you evaluate a particular statement or behavior as "unethical," what are you really saying? What ethical principle or principles undergird your judgment? What must you know about a context or situation to fairly evaluate the ethics of its participants? Or doesn't the context matter? What are your personal ethical standards, and how do they influence or color what you observe and write about in the field? Write your responses to these items and share them with your class. No doubt, the resulting discussion should prove *very* interesting.

5. What is meant by the expression "poetic (or artistic) license"? Are there ethical limits to the application of this license in sculpture, painting, fiction, or dramatic art? What about in writing the new ethnography? If you believe there are limits, what are they? If you believe there should be no limits, what ethical standards could you use in the accomplishment of such work?

For Further Reading

The works listed below should help you extend and apply the material in this chapter. Some of the pieces address theoretical and conceptual issues involved in fieldwork and writing ethical criticism of cultures (see especially Conquergood, Hastrup, Said, and Wolcott). Others involve the ethics of relationships—both in the field and on the page (see especially Charmaz and Mitchell, Mykhalovskiy, and Rawlins). And others explore the ethical dimensions of engaging "otherness" and the obligations this places on the writer to explore her- or himself (see especially Behar, and Kellett and Goodall).

Behar, R. 1996. *The vulnerable observer: Anthropology that breaks your heart.* Boston: Beacon.

Charmaz, K., and Mitchell, R. G. 1996. The myth of silent authorship: Self, substance, and style in ethnographic writing. *In Reflexivity and voice,* edited by R. Hertz. Thousand Oaks, CA: Sage.

Conquergood, D. 1991. Rethinking ethnography: Towards a critical cultural politics. *Communication Monographs* 58: 179–194.

Hastrup, K. 1995. *A passage to anthropology: Between experience and theory.* London: Routledge.

Kellett, P. M., and Goodall, H. L. 1999. The death of discourse in our own (chat)room: "Sextext, learning organizations, and virtual communities," in *Soundbite culture: The death of discourse in a wired world,* edited by D. Slayden and R. K. Whillock. Thousand Oaks, CA: Sage.

Mykhalovskiy, E. 1997. Reconsidering "table talk": Critical thoughts on the relationship between sociology, autobiography, and self-indulgence. In *Reflexivity and voice,* edited by R. Hertz. Thousand Oaks, CA: Sage.

Rawlins, W. 1992. *Friendship matters.* New York: Aldine de Gruyter.

Said, E. 1983. *The world, the text, and the critic.* Cambridge: Harvard University Press.

Wolcott, H. F. 1995. *The art of fieldwork.* Walnut Creek, CA: AltaMira Press.

6 | The Future of New Ethnographic Writing

This rethinking of ethnography is primarily about speaking and listening, instead of observing.... [This] shifts the emphasis from space to time, from sight and vision to sound and voice, from text to performance, from authority to vulnerability.

DWIGHT CONQUERGOOD
"Rethinking Ethnography"

Why do we *read* ethnographies?

What does it mean, "to read" them?

What are we reading them *for?*

What *standards* should we use to evaluate their scholarly worth?

How can we use our answers to these questions to inform how we write the new ethnography?

In this final chapter I examine the above questions about reading and writing. I try to answer them by providing exemplars of good ethnographic prose. I believe these exemplars challenge readers to explore new scholarly and personal dimensions of storytelling and reading. They also reveal scholarly possibilities of new writing in our field.

I begin with *questions* drawn from conversations I've heard or participated in over the past few years. These are difficult questions, sometimes troubling ones, about writing, reading, academic culture, and the purpose of the new ethnography. In the context of these questions, I provide excerpts from scholarly work that inspired them, as well as writing that attempts to answer them. Rather than explain how *I* think each piece answers the questions, I will ask *you* to. Think of these sections as individual *thought experiments,* wherein the central problematic has to do with what forms of writing best advance the prospects of ethnography in the twenty-first century. You may wish to read the stories in full and write about them, and your responses to them, in your professional journal or notebook.

Experiments with writing characterize the new ethnography. At the same time, these experiments challenge traditional standards for evaluating scholarship. For this reason, I conclude this chapter with a critical and cultural examination of the evaluative standards used to judge the scholarly worth of new ethnographic writing.

⌐   ⌐

To understand our purposes for writing, we must understand our purposes for reading. Let's begin with some questions about reading— specifically, questions about why, and how, and what, you read.

When you receive a fresh copy of your favorite academic journal, what *motivates* you to open the cover and peruse the contents? A sense of professional obligation? Available time? Participation in the scholarly community? The pursuit of pleasure? The avoidance of some other task, such as cleaning your apartment, doing laundry, calling your mother, or tracking down that missing reference in the library?

Or, is it the *prose that constitutes the first line,* the language and style that is found in an opening paragraph, like this:

> I cruise theories. A look, a glance, a turn of the head. I walk away, pause, wait for the theory to follow. I let theories pursue me, and when I am ready, I turn to say hello, to ask, "Are you ready?" Some theories are better for cruising than others. Theories of desire are most thrilling, unpredictable, moist in all the right places (Corey and Nakayama, 1997, p. 58.).

What *reading practices* characterize how you read? Do you read a text from beginning to end? Do you always read the abstract first? Or, do you read the introduction and conclusion, and then, if properly stimulated, back up and read the rest/more/some of it? Or, do you start with a quick perusal of the references, figuring that if the author aligns herself or himself with the same discourse community as you do, it's worth reading, and if not, well, there's really not much point in even trying? What I am asking is: Do you too "cruise" readings?

Or is it deeper than that? Are there cultural reasons for your reading practices? For example, do you consider yourself to be a member of a particular scholarly community, one that requires its members to read *whatever* new piece of work is done within it and for it? If so, do you consider yourself to be motivated to read by your ability to identify with the author's references? What if there are none?

Consider the following list of references. Would you want to read the essay it's attached to? Why or why not?

Shotter, J. 1993. *Cultural politics and everyday life.* Toronto: University of Toronto Press.

Shotter, J., and Gergen, K. 1994. *Texts of identity.* Newbury Park, CA: Sage.

Shulman, D. 1994. Dirty data and investigative methods. *Journal of Contemporary Ethnography* 23: 214–253.

Stocking, G. 1983. *Observers observed.* Madison: University of Wisconsin Press.

Stoller, P. 1989. *The taste of ethnographic things.* Philadelphia: University of Pennsylvania Press.

Strine, M., Long, B., and Hopkins, M. F. 1990. Research in interpretation and performance studies: Trends, issues, priorities. In *Speech communication: Essays to commemorate the 75th anniversary of the Speech Communication Association,* edited by G. M. Phillips and J. T. Wood. Carbondale: Southern Illinois University Press.

Taylor, B. 1997. Home zero: Images of home and field in nuclear-cultural studies. *Western Journal of Communication* 61: 209–234.

Todorov, T. 1977. *The poetics of prose.* Ithaca, NY: Cornell University Press.

Trujillo, N. 1997. Ethics and ethnography. National Communication Association annual convention, Chicago, November 1997.

Turner, V. 1969. *The ritual process.* Ithaca, NY: Cornell University Press.

Tyler, S. A. 1992. On being out of words. In *Rereading cultural anthropology,* edited by G. E. Marcus. Durham, NC: Duke University Press.

Let's consider the *functions of reading* in your everyday life.

Do you read because you have nothing better to do? Or, do you read because you believe there *is* nothing better to do *than* to read? Do you read to find yourself connected to someone through their story?

Maybe because the story asks the same questions about life that you do, and maybe because someone is seeking the same answers as you are? Mark Neumann observes that ethnography "renames a familiar story of divided selves longing for sense of place and stability in the fragments and discontinuities of modernity" (1996, pp. 173–174).

What do you think?

What is it, exactly, that you *get out of* reading?

How ABOUT THE LOGIC implied by this question to guide reading practice: Do you only read work by authors you know or admire?

Do you only read women (or men) authors? *Contemporary* men (or women)?

Only feminists? Critical theorists? Gays/lesbians/bisexuals? Postcolonials? Modernists? Postmodernists?

Performance studies authors?

Org. Comm. writers?

People you went to grad school with? Or, folks you are likely to run into at conventions?

Perhaps you read only those works that can advance an argument you are trying to make in your own work. Or, texts you can criticize. Or footnote. Or one-up your colleagues with. Does the cultural status and name of the scholar inform your decisions to read?

What if I told you that one of the best new ethnographies I've read in a long time came from the thesis work of a then-*master's* student? Would you want to read it? Her name is Stacy Holman Jones. My bet is you don't recognize her name. Yet. Does the absence of instant name recognition discourage you from reading her work? Her study is about women's music communities. Interested? Yes/no? What if I further explained that part of her work reports on and interprets her struggle to gain acceptance writing new ethnography in academic culture, namely her struggle with her thesis committee members? Have you had a similar experience? Interested yet? Here is an excerpt:

I am waiting.

My fingers have gone cold and thin, blood pounds in my ears. I stare at my colleagues—teachers, friends, scholars, women—across the conference room table, its faux wood a sea of separation. Bronzed lips smile, but my eyes return an empty stare. Motherly, sisterly concern wraps silently around me and I push it off.

Footsteps and laughter. Here they come. Bill first, his wavy hair and deliberate gait somehow entering the room before him, wistful grin trailing behind. Then Gerri, smiling and warm in white. She looks at me, wills me confidence. And Nick, his baseball cap and shorts camouflaging serious questions.

My final performance. A play in justification and explanation—of my words about other people, presented to still other people. A parody in which I defend my choices, including the choice to include myself. A simulacra of the ethnography, the performances, the writing, the ethnographer and the participants. Conjuring them all up in a sterile room before the tribunal of hyperreality (Jones, 1998, p. 13).

Do you read sentences like these, perhaps as you did as a child, with a sense of *wonder?* How about with *anticipation?* Awe? Or, is your typical emotional response, or rhetorical and narrative involvement, likely to be one of routine to which you append personal and professional frustration, jealousy, aggravation, anxiety, or boredom, or all of these emotions? Or, is *how you respond emotionally* the key to what you read? Or, is it how the writing appeals to your imagination? Level with me: Is reading *fun* anymore?

Would you be intrigued to read a piece that begins (see left-hand column) and ends (see right-hand column) like this one does?

Like "public" and "private," the terms "home" and "field" traditionally have been opposed in cultural vernacular. *Home* has connoted a private and familiar space of refuge, whose inhabitants are legitimated as a "family" by custom and law. *Field* has connoted a public and chaotic space of labor, in which workers negotiate both risk and opportunity to produce valued commodities. These spaces have been viewed as relatively separate and distinct, and as circumscribing the routines of many cultural members (such as commuters).

Recent cultural history and theory, however, have compelled scholars to reconsider the relationship between these two terms, and their highly-charged associations....

"You're a *slob!*" she shouted. "You're *irresponsible* and *unclean!*"

Spit actually flew from her mouth, and her hair stood out on end.

"You don't seem to do any *work!*" she continued. *"You have a lifestyle like a teenager!"*

Caught off guard, I stood transfixed as Bonnie worked her way through a litany of my sins (including: I had kept *two* jugs of filtered water by her coffee maker)....

After attempting to defend myself, I bolted from the house, shaking with adrenaline. Instinctively, she had found my weakest point—my self-image, my doubts about my own authority—and had spilled blood.

Are you wondering how this author, Bryan Taylor (1997, pp. 209, 227), manages to bridge the traditional academic opening on an essay about "nuclear weapons sites" and "nuclear families" with the personal, violent explosion and its aftermath, toward the end? Aren't you *curious* about his metaphorical linking of theory and practice? What if I told you that the underlying tension lies between his supposedly "safe" work as an ethnographer at Los Alamos and his admittedly "unsafe" boyhood home in Massachusetts? And, furthermore, told you that he uses this tension to explore the cultural dimensions of personal and academic experiences? The purpose of this new ethnography is to link these experiences, these literatures, to produce new insights about the terms of atonement for oppressors and the oppressed.

Do you read for literary style, for interesting uses of language? What do you make of attempts at linguistic relativity? How about of humor? Irony? Word-play?

Have you read any Kenneth Burke?

You *have?* Good. What follows is an example of a new ethnography by Dean Scheibel about "Surf-Nazi" culture that derives its theoretical joy from reading Burke into the language of surfers. Like this:

> Joe Terrene, a surfer for over 25 years, sits atop his surfboard and rocks gently in the chilly water at Malibu Surfrider Beach. At 5:30 A.M., Malibu wears the gray morning fog as a winter shroud. Joe notes the comings and goings of surfers; the night surfers are leaving the water, even as members of the "dawn patrol" are grabbing the few remaining spaces of free-parking area on Pacific Coast Highway. The practice of night surfing is the result of insanely large crowds of surfers vying for too few waves during the day. The crush of surfers leads to frustration for many, and anger for some. "Wave etiquette" is not always observed, and both the uncultured, as well as the possessive locals, "snake" other surfers who have legitimate rights to the wave....
>
> And Joe is not alone: few surfers bless water snakes. The symbolic action of "snaking" or being "snaked" brings with it the quality of treachery. The "snake" is symbolically linked to the serpent in the Garden of Eden. Thus, to "snake" someone is to assume the mythic role of Satan, who assumed the form of a snake to tempt Eve. To have been "snaked" is to have been sinned against by someone who has not resisted the temptation of acting improperly (1995, p. 253).

What do you make of deeply personal symbolic inflections such as these in an otherwise theoretical journal article? Do you maintain that "the personal" and "the professional" in scholarly writing (and reading) should be mutually exclusive? Or, is the prose better, the reading experience more enjoyable, the learning better, *for you,* when they are fused?

WHAT DO YOU LEARN from what you read? How do you learn it?

Do you enter into a conversation with it/the author via dialogue or dialectic? Is it your practice to do both? Might that practice be necessary to attain comprehension and understanding?

Do you learn best from a well-told tale, or from a traditionally argued and theoretically warranted series of well-supported claims? Do you learn *differently* from these genres? If it is different, *how* is it different? If it isn't different, then *why* isn't it?

Do you think the answer you just gave is unique to you, or generalizable to other readers in the field? Are you *sure* about that? These days, can you really say for certain that *anything* is generalizable to the field?

Do you think the response you just uttered sums up what "counts," *for you,* as scholarship?

DO YOU BELIEVE what you read, and then expose it to doubt? Or, is it the other way around?

Do you attribute more credibility to narratives of personal experience, or to well-documented, neatly framed scholarly arguments? Can one do the other? How does your answer to this question carry over into your personal life? What have been its *consequences?*

Let's examine writing that connects personal consequences to a scholarly purpose. Would you be interested in reading an ethnography of demolished baseball parks? Don't *look* at me like that. What if I told you that what you were about to read was an excerpt from a *serious* piece of scholarly work? Interested? Still not interested? What if I read this paragraph to you:

> This study helped to expose and to express my grief. The emotion I had
> kept inside of me for the year and a half after his [the writer's father]
> death poured out during the research experience. Interestingly, I discov-
> ered my own feelings and emotions about my own father when I recorded
> and analyzed the language of other fans, many of whom also went to
> the final game at Old Comiskey to be with their fathers, grandfathers,

husbands, and other loved ones, in person or in spirit. In this way, this ethnographic research has guided me to an understanding about others and about myself. It has been both painful and cleansing. The relationship with my father that I never quite understood has become a bit clearer. I only wish that the 6-year old boy still within me had a place to visit him. Goodbye dad, goodbye old friend (Trujillo and Krizek, 1994, p. 318).

Didn't expect *that*, did you?

Is part of the appeal of *any* piece of scholarly writing its *ability to surprise you?* Surprise you into awareness? Into being interested? Surprise you into sense-making?

ARE YOUR READERLY PRACTICES turned on by exotic settings and the stories that emerge from them?

What if I told you that one of the best ethnographies I've ever read dealt with one man's experiences in Africa, when he witnessed the following scene:

> The Baro River was wide and swift and muddy. One day we stood on its bank and contemplated swimming. Other Peace Corps Volunteers had come to Gambella by Land Rover. There were six of us, four men and two women. I don't remember names except for the fourth man. Maybe there were only five of us. Two women. Three men. All young. Early 20s.
>
> We stood on the bank and watched the muddy river. The brown liquid swirled and increased its speed around two large rocks. One rock was across from us in the middle of the river. The other rock was a hundred yards or more downstream from the first. The heat and the humidity encouraged us into the water.
>
> The current was strong and it was difficult to swim. So, we devised a game. First, each of us in turn fought our way through the fast water to the upstream rock. The water accelerated when it divided to pass around the rock. It wasn't easy to pull ourselves from the current. Most of us had bloody arms because we didn't want to be swept further down the river.... A growing number of natives watched all this with great interest.
>
> The game became hypnotic. The heat. The humidity. The brown water. Hypnotic. Each cycle of the game deepened the spell. The constant sound of rushing water was like the white noise of sensory deprivation. Our casual conversations became strangely disembodied. The natives watching us with interest shimmered on the shore. We were out there. In the sun. On a rock. Hypnotic.

182

Suddenly, the trance was broken when someone suggested that we swim to a sandbar. We were all together and resting on the upstream rock.... We liked the idea. It was time to change the game. The sandbar was upstream. I silently wondered if I could make it.

Tim volunteered to go first. He was probably the strongest swimmer. Six feet. One hundred eighty pounds. He dove into the water and swam hard and made a diagonal toward the sandbar by swimming for a point far upstream beyond it. Those of us on the rock cheered and shouted our encouragement as he slowly veered in the direction of the sandbar. "Come on, Tim! You can do it! Nice Job! You're almost there!"

The intensity of our excitement increased. We watched Tim get closer and closer to the sandbar. Such a simple thing to be caught up in such a simple struggle. Archetypal. We wanted him to make it. We wanted him to pull himself from the water and stand on the sandbar, exhausted, smiling, and waving to us to join him.

Tim inched his way against the current toward the sandbar. Finally, he was able to stop swimming and drop his feet. All of us on the rock let out a hoot! as he began to swing his body with powerful strides against the rapidly flowing river. The water was just below his chest.

Suddenly, Tim wasn't there. One moment he is nearly to the sandbar and the very next instant he is gone. Completely vanished. It seemed like he took a lightening-fast backflip into the water. Just before Tim disappeared I thought I saw his face go into a bunch of o's. His eyes made o's. His mouth made an o. A big o. Oh! But no sound. We were stunned. We stood paralyzed by our total absorption in what had happened. We weren't comprehending what we witnessed. No one moved. No one spoke.

When Time vanished I became fully focused in the present. Nothing else existed. The eternal now. All my perceptions were heightened. The roar of the water was overwhelming. In this state, for this moment, I was the Baro River.

Tim's right arm raised from the river. It stayed suspended and motionless for what seemed a long time. His hand appeared to quiver ever so slightly before disappearing once again beneath the surface of the water. Still, no one made a sound. I think I was the first to say "crocodile."

...Now the natives on the shore made more sense to me. They had come to watch the crazy "foreign-gies" swim in the Baro River with the crocodile (Crawford, 1991, pp. 5–6).

Would this account make you want to read the whole article? Is it the power of the *story*, or the puzzle about how it might be used to advance a *theory* of ethnographic practice, that motivates you *more*? Are these two goals mutually exclusive, or mutually reinforcing?

How you answer this question is key to understanding what narrative style works for you. And why it works. It is also an important question to raise about scholarship in general. What is a narrative style in scholarship *for*? What is new *ethnographic* scholarship *for*? Is there a difference? Is your definition of scholarly purpose large enough, accommodating enough?

Or should it *not* be too large, or necessarily accommodating?

What standards for ethnographic scholarship are *you* willing to live with? To write *within*? To *apply* to all the writing that you read?

❏   ❏

Perhaps it is not the exotic that draws you to ethnographic reading. Perhaps you are more persuaded to read something closer to home, say one woman's experiences with men on a college campus? You are intrigued by prose that illuminates the ordinary, the everyday. You are rhetorically pulled into accounts that explain a particular communication practice or behavior. Maybe you are induced to respond to it because what happens in it mirrors your personal experiences.

Below is a frank excerpt from a new ethnography of remarkable rhetorical intensity. Written by Annette Markham, it tells a story about using conversations to acquire cultural knowledge about a college sweatshirt that displays the message "Go Ugly Early":

> Stacy: "Go Ugly Early" means since it's inevitable that a guy's gonna get drunk and make a poor judgment about who to take home to fuck, he might as well get drunk quickly and choose the ugly girl early—make that poor judgment sooner rather than later.... It's indicative of a kind of general lack of respect for a woman's personhood. It seems to me to be sign-evidence of a tendency to take women as nothing more than sexual objects, whose sexuality is defined in terms of fairly constrained notions of attractiveness.... I think it says to men, "Fuck anything you can...any hole is a good hole," that's what I think this message says. Ideally, you would not want to fuck something that you don't want to face in the morning, but, you know, if you have to...
> (Markham, 1999, p. 5).

Markham collects data from bars, from colleagues, and from her reading of Foucault. She links the culturally inscribed meanings of this expression to issues of gender, of age, of self. She opines:

> If I am that which I study, or if I am part of that which I study, then my own understanding must be acknowledged, can be interpreted, should be scrutinized. The expression, as many have pointed out, does not live only on the backs of Jake's sweatshirts, although from this place it appears and addresses the observer as well as the wearer. As we encounter the phrase, it somehow enters out sense-making mind and influences the way we know and understand our worlds. But the expression also lives in the attitudes and behaviors of those who execute the directive "Go Ugly Early," whether or not they utter the phrase or wear the sweatshirt. And as they live it, we live it, because our lives are inextricably linked in a dense tapestry of interconnected threads.
>
> So to study my understanding is to know a bit more about how this expression gets played out and how it plays with our knowledge of self and others and our enactment of everyday life (Markham, p. 15).

From an outward expression emerges an inward path. Does her journey appeal to you?

Do you *learn* from it?

WHAT IS IT ABOUT ethnographic writing that induces you to learn?

Do you learn best when you are *emotionally* involved in the story, *intellectually* engaged, or both? Is there some necessary categorical or experiential difference between the two? Or, is this ordinary distinction merely arbitrary, brought on by a lifetime of cultural brainwashing about the ways of minds and hearts? Does this Cartesian division add to, detract from, or just interfere with your reading practices? With what you think you should learn from scholarship?

Consider the following excerpt from an ethnographic account written by Nick Trujillo about his own grandmother:

> I was devastated when I learned about the death of my grandmother, whom my sisters and I called "Naunny." I vividly remember when I heard the message from my dad on the answering machine that January evening in 1994. I instantly fell to my knees and started crying and praying for her. I knew she had been moved to a nursing home because of her dementia and that she had developed a case of the flu, but I had no idea that her flu had turned into serious pneumonia. To this day, I still wish that my

dad had called me earlier so that I could have traveled to Los Angeles to see Naunny one more time; instead, I went there to attend her funeral and deliver her eulogy.

Two summers later, I visited relatives in Los Angeles for the first time since her death. Whenever I visited L.A. in past years, I would always spend time with Naunny and Pete, her second husband, and it felt very empty not being able to visit her in her little apartment in East L.A. So instead of visiting her there, I decided to visit her at her gravesite (Trujillo, 1998, p. 344).

Trujillo uses this framing to account for how he responded to a death in his family, but also to bring life to the narratives about "Naunny" that defined her life. Ethnographically, he critically examines family stories about identity, using collected narrative accounts, metaphors, and memorable moments as the rhetorical foundation for a larger argument about how women, in general, are interpreted by their family members.

Now, what interests you more: the opening narrative, or my explanation of Trujillo's ethnographic purpose? Or, is it the way the rhetorical and narrative foundations—the argument and the metonym—intertwine to produce knowledge? Is there something important to be learned from this powerful collaboration between rhetorical devices used to construct, or to produce, *interest, empathy*, and *knowledge?*

But there is more to examine in the above excerpt. Everyone has a family, and, in most cases, everyone has a personal experience of a family member's death. Does the feeling that you might *closely identify* with an author's personal account *worry* you as you read, or does it *help* you, does it enable the reading in some way? Why is that?

What do you expect *to learn* from reading scholarship, anyway?

What are you going *to do* with ethnographic knowledge?

What is the role, and function, of storied knowledge in the world?

TELL ME THE LAST IMPORTANT THING you learned from reading an ethnography.

Don't sidestep this question, or ambush it, or strategically adapt your answer to fit what you think I am after, or your professor is after. Just tell me. I don't care if you learned it from a book or an article, from a magazine, or from a dramatic performance. I don't care if it was fiction, or nonfiction, or autobiography, or autoethnography, or a performance, or advertising copy. What I do care about is your *answer.*

I want to know what you learned. That's all.

You want me to go first?

Okay, I'll share. The last best thing I learned from reading an ethnography came from combining the insights from Carolyn Ellis's brave, beautiful, and evocative account, *Final Negotiations* (1995), with those of her husband, Art Bochner's, painful and conflicted account of the death of his father (1997). I can't excerpt passages from both works and do justice to either of them or to the joint relational dialogue they provide. I can't let you cruise them, either.

You'll just have to read them for yourself. Ellis's account is a book about many things, but specifically about her relationship with her mentor/lover as he died. About the academic and professional culture they lived with, and within. About the emotions associated with living a life of the mind, and the minds associated with living a life in academic culture that often denies our emotions. Bochner's account is written as an article about the "divided self" that is produced in the academy, and that is, for him, brought into view when his father dies while he is attending a professional convention.

What did I learn from these independent yet ethnographically and theoretically collaborative works?

The easy answer is, I learned more about the human experiences of love and death, and how they are intimately connected. *Big* stuff.

I also learned about love in death in Trujillo's piece, and in Crawford's. I am drawn to writing that isn't afraid to ask the big questions about life, and to writing that links those big questions to how I can understand my life in this cosmos, on this blue planet, a bit better.

But between Ellis's and Bochner's elegant prose accounts is something else I am hungry for. Something I narratively *desire*. Something I think maybe I can contribute to. That is: writing about life in the academy. I am, lately, interested in writing ethnographic accounts of women and men who, like myself, lead institutional lives within the peculiar subcultural framing of a university or college. People who live life with passion and energy, who are excited about ideas, and who view their work as the expression of their lives.

I don't think we have scratched the proverbial surface in our critical and cultural appreciation for the ordinary, everyday—as well as the extraordinary—experiences of this group. Nor do I think we have adequately turned our critical attention toward the stuff of our lives, and our selves, in these institutional contexts. Not only do I believe we will find "news" there, I also believe we will find resources for personal, social, professional, and institutional liberation.

So that's what I learned recently.

Your turn.

◻   ◻

Big, Important Questions. Let me dwell on this idea, and its place in the new ethnography, a little longer.

Some years ago, I wrote an ethnographic study about the spirituality of community (Goodall, 1996). I had a hard time writing it. In part, it was hard because I was writing about spirituality, and finding language to express the experiences of the ineffable is difficult. But it was also difficult because for a long while I couldn't find the *nerve* to talk about the Big, Important Stuff. Fortunately, I ran across an article in the *Western Journal of Communication* by Janice Hocker Rushing (1993). Her article makes an intriguing case for understanding the narrative tensions among the rhetorical characters of Power, Other, and Spirit as *three historical figures* engaged in an unfolding drama in and about Western civilization. She uses these figures to discuss cultural themes, but I read into her account a way to *adapt* them to my ethnographic project. Here was a scholar unafraid to tackle the Big Stuff.

I used this pioneering study to further my own explanatory language and narrative development. I was empowered by her prose to ask larger questions, and, as a result, to explore ways of writing spirit into a community. The questions that dominate that particular text are: Who are we when we "do" community? Why are we *here,* doing or performing, these communal practices? Why are we the beings who use symbols to communicate, and use communication to build communities? What are the studies and practices of communication teaching us about *who* we are? About what communication is *for?*

I couldn't answer a lot of these questions. But raising them, and finding narrative methods of inquiry to explore them, opened my ethnographic self to a new *rhetorical* frontier of inquiry. I found a way to write about how experiences of the ineffable shape the everyday. I learned what it means to "read" between the lines of lived experience a variety of alternative interpretive possibilities. I became narratively involved in how individual life quests and communal participation figure into a larger puzzle about human purpose and agency.

Since then, I have been on the lookout for ethnographic studies that go after the Big Questions. One very interesting book (and accompanying video) is Mara B. Adelman and Lawrence R. Frey's *The Fragile Community: Living Together with AIDS* (1997). The book and video are remarkable in that they use shared symbolic codes as the basis for understanding the everyday dialectics of communities. But, moreover, I am taken by the narrative style used to accomplish a larger purpose: the intense display of communally constructed, diverse voices create a vision for community that simultaneously celebrates life while preparing its members for their inevitable deaths. Most of the informants in the Alexian House—persons we get to know through the writing and video—"pass" by the end of the book and film. Again, there is no particular excerpt to demonstrate the power of these narrative choices, but the ability to show the imminence of death in life, and of the relationship of our stories about our identities to it, is a fine example of text-making that evokes the Big Questions about life.

OKAY, SO MAYBE YOU AREN'T as interested as I am in ethnographies that go after the Big Questions. Fair enough. But let me ask you this: What is supposed to be the scholarly worth of a text?

The obvious answer is that it is supposed to be a "contribution to knowledge." *Whose* knowledge? And how do you know "a contribution" when you read it?

Spell out the exact terms of that rhetorical knowing for me, would you?

Is the basic thing here simply the acknowledged role of *critique* in our culture? Is a "contribution to knowledge" essentially a comparison of what you knew *before* you read to what you know *after* it? Or, is that only ever part of it?

Is it more likely that the art of critique is a *comparison,* not of what you learned to what you didn't know, so much as how well the writing *conforms to what you think writing ought to be or do?* A comparison of the writing to its *form* as an identifiable document of some kind. As an essay, or poem, or scholarly monograph? As a member of a class or genre of work? Is that it? Is that *really* it? And is it so *because* once you know what genre a piece of writing conforms to, you know what standards to use to evaluate it?

What about writing that challenges the textual boundaries of such conventions? What do you make of them? How do you make sense out of them? What does what you make of them *do* to your ideas about scholarship, to your applicable standards for evaluation? To your idea of making "a contribution to knowledge"?

How DOES, or how should, the new ethnography make contributions to knowledge? What are the relevant evaluative standards for new ethnographic writing?

By now, you know that by using the term "new ethnography," I am referring to an emerging, alternative style of qualitative writing. Specifically, I am referring to writing that combines the personal and the professional (for example, autoethnography, autobiography), as well as work that may be rendered as a story (for example, fiction or nonfiction), or an account that derives rhetorical force from a blurring or blending of literary genres.

Objections to these new forms of ethnography include: worry about the role of the emotions in scholarly writing, concern for revealing what is personal in what is supposed to be professional, the ethics of writing stories that get readers to closely identify with them. However, I think of these objections as indicative of a scholarly *misperception* or disciplinary *misunderstanding* of the goals, values, and ethics of new ethnographic writing.

As we saw in Chapters 1 and 2, the challenge of new ethnography is borne of a strong, paradigmatic historical association of written scholarship with: (1) the ethics and values of argumentation and debate, (2) a connection between the prescribed form of academic writing and effective public speaking, and (3) a preferred idiom for scholarly expression derived from describing, categorizing, and analyzing nonsymbol-using, unemotional phenomena, in the physical sciences.

Scholarly writing, therefore, is supposed to present clear, well-reasoned arguments to culturally like-minded readers. Its author is supposed to be superior to, distanced from, and objective about his or her subject. Its value is derived from contributing "findings" about the observed subject to an additive body of previous work. When done properly, findings lead to systematic generalizations.

Scholarly writing features prose that is largely self-less. It is writing that avoids references to a self, or doubt, or procedural ambiguities, or personal vulnerabilities. As well, it is writing that makes no references to the quality of lived experiences as a person, an academic, or a field researcher. It is writing that, looked at one way, is ungendered, divorced from class consciousness, and is unable or unwilling to give voice to its own racial or sexual subjectivity. It is writing disconnected from its cultural and institutional contexts. Yet viewed another way, to date it has been writing that privileges a masculine, middle-class, heterosexual, and white set of rhetorical and critical standards; it is writing that above all has displayed the values of academic culture and institutional life. Viewed either way, it is writing that dismisses personal preferences and matters of taste, ignores issues related to sexual orientation, and denies the importance of the vast human landscape of emotions.

New ethnography, ideally, does *not* behave in any of these ways. It is writing that is untamed, and in some rhetorical ways undisciplined. It overtly privileges the personal over the so-called objective, and if it is good, it dissolves any idea of distance, doesn't produce "findings," isn't generalizable, only has credibility when self-reflexive and authority when richly vulnerable. Rather than being governed by an ethic derived from British colonial sportsmanship as practiced by combative, individual, self-denying, self-sacrificing men, ours is an ethic derived from a more evolved *dialogic* standard. I mean "dialogic" here in the sense that refers to how women and men can use diverse narrative forms and personal language to share, and *to learn from,* the full communicative range of human questions, experiences, and meanings. Which is to say that ours is an ethic dedicated to the singular proposition that *close textual identification between consenting writers and readers is a very good thing.* It is a very good thing *not* because self-disclosure is in itself a good thing, and *not just* because it exposes our vulnerabilities and emotions, and *not* because it challenges the authority of traditional forms of reporting. It is a good thing because when it is done well, we can *learn previously unspoken, unknown things about culture and communication* from it.

⌗   ⌗

Allow me to explain. First, let us revisit the narrative premises of—and purposes for—the new ethnography.

New ethnography is a cultural way of coding academic attempts to author a *self* within a *context* of *others.* It is a way of writing to get to the *truth* of *our* experiences. It is a method of inquiry, scholarly inquiry, that privileges the exploration of a self *in response to questions that can only be answered that way,* through the textual construction of, and thoughtful reflection about, the *lived experiences of that self.*

191

As a form of *writing,* its intended goal is to craft words into stories and accounts capable of accomplishing those purposes. Because it is *not* about describing and explaining others or otherness beyond that which is necessary to the central task (or is implicit in any rendering of the self), the fact that it can achieve its purposes should not be confused with simple narcissism or academic navel-gazing. The criticism that the new ethnography is narcissistic applies largely to writing that *doesn't* achieve its purpose. If the questions raised about the inspected self are not highly important, and if the prose used to answer it is not rhetorically and stylistically compelling, chances are good that bad thinking and bad writing are at fault—not the goals of new ethnography itself.

This is not only a problem with ethnography. We live and participate happily in an academic culture that rejects about 90 percent of all work submitted as scholarship on the grounds that it represents bad thinking or bad writing. An even higher rejection rate may be applied to all the novels, poetry, plays, and collections of essays submitted to publishers every year. But I don't hear anyone screaming that as a result of poor execution, novels, poetry, and essays in general have no worth, or that they shouldn't be published.

Our problem is pretty easy to diagnose. Just because an author claims to have written a new ethnography doesn't mean it is *good* new ethnography. Or just because some ethnographer pens a narcissistic account doesn't mean that *all* new ethnography consists of narcissistic accounts. As some famous somebody once put it: "The problem with Narcissus was *not* that he looked at the reflected image of himself in the water, but that he didn't look long or hard enough at it. Had he done that, his critique would have been more *self-reflexive* and the lessons learned from it more worthwhile."

Ethically then, my obligation *to readers* depends on whether I think there is educational worth—another way of saying "scholarly value"—in what I have written. Am I posing interesting *research questions?* Are my questions and concerns *important?* Is my work *informed by the current literature?* Can my writing help readers *learn?* Does the narrative style help *fulfill my purpose?* Personally, I write down a lot of ethnographic things that never become public; they may begin as good ideas but become too weird, or too shallow, or just not very well rendered. I may write myself into something—some narrative place, rhetorical dead-end, or theoretical silliness—that I can't write my way out of. I may complete a piece of work, circulate it to friends and colleagues, and receive feedback that either encourages me to rethink and rewrite it, or to abandon it altogether. But what I *do* choose to share as a work of new ethnography, I do so because I think it may help inform and inspire *readers*. The narrative form and informational content work *together*. The rhetoric *achieves* its desired purpose.

I think of the intent to inform and inspire as *writerly* obligations. I conceive of them in much in the same way as Bill Rawlins (1998) describes the *communicative* obligations that close friends share: *Friends bust friends out of jails*. If that "jail" happens to be constructed out of a narrative of denial, or a of lack of self-awareness, or out of fear, or anxiety, over the content of a life, then I believe my ethical purpose is to help readers *find the strength to deal with it*. Which is to say, I want to rhetorically craft words capable of helping them to explore, to create, and to build a new language pattern for expressing, for liberating, that "jailed" part of themselves that has been "unsentence-able."

One dialogic problem with this approach is that vulnerable readers may find that what is brought out of them by the prose *may not always be pretty*. Or *tame*. The process of self-discovery I aim to inspire may prove *painful*. It may unlock experiences that some readers don't want to unlock, take them to places within themselves they don't really want to explore, or at least not explore *again*.

A related problem is that new ethnography sometimes challenges a reader's sensibilities. For example, readers with a heteronormative sensibility may be confronted with a homonormative tale. Such was certainly the case with the publication of a study of a cultural performance called "Sextext" (Corey and Nakayama, 1997). Some of the objections to that essay's being part of our scholarly literature reminded me of how men used to object to the idea that women should hold property or vote. Or that black people should sit anywhere but in the back of the bus. I don't doubt that some people are offended by this scholarly display of democratic values, but to deny that homonormative writing ought to have a place in our culture is an *egregious* form of censorship. Perhaps scholars can reach a tolerant middle ground if new ethnographers agree that our work should be marketed with a warning from the Surgeon General: "This form of writing may be dangerous to you! *It may mess with your head!*"

Frankly, I don't think messing with your head is a problem. I think messing with your head is what *all* scholarship should be and do. It should be *dangerous*. It should *expand your mind*. It should open locks, provide pathways, offer a language capable of inspiring personal, social, and institutional liberation. I think it should help people think and behave differently, if they choose to. *Writing that doesn't mess with your head isn't very good writing.*

THE SECOND CULTURAL OBJECTION based on a misunderstanding of new ethnographic goals is that what we publish, as informational products, are highly suspect, at least to some readers. The question is often asked: How are we supposed to judge the worth of somebody's personal story, anyway? Or, of what theoretical or methodological value is one person's anecdotal experience?

As I've said, one of the most "disturbing" characteristics of new ethnography to traditional academic readers is a prose style at odds with the clear, scholarly preference for an impersonal, nonemotional, argumentative, idiom of representation. But I agree with what Clifford Geertz says: "The strange idea that reality has an idiom in which it prefers to be described, that its very nature demands we talk about it without fuss—a spade is a spade, a rose is a rose—on pain of illusion, trumpery, and self-bewitchment, leads to the even stranger idea that, if literalism is lost, *so is fact*" (1988, p. 140; emphasis mine).

I don't buy the idea that alternative forms of writing sacrifice information value, and neither did Geertz. Humans are symbol-users, creatures *born to* use the gift of language, *storytellers* from the very origins of articulation. We learn from accounts of our experiences, and from the experiences of others, by exploring *the language* that shapes and guides *the storying* of those experiences. The more natural the story, the easier it is to read—and to get close to, or identify with—the facts and the feelings of what is being said. The more closely we can narratively identify with the facts and feelings, the nearer we are to getting to an experience of *truth* in what is being said. If the question we ask is worthy enough, if the issue is compelling enough, then *whatever story form* that evokes or answers it should be good enough, too. Do scholars really have a place to stand—epistemologically, ontologically, rhetorically, or pragmatically—that licenses a *dis*regard for revealed truth because of the *form* of its expression? Or, is there a theoretical posture that allows us to negate the *value of information* because of its *poetics?* Regardless of the idiom chosen, scholars, poets, fiction writers, dramatists, and performance artists organize theories, methods, facts, and feelings—*the information we use to make* *sense of our lives, cultures, and communication*—into many different types of stories and into variously genred accounts.

But scholarly objections are also raised about the seeming inability of reviewers and readers to judge the *worth* of a personal story. If it makes us weep, or shout, or laugh, is this enough? If it is written in an appealing way, if its poetry is sensuous, and its story sublime, is this enough? If it speaks directly to my heart, but leaves my colleague next door cold, how should I evaluate its scholarly effectiveness and heuristic worth?

In other words, how do we know when new ethnography is good scholarship?

WHAT ARE OUR CULTURAL STANDARDS for evaluating the worth of stories in general?

First and foremost, a good story is decidedly more *metonymic* than argumentative. In other words, good stories strive to use *relational* language and narrative styles to create a purposeful *dialogue* between the readers and the author. This dialogue proceeds through close, personal identification—and recognition of difference—of the reader's experiences, thoughts, and emotions, with those of the author. This dialogic process is dependent on a mutual investment and mutual risk-taking, as well as a shared belief that how we end up (at the end of the essay or book) is going to be based on the *quality* of what we share through the writing/reading experience.

A good story is a good *read*. It gives pleasure, enlivens the imagination, and delights the senses. It appeals as a form of literature as well as a way of knowing. It teaches through its manner of expression as well as through its claims about the world.

What makes a good story a *scholarly* good story?

Second, good scholarly new ethnographic writing *affects* and *influences* us. As I've said, it tells a good story—that is part of it—and, like a good story, it also induces us to think, to reflect, and to feel. But in its telling, good new ethnography also asks us to examine, or to reexamine, taken-for-granted assumptions, theoretical orientations, and scholarly meanings we associate with cultures. In the field of communication studies, scholarly reexaminations of meanings are most directly applicable to communication practices, activities, and performances. A piece may reveal choices that we find inspiring, troubling, funny, smart, or sad, but the purpose of that revelation is thematically linked to advancing "knowledge" by addressing a "research question."

Third, good scholarly new ethnography is *self-reflexive*. It is told through the voice of a narrator who isn't shy about examining her- or himself as she or he examines others and contexts. This is accomplished by the development of a persona capable of thinking, reflecting, and examining the self on the page. Self-reflexive moments are used to add personal background information to an account, reveal the author's complicity in how something happened, or pose difficult questions that do not necessarily have clearly defined answers.

Such scholarly new ethnographic prose may induce in us a sense of human connection, achievement, potential, personal loss, envy, pride, compassion, or uniqueness, among many other emotions. But such relational inducements serve the greater purpose of getting us to read in ways that challenge or further what we know. We may identify closely with the writer, or not, or just feel deeply for her or his plight. But our identifications should do something other than establish connections; they should *use those connections* to give us what Kenneth Burke (1989) calls "equipment" to think, and to feel, with.

So, yes, we may laugh, cry, or not know whether to laugh or cry. Because these responses are human, they should be welcome in our scholarly community. But these responses are not enough to warrant a particular piece of writing's being called a *scholarly* contribution. To reach that level requires that an author write about the self in ways that lead to readers' *personal reflection*. Within that reflection, we may be convinced of the truth of something we used to be uncertain about, or suspicious about a truth we never before thought to question. We may learn something entirely new, or overturn something we have long believed. Or even this: We may suddenly turn around in our own earthly space and realize that we will never again be able to turn around in that space in quite the same way.

Finally, good scholarly new ethnography usually *produces scholarly talk and editorial controversy*. One of the uneasy lessons I've learned from serving on editorial boards is that it is a myth to assume that our field—or perhaps any of the humanities fields—has a common litera-ture, much less a common theoretical or methodological ground. What we *do* have is a series of seemingly required references that differ radi-cally from subspecialty to subspecialty, from journal to journal. One cultural commonplace is that there appears to be a correspondence between scholarly citations and the lists of names on our editorial mast-heads. But ours is a status hierarchy, a meritocracy, in which scholarly publication is equated with critical skills. Entry into the ranks of the Often Named depends on publication success. The more we publish, the more Often Named we become. The more Often Named we become, the better the proof of our status as scholars in the field. Then, as it is with the election of all scholarly elites, journal review boards are formed, and the women selected for inclusion cut their hair, while the men selected for inclusion grow whiskers.

Pardon me. I can't help myself sometimes.

Anyway, that's just the way it *appears* to be. It is the way it appears to be because we have decided to act as if it has been written down somewhere. Funny, I can't seem to find that old stone tablet. What I *have* found is that work that lives the longest in our texts tends to inspire talk among colleagues and, in some cases, become highly controversial. This means, put simply, that other scholars can present convention papers, organize panels, and publish articles talking, learning from, critiquing, and fighting about it. Anything that causes us to behave in these ways is probably an honest clue to what a realistic standard ought to be for perceiving and measuring scholarly worth.

In this regard, I've rarely seen a set of reviews that said exactly the same things about a potentially publishable piece, but I have seen a lot of commonality in critiques about work that was rejected. What we apparently *do* know is what *bad* writing and *bad* thinking read like. Bad writing *re-presents* bad thinking. It is writing that fails to capture and sustain our interest, doesn't tell a good story or make a good case, falls short of describing or analyzing its characters or texts well, and doesn't amount to informed relevant literature in the field.

It's bad. It's bad *writing.*

Probably the best measure of what good scholarly writing is—whether it is traditional, new ethnographic, or otherwise—can be summed up this way: We will recommend it enthusiastically to people we call our friends, colleagues, and students.

❏   ❏

In summary, I think the major problems or challenges facing writers of new ethnographies are those derived from a deep, disciplinary misunderstanding of our purpose. I think this misunderstanding is made worse by trying to associate the evaluative and ethical standards for traditional scholarly work with what is clearly an interpretive genre that does not share the narrative goals or argumentative values of traditional scholarship.

New ethnographers aren't writing to argue with anyone. We don't want to fight. We aren't aiming to win some kind of infantile war of who knows the bigger words. We aren't playing childish games such as "*My* [theoretical] daddy is bigger than *your* [theoretical] daddy!" or participating in the usual disciplinary comparisons about the length of our scholarly cigars. New ethnography isn't about establishing an additive line to an established body of research whose contributions can be easily articulated as objective "findings." And, we will never agree that what makes work "scholarly" has any necessary relationship to the idiom of its natural expression.

What I hope we are doing through the practice of new ethnography is *evolving to a higher state of scholarly consciousness.* The measure of our human worth will be in the quality, and the difficulty, of writing through the questions we ask, as well as in the ways in which our stories speak to the communicative needs—to the souls and hearts and minds—of other human beings. We want to use our work to build closer relationships with our readers and a stronger, more open, more diverse, and certainly a more thoroughly humane, scholarly community.

Ours is a *dialogic* ethic, and a *transformational* vision.

The time has come in the academy to change some of our academic standards, for the *better.* To improve what and how we know, as well as whom we know it *for,* and why we know it *at all.* To enable an intellectual evolution in our field away from sponsoring knowledge for its own sake, to sponsoring knowledge for the sake of humankind. To use what we write, and what we write about, to make differences—positive, productive differences—in the lives of people.

In my view, how we learn to read and write the new ethnography will help make these changes in the world, and in the academy.

References

Adelman, M. B., and Frey, L. R. (1997). *The Fragile Community: Living together with AIDS*. Mahwah, NJ: Lawrence Earlbaum.

Agar, M. (1994). *Language shock: Understanding the culture of conversation*. New York: Morrow.

Agee, J., and Evans, W. (1941, 1984). *Let us now praise famous men*. Birmingham, AL: Southern Living Galleries.

Anderson, C. (1987). *Style as argument*. Carbondale: Southern Illinois University Press.

Anderson, J. A., and Goodall, H. L. (1995). Writing the body ethnographic: From a rhetoric of representation to a poetics of inquiry. In *Building communication theories*, edited by F. Casmir. Hillsdale, NJ: Lawrence Earlbaum Associates.

Anderson, W. T. (1990). *Reality isn't what it used to be: Theatrical politics, ready-to-wear religion, global myths, primitive chic, and other wonders of the postmodern world*. New York: HarperCollins.

Atkinson, P. (1990). *The ethnographic imagination: Textual constructions of reality*. London: Routledge.

Bahktin, M. (1984). *Problems of Dostoevsky's poetics*. Ed. and trans. C. Emerson. Minneapolis: University of Minnesota Press.

Banks, A., and Banks, S. P. (1998). *Fiction and social research*. Walnut Creek, CA: AltaMira Press.

Barthes, R. (1972). *Mythologies*. New York: Hill & Wang.

Barthes, R. (1979). From work to text. In J. V. Harari (ed.), *Textual strategies: Perspectives in post-structuralist criticism*. Ithaca, NY: Cornell University Press.

Bazerman, C. (1988). *Shaping written knowledge: The genre and activity of the experimental article in science*. Madison: University of Wisconsin Press.

Behar, R. (1993). *Translated woman: Crossing the border with Esperanza.* Boston: Beacon.

Behar, R. (1996). *The vulnerable observer: Anthropology that breaks your heart.* Boston: Beacon.

Benson, T. (1980). Another shootout in cowtown. *Quarterly Journal of Speech 67:* 347–406.

Blair, C., Brown, J., and Baxter, L. (1995). Disciplining the feminine. *Quarterly Journal of Speech 81:* 1–24.

Blythe, W. (1998). *Why I write: Thoughts on the practice of fiction.* Philadelphia: Little, Brown, and Company.

Bochner, A. (1994). Perspectives on inquiry II: Theories and stories. In *Handbook of interpersonal communication,* edited by M. L. Knapp and G. R. Miller. Newbury Park, CA: Sage.

Bochner, A. (1997). It's about time: Narrative and the divided self. *Qualitative Inquiry 3:* 418–439.

Brockriede, W. (1972). Arguers as lovers. *Philosophy and Rhetoric 5:* 1–11.

Brown, R. H. (1997). *Postmodern representations.* Urbana: University of Illinois Press.

Buber, M. (1985). *Between man and man.* 2nd ed. New York: Macmillan.

Bullis, C., and Bach, B. W. (1989). Socialization turning points: An examination of change in organizational identification. *Western Journal of Speech Communication 53:* 273–293.

Burke, K. (1935). *Counter-statement.* New York: Bobbs-Merrill.

Burke, K. (1957). *The philosophy of literary form.* New York: Vintage.

Burke, K. (1969). *A rhetoric of motives.* Berkeley: University of California Press.

Burke, K. (1989). *Symbols and society.* Chicago: University of Chicago Press.

Charmaz, K., and Mitchell, R. G. (1996). The myth of silent authorship: Self, substance, and style in ethnographic writing. In *Reflexivity and voice,* edited by R. Hertz. Thousand Oaks, CA: Sage.

Chiseri-Strater, E., and Sunstein, B. S. (1997). *Fieldworking: Reading and writing research.* Upper Saddle River, NJ: Blair Press/Prentice Hall.

Clifford, J. (1983). On ethnographic authority. *Representations 1,* no. 2: 118–146.

Clifford, J., and Marcus, G. (1986). *Writing culture: The poetics and politics of ethnography.* Berkeley: University of California Press.

Communication Studies 298, California State University, Sacramento (1997). Fragments of self at the postmodern bar. *Journal of Contemporary Ethnography 26:* 251–292.

Conquergood, D. (1991). Rethinking ethnography: Towards a critical cultural politics. *Communication Monographs 58:* 179–194.

Conquergood, D. (1993). Homeboys and hoods: Gang communication and cultural style. In *Communication in context: Studies of naturalistic groups,* edited by L. Frey. Hillsdale, NJ: Lawrence Earlbaum Associates.

Conquergood, D., and Siegel, T. (1990). *The heart broken in half.* Video-documentary (58 mins.). Chicago: Siegel Productions; New York: Filmmakers Library.

Corey, F., and Nakayama, T. K. (1997). Sextext. *Text and Performance Quarterly 17:* 58–68.

Crapanzano, V. (1986). Hermes' dilemma: The masking of subversion in ethnographic description. In *Writing Culture,* edited by J. Clifford and G. E. Marcus. Berkeley: University of California Press.

Crawford, L. (1991). Personal ethnography. Paper presented at the Alta Conference on Organizational Communication, Alta, UT, July.

deCerteau, M. (1984). *The practice of everyday life.* Berkeley: University of California Press.

deCerteau, M. (1996). *The practice of everyday life, volume II: Living and cooking.* Berkeley: University of California Press.

Denzin, N. K. (1989). *Interpretive interactionism.* Newbury Park, CA: Sage.

Denzin, N. K. (1996). *Interpretive ethnography.* Walnut Creek, CA: AltaMira Press.

Eisenberg, E. M. (1998). From anxiety to possibility: Poems 1987–1997. In *Fiction and social research,* edited by A. Banks and S. P. Banks. Walnut Creek, CA: AltaMira Press.

Eisenberg, E., and Goodall, H. L. (1997). *Organizational communication: Balancing creativity and constraint,* 2nd ed. New York: St. Martin's.

Ellis, C. (1993). "There are survivors": Telling a story of sudden death. *Sociological Quarterly 34:* 711–730.

Ellis, C. (1995). *Final Negotiations.* Philadelphia: Temple University Press.

Ellis, C., and Bochner, A., eds. (1996). *Composing ethnography.* Walnut Creek, CA: AltaMira Press.

Ellis, C., and Flaherty, M., eds. (1993). *Investigating subjectivity.* Newbury Park, CA: Sage.

Ellis, C., Keisinger, C., and Tillmann-Healy, L. (1997). Interactive interviewing: Talking about emotional experience. In *Reflexivity and Voice,* edited by R. Hertz. Thousand Oaks, CA: Sage.

Emerson, R. M., Fretz, R. I., and Shaw, L. L. (1995). *Writing ethnographic fieldnotes.* Chicago: University of Chicago Press.

Fisher, W. (1987). *Human communication as narration.* Columbia: University of South Carolina Press.

Geertz, C. (1973). *The interpretation of cultures.* New York: Basic Books.

Geertz, C. (1983). *Local knowledge.* New York: Basic Books.

Geertz, C. (1988). *Works as lives: The anthropologist as author.* Stanford: Stanford University Press.

Geertz, C. (1995). *After the fact.* Cambridge: Harvard University Press.

Goffman, E. (1959). *The presentation of self in everyday life.* Garden City, NJ: Anchor/Doubleday.

Goffman, E. (1967). *Interaction ritual.* Harmondsworth, Eng.: Penguin.

Goffman, E. (1974). *Frame analysis.* Philadelphia: University of Pennsylvania Press.

Goffman, E. (1980). *Forms of talk.* Philadelphia: University of Pennsylvania Press.

Goodall, H. L. (1980). *Courtship as a rhetorical form: An analysis of the interpersonal communication of Zelda and Scott Fitzgerald.* Dissertation, Pennsylvania State University.

Goodall, H. L. (1983a). *Human communication: Creating reality.* Dubuque, IA: Wm. C. Brown.

Goodall, H. L. (1983b). The nature of analogic discourse. *Quarterly Journal of Speech 69:* 171–179.

Goodall, H. L. (1989a). On becoming an organizational detective: The role of context sensitivity and intuitive logics in communication consulting. *Southern Communication Journal 55:* 42–54.

Goodall, H. L. (1989b). *Casing a promised land: The autobiography of an organizational detective as cultural ethnographer.* Carbondale: Southern Illinois University Press.

Goodall, H. L. (1990). A theatre of motives and the meaningful orders of persons and things. In *Communication Yearbook 13,* edited by J. A. Anderson. Newbury Park, CA: Sage.

Goodall, H. L. (1991). *Living in the rock n roll mystery: Reading context, self, and others as clues.* Carbondale: Southern Illinois University Press.

Goodall, H. L. (1993). Mysteries of the future told: Communication as the material manifestation of spirituality. *World Communication Journal 22:* 40–49.

Goodall, H. L. (1994a). *Casing a promised land, expanded edition.* Carbondale: Southern Illinois University Press.

Goodall, H. L. (1994b). Living in the rock n roll campaign, or, myth, media, and the American public imagination: An intertextual quest. In *Bill Clinton on stump, state, and stage: The rhetorical road to the White House,* edited by S. A. Smith. Fayetteville: University of Arkansas Press.

Goodall, H. L. (1996). *Divine signs: Connecting spirit to community.* Carbondale: Southern Illinois University Press.

Goodall, H. L. (1997). Transforming communication studies through ethnography. In Judith Trent (ed.), *Communication for the 21st century.* Boston: Allyn & Bacon.

Goodall, H. L. (1999). Casing the academy for community. *Communication Theory 9:* 1–30.

Hall, S. (1997). *Representation and the Media.* Video (55 mins.). Northampton, MA: Media Education Foundation.

Hastrup, K. (1995). *A passage to anthropology: Between experience and theory.* London: Routledge.

Hertz, R. (1997). *Reflexivity and voice.* Thousand Oaks, CA: Sage.

Hillman, J. (1991). *Blue fire: Selected writings of James Hillman.* New York: HarperPerennial.

Homans, G. C. (1961). *Social behavior: Its elementary forms.* New York: Harcourt, Brace, & World.

Hopper, R. (1992). *Telephone conversation.* Indianapolis: Indiana University Press.

Hopper, R. (1998). Flirtations: Conversation analysis from fiction and life. In *Fiction and Social Research,* edited by A. Banks and S. P. Banks. Walnut Creek, CA: AltaMira Press.

Jackson, M. (1989). *Paths toward a clearing.* Indianapolis: Indiana University Press.

Jones, S. H. (1998). *Kaleidoscope Notes.* Walnut Creek, CA: AltaMira Press.

Kellett, P. M. (1999). Dialogue and dialectics in managing organizational change: The case of a mission-based transformation. *Southern Communication Journal 64:* 211–231.

Kellett, P. M., and Goodall, H. L. (1999). The death of discourse in our own (chat)room: "Sextext," learning organizations, and virtual communities. In *Soundbite culture: The death of discourse in a wired world*, edited by D. Slayden and R. K. Whillock. Thousand Oaks, CA: Sage.

Knapp, M. L., and Vangelista, A. L. (1992). *Interpersonal communication and human relationships*. 2nd ed. Boston: Allyn & Bacon.

Kreiger, S. (1991). *Social science and the self: Personal essays on an art form*. New Brunswick, NJ: Rutgers University Press.

Langellier, K. M. (1989). Personal narratives: Perspectives on theory and research. *Text and Performance Quarterly 9:* 243–276.

Louis, M. (1980). Surprise and sense-making: What newcomers experience in entering unfamiliar organizational settings. *Administrative Science Quarterly 23:* 225–251.

Lyotard, J. (1984). *The postmodern condition: A report on knowledge.* Minneapolis: University of Minnesota Press.

Mailer, N. (December 1997). Man at his best. In *Esquire,* p. 122.

Maines, D. 1997. On teaching tools and data in the use of biographies and autobiographies. National Communication Association, November 1997.

Malinowski, B. (1922). *Argonauts of the Western Pacific.* New York: Dutton.

Malinowski, B. (1967). *A diary in the strict sense of the term.* London: Routledge and Kegan Paul.

Manganaro, M. (1990). *Modernist anthropology: From fieldwork to text.* Princeton, NJ: Princeton University Press.

Manganaro, M. (1991). *Modernist anthropology.* Princeton, NJ: Princeton University Press.

Marcus, G. E., and Fischer, M. M. J. (1986). *Anthropology as cultural critique.* Chicago: University of Chicago Press.

Markham, A. (1999). "Go Ugly Early": The ethnography of an expression and the expression of an ethnography. Unpublished manuscript.

Mumby, D. (1993). *Narrative and social control.* Newbury Park, CA: Sage.

Mykhalovskiy, E. (1997). Reconsidering "table talk": Critical thoughts on the relationship between sociology, autobiography, and self-indulgence. In *Reflexivity and Voice,* edited by R. Hertz. Thousand Oaks, CA: Sage.

Nelson, C., and Watt, S. (1999). *Academic keywords.* New York: Routledge.

Neumann, M. (1996). Collecting ourselves at the end of the century. In *Composing ethnography: Alternative forms of qualitative writing,* edited by C. Ellis and A. P. Bochner. Walnut Creek, CA: AltaMira Press.

Okely, J., and Callaway, H. (1992). *Anthropology and autobiography.* London: Routledge.

Pacanowsky, M. E. (1988). Slouching towards Chicago. *Quarterly Journal of Speech 74:* 453–467.

Pacanowsky, M. E., and O'Donnell-Trujillo, N. (1983). Organizational communication as cultural performance. *Communication Monographs 50:* 126–147.

Paget, M. (1995). Performing the text. In *Representation in ethnography,* edited by John Van Maanen. Thousand Oaks, CA: Sage.

Pearce, B. (1989). *Communication and the human condition.* Carbondale: Southern Illinois University Press.

Philipsen, G. (1975). Speaking "like a man" in Teamsterville: Culture patterns of role enactment in an urban neighborhood. *Quarterly Journal of Speech 61:* 13–22.

Philipsen, G. (1976). Places for speaking in Teamsterville. *Quarterly Journal of Speech 62:* 15–25.

Philipsen, G. (1992). *Speaking culturally: Explorations in social communication.* Albany: State University Press of New York.

Rabinow, P. (1986). Representations are social facts: modernity and post-modernity in anthropology. In *Writing culture,* edited by J. Clifford and G. E. Marcus. Berkeley: University of California Press.

Rabinow, P., and Sullivan, W. M. (1987). Interpretive social science: A second look. Berkeley: University of California Press.

Rawlins, W. (1992). *Friendship matters.* New York: Aldine de Gruyter.

Rawlins, W. (1998). From ethnographic occupations to ethnographic stances. In *Communication: Views from helm for the 21st century,* edited by J. S. Trent. Boston: Allyn & Bacon.

Reissman, C. K. (1993). *Narrative analysis.* Newbury Park, CA: Sage.

Richardson, L. (1997). *Constructing the academic life.* New Brunswick, NJ: Rutgers University Press.

Rosaldo, R. (1989). *Culture and truth.* Boston: Beacon Press.

Rose, D. (1990). *Living the ethnographic life.* Thousand Oaks, CA: Sage.

Rothenbuhler, E. W. (1998). *Ritual communication: From everyday conversation to mediated ceremony.* Thousand Oaks, CA: Sage.

Rushing, J. H. (1993). Power, other, and spirit in cultural texts. *Western Journal of Communication 57:* 159–168.

Sacks, H. (1984/1970). On doing being ordinary. Edited transcript of lecture 1. University of California.

Sahlins, M. (1976). *Cultural and practical reason.* Chicago: University of Chicago Press.

Said, E. (1983). *The world, the text, and the critic.* Cambridge: Harvard University Press.

Sanjek, R. (1990). *Fieldnotes: The makings of anthropology.* Ithaca, NY: Cornell University Press.

Scheibel, D. (1995). "Making waves" with Burke: Surf Nazi culture and the rhetoric of localism. *Western Journal of Communication 59:* 251–269.

Scott, J. (1990). *Domination and the arts of resistance: Hidden transcripts.* New Haven, CT: Yale University Press.

Senge, P., et al. (1994). *The fifth discipline fieldbook.* New York: Doubleday/Currency.

Shorris, E. (1984). *Scenes from corporate life: The politics of middle management.* New York: Penguin.

Shotter, J. (1993). *Cultural politics and everyday life.* Toronto: University of Toronto Press.

Shotter, J., and Gergen, K. (1994). *Texts of identity.* Newbury Park, CA: Sage.

Shulman, D. (1994). Dirty data and investigative methods. *Journal of contemporary ethnography 23:* 214–253.

Stocking, G. (1983). *Observers observed.* Madison: University of Wisconsin Press.

Stoller, P. (1989). *The taste of ethnographic things.* Philadelphia: University of Pennsylvania Press.

Strine, M., Long, B., and Hopkins, M. F. (1990). Research in interpretation and performance studies: Trends, issues, priorities. In *Speech Communication: Essays to commemorate the 75th anniversary of The Speech Communication Association,* edited by G. M. Phillips and J. T. Wood. Carbondale: Southern Illinois University Press.

Tannen, D. (1990). *You just don't understand: Men and women in conversation.* New York: William Morrow.

Tannen, D. (1994). *Gender and discourse.* New York: Oxford University Press.

Taylor, B. (1997). Home zero: Images of home and field in nuclear-cultural studies. *Western Journal of Communication 61:* 209–234.

Tedlock, B. (1991). From participant observation to the observation of participation: The emergence of narrative ethnography. *Journal of Anthropological Research 47:* 69–94.

Tillmann-Healy, L. (1996). A secret life in a culture of thinness. In *Composing ethnography,* edited by C. Ellis and A. Bochner. Walnut Creek, CA: AltaMira Press.

Todorov, T. (1977). *The poetics of prose.* Ithaca, NY: Cornell University Press.

Trenholm, S. (1996). *Thinking through communication.* Boston: Allyn & Bacon.

Trujillo, N. (1997). Ethics and ethnography. National Communication Association annual convention, Chicago, November 1997.

Trujillo, N. (1998). In search of Naunny's grave. *Text and Performance Quarterly 18:* 344–368.

Trujillo, N., and Krizek, B. (1994). Emotionality in the stands and in the field: Expressing self through baseball. *Journal of Sport and Social Issues 18:* 303–325.

Turner, V. (1969). *The ritual process.* Ithaca, NY: Cornell University Press.

Tyler, S. A. (1988). *The unspeakable: Discourse, dialogue, and rhetoric in the postmodern world.* Madison: University of Wisconsin Press.

Tyler, S. A. (1992). On being out of words. In *Rereading Cultural Anthropology,* edited by G. E. Marcus. Durham, NC: Duke University Press.

Van Maanen, J. (1995). *Representation in ethnography.* Thousand Oaks, CA: Sage.

Van Maanen, J., and Barley, S. R. (1984). Occupational communities: Culture and control in organizations. *Research in Organizational Behavior 6:* 287–365.

Walcott, H. F. (1995). *The art of fieldwork.* Walnut Creek, CA: AltaMira Press.

Watzlawick, P., Beavin, J., and Jackson, D. (1967). *The pragmatics of human communication: A study of interactional patterns, pathologies, and paradoxes.* New York: Norton.

Weick, K. (1995). *Sense-making in organizations.* Newbury Park, CA: Sage.

Welker, L. S., and Goodall, H. L. (1997). Representation, interpretation, and performance: Opening the text of *Casing a Promised Land*. *Text and Performance Quarterly 17:* 109–122.

Wilkes, J. (1998). *The star chamber: The Independent Counsel's investigation of the President.* Fayetteville, AR: Pepperdine Press Books.

Wood, J. T. (1996). *Gendered lives.* Belmont, CA: Wadsworth Publishing Company.

Index

About the Author

H. L. (Bud) Goodall, Jr., is Professor and Head of the Department of Communication at the University of North Carolina–Greensboro. He is the author, or coauthor, of eighteen books about communication, organizations, and culture, including the classic ethnographic trilogy *Casing a Promised Land; Living in the Rock n Roll Mystery*; and *Divine Signs: Connecting Spirit to Community*. He has been selected for the Gerald M. Phillips Award for Mentoring from the American Communication Association, a "Texty" from the International Association of Textbook Authors, and an "At the Helm" in Ethnography address by the National Communication Association.

Madison could just see one of the spires of the cathedral on the far side of the park-like square across the street. She hoped Adam was up for exploring the building. She loved architecture. She couldn't remember ever telling him that. They spent most of their time together in the bedroom, and as much as she enjoyed every moment spent exploring his body, it might be nice to discover other interests they had in common. Did he like old buildings? She knew he drew animals in ink and charcoal—did that mean he liked nature? There was still so much she wanted to learn about him, but she knew as soon as he reappeared, her hormones would kick into high gear and her thoughts would wind up straight in the gutter. As usual.

Nearby, a musician played a low, haunting melody on the saxophone. Blues was not a type of music she listened to, but she couldn't deny that the sound tugged at her soul. She watched a horse pulling a buggy trot by, admiring the graceful stride of the beautiful animal. She needed to find some time to ride Ginger. She supposed that now that she was jobless, she'd have plenty of time to exercise her trusty mare. Elbow on the sticky table, she rested her chin on her fist and frowned. She still couldn't figure out how Joanna had found out about her relationship with Adam. Adam hadn't been to the office for several months. He'd finished his year-long probation and because he'd stayed out of trouble, he was no longer required to go to counseling. Had Joanna been sitting on the information about Madison's affair for that long? It seemed strange her relationship with Adam would become an issue now and not when the two of them had first taken their liaison to a deeper level. Thinking about having sex with Adam in her office had Madison crossing her legs. Damn, that had been hot. Even hotter than New Orleans in June. Not that central Texas was much cooler, but the humidity here was liable to give her heatstroke. She turned her face toward the gentle breeze coming in from the gulf and closed her eyes to relish the mild cooling sensation.

"Madison?"

She opened her eyes at the sound of her name on a stranger's lips. She was none too happy to discover who in New Orleans knew her by name. She frowned. The guy who'd

followed her through the airport was not on her list of people she wanted to hang out with.

"Hello, Chris," she said, her upbringing forcing her to be friendly to the guy. Dammit. "Are you enjoying the city?"

"Very much," he said. "Hey, I was wondering if you'd like to go out tonight."

"I already have plans with my boyfriend," she said.

Chris eyed the empty chair next to her skeptically. "Not sure what you see in him," he said and laughed.

"He's inside ordering."

"Whatever you say, sugar lips," Chris said. He saluted her with one finger and quickly disappeared into the crowd.

Madison shook off the feeling of uneasiness brought on by seeing the guy again. What were the chances? She supposed the odds weren't astronomical. They were both tourists in a very touristy part of the city, but she had to admit that running into him set her on edge. He didn't seem dangerous or particularly creepy, just interested. A bit too interested. Or maybe she was flattering herself. Chris hadn't tried to push himself on her much at all this time.

"Beignet for your thoughts," Adam said.

She straightened in her chair and smiled up at him, ridiculously glad to see him. He set a basket with three square pastries before her. The donut-sized treats were completely covered with powdered sugar.

"Oh," she said, "those look good!" She inhaled deeply, and her mouth watered. "And they smell even better."

Her stomach growled in agreement. And upon the first bite, her taste buds concurred. The beignet was similar to a donut, only chewier. And a bit messier. She soon had powdered sugar everywhere. Adam sat across from her and sipped his coffee.

"Something wrong?" he asked. "You were frowning when I walked up."

She shook her head. "Just thinking." She grinned at him. "I can actually do that when you're out of sight."

"Well, if thinking makes you frown, I guess I better stick around fulltime."

"You'll hear no complaints out of me," she said.

"You thinking about your job?" He pinched a corner off

one of her beignets and popped it into his mouth.

"Yeah," she said. "Just wondering why Joanna waited until now to fire me. You haven't been to the office for a few months. How long did she know about us?"

Adam shrugged. "It is strange. I wish you'd allow me to have a little chat with her."

"I think I'll try talking to her again," Madison said. "I was so stunned when she fired me, I didn't plead my case very well. Now that I've had a little time to digest the situation, I might be able to get my job back."

Adam reached across the table and squeezed her hand. "If that's what you want. If you change your mind about needing me, just say the word and I'm there."

She turned her hand over and laced her fingers through his. "I do need you," she said. "I just think this situation requires a little finesse."

He licked the sugar off the fingertips of his free hand. "You don't think I'm capable of finesse?"

Uh, no. She knew he wouldn't be able to maintain his composure if her boss talked to him the way she had talked to Madison. "She basically called me a slut and said I should have kept my legs closed."

Adam slammed a fist on the table, sloshing coffee from their cups. "That fucking bitch. She better not talk to you like that in front of me unless she wants a fist in her mouth."

She smiled, knowing he was mostly talk, but also knowing his attitude wouldn't help her cause. "Exactly the finesse I was talking about, sweetie."

She took a sip of her coffee, surprised by the rich, somewhat spicy flavor of the brew. "This is really good," she said, taking another sip.

"It's the chicory."

"No idea what chicory is, but I approve."

The beignets were fantastic as well and now that Adam was near, her thoughts turned away from her problems and focused once again on him. Maybe it wasn't practical to center her world around him, but she much preferred it to sulking about her reality. Even though her eyes were on the fascinating people strolling by and her ears were treated to the practiced

horn of the nearby musician, she was aware of Adam on a level she'd never experienced with another person. It was similar to how she knew her twin sister was near, but the awareness tugged at her from a different place. Only part of the reaction was sexual; she didn't have a name for the rest of it.

"Madison?"

She turned her head to meet his gaze, and was instantly drowning in his smoky gray eyes.

"You have a little something . . ." He leaned across the table and kissed her, his tongue trailing lightly over her lips.

Completely under his spell, she leaned forward, groaning in protest when he drew away.

"Sugar lips," he said with a grin that showed off the deep dimple near one corner of his sensual mouth. "Even sweeter than usual."

Sugar lips. That guy, Chris, had called her that earlier. She'd completely forgotten about his unexpected reappearance. Should she mention him to Adam? No. There wasn't really anything to tell. It wasn't like the guy had harassed her. And seeing him had just been a coincidence. Half the tourists in New Orleans were probably in the French Quarter at any given moment.

Having already devoured her first beignet, she picked up another and rubbed powdered sugar all over her mouth. "Oh," she said, "I seem to have a little something . . ."

Adam chuckled and leaned in for another kiss. She melted beneath his attention, kissing him back with as much passion as he showed her. Beneath her skirt, his hand moved to the bare skin of her knee. She was already so fired up that the simple touch of his fingertips against her skin sent waves of tingling pleasure up her thigh to pulse deep within her pussy.

"Is it time to go to that club yet?" she asked breathlessly when he tugged his lips from hers.

"Not yet."

Damn.

"So any luck with your writer's block?" Madison asked, hoping to distract herself from the very definition of distraction seated across from her.

"It will come," he said, picking at the corner off her spare

beignet and popping a piece into his mouth. She couldn't help but wonder if he was intentionally avoiding her eyes. "Today I just want to focus on you."

"I'm okay with that."

After brunch he took her hand and they headed across the street. Artists and fortune-tellers were set up along the sidewalk outside Jackson Park, which Adam said was named after Andrew Jackson. The park featured a statue of Jackson, the hero of the Battle of New Orleans, at its center.

They stopped short when a tall and lanky man, who reminded Madison of a clean-shaven Abraham Lincoln, stepped into their path. He touched Madison's shoulder and examined her face.

"What the hell?" Adam said, shoving the guy's hand away from her.

"I have to draw you," the guy said.

"You don't have to draw shit," Adam grumbled.

While Madison was fascinated by the motley bunch of street vendors, Adam seemed annoyed by them. But then this wasn't his first time in New Orleans, so every nuance wasn't necessarily a grand adventure for him. Madison examined the artist's caricatures and giggled at his interpretation of Morgan Freeman's freckles and Nicole Kidman's forehead.

"I want him to draw me," Madison said and promptly sat on the stool next to the artist's easel.

"He's a caricaturist," Adam said, as if the vocation was synonymous with roadkill.

"I know."

The artist took a seat and began to sketch.

"If you want someone to draw you, I'll do it," Adam said.

And she'd love to see what he came up with. "Get to work then," she said. "We'll see who does a better job."

Adam turned to the street artist. "How much for a blank sheet of paper and a charcoal pencil?"

"Uh . . . twenty bucks?"

Adam's glare indicated he knew he was being robbed, but he paid the man, collected his supplies, including a clipboard, and sat on the sidewalk near a wall. He didn't even look at Madison as he worked, but she couldn't take her eyes off him.

Nor was she interested in Mr. Lincoln's small talk. The caricaturist refused to give Madison a peek at his finished work while they waited for Adam to complete his drawing. Madison fanned herself with her hands. Even in the shade, she was growing uncomfortably warm. Adam must be dying in his jeans if she was this hot in a skirt. She was admiring Adam in those jeans when he looked up at her unexpectedly. He added a small touch to his drawing and held it at arm's length to examine it. After a few more scratches with his pencil, he climbed to his feet.

"I couldn't remember which side your beauty mark was on." Adam kissed the small mole under her left eye. "I can't believe I forgot."

He'd just drawn her from memory and felt bad about forgetting such a small detail? She wasn't sure if she wanted to see what he'd drawn. She decided no matter how bad it was, she'd fawn over it.

"You first," Adam said to Mr. Lincoln.

The artist turned his easel around. The man's talent was obvious, though the large gap between Madison's front teeth, her overly long neck, the alien-sized eyes and the bushy mess of hair more expansive than the state of Texas made her a bit self-conscious.

"Doesn't even look like her," Adam said.

"It isn't supposed to," Madison reminded him. "Well, not exactly."

"Let's see yours," Mr. Lincoln said.

Adam turned the clipboard around, and Madison's mouth dropped open in shock. Shock from the unquestionable skill it had taken to create such a perfect likeness of her. Further shock from the fact that she was entirely naked. Her face went hot as she took in the sight of her fingers buried in the expertly drawn folds between her legs, her breasts pushed together into cleavage with nipples hard and straining. Her facial expression could only be described as her O-face.

"Adam!" she managed to squeak before grabbing the clipboard and hiding the drawing from passersby by holding it against her chest.

"You win," Mr. Lincoln said. "How much do you want for

it?"

Madison's face went even hotter.

"It's not for sale," Adam said.

Madison wandered away from the passing pedestrians and took another peek at Adam's work. He was so talented, tears filled her eyes. Sure, she looked like a porn star and yes, she had to wonder if this was how he saw her every time he looked at her—if so, no wonder he was always horny—but every detail of her body had been captured to perfection. From memory. Not only was she astonished that he knew her body that well, but she was hopelessly flattered.

"Are you ashamed of me for drawing it?" Adam asked, his voice uncharacteristically gruff. He peered over her shoulder at the page.

"*Ashamed?*" she said. "Of course I'm not ashamed of you. It's the most amazing thing I've ever seen in my life. I just don't want strangers to see me like that."

"So it would bother you if other people saw you naked and coming, even though it's the most beautiful sight in the world?"

"Of course it would bother me."

"Well, hell. We should probably head back to the hotel for some more teasing then," he said and took her hand.

"What?"

"Or maybe it's best to do it here." He meandered down the street, holding her hand to keep her in step with him.

"Do *what* here?"

"Oh, nothing," he said. "Do you want me to carry that for you?"

He extended a hand toward the clipboard she held. Her eyes widened when she realized anyone could have gotten an eyeful while she was trying to figure out why *more* teasing was in order. Pausing under a moss-draped tree, she released the page from the clipboard and flipped it over so that the blank backside was facing outward. That was better. Now she could prevent it from being wrinkled *and* from being seen.

"Fortunes told, palms read," a deeply tanned and wrinkled woman called from a nearby table that was covered with a gold-fringed purple satin tablecloth, a crystal ball sitting in its

center.

"Is that something you're interested in?" Adam asked, nodding toward the fortune-teller.

Madison didn't believe in fortune-telling and the occult, but it might be fun to play along. "I'll get my fortune told if you get your palm read."

"No thanks," he said.

She grabbed him by the T-shirt and tugged him toward the table. "He'd like his palm read," Madison said.

Adam shook his head in annoyance but extended his hand toward the mystic.

"Very interesting," the woman said, pouring over Adam's palm. "You have multiple talents, I see."

Which was probably given away by the calluses on his fingertips earned from playing guitar and the smudges of charcoal on the side of his hand, Madison decided.

"The road behind you was much rockier than the one ahead."

"I should hope so. Anything else?"

"Your love line is unwavering."

"Which means?"

"You will love one special person above all others for all your years."

He rubbed his unoccupied hand over his hip pocket and then glanced up at Madison. "Fine with me."

He gladly paid the woman's fee and tugged Madison toward the table. She didn't understand why her tummy was fluttering with nerves when she sat across from the woman and her crystal ball.

After some seemingly unnecessary stroking of the clear orb on her table, the woman said, "You've been betrayed by someone close to you."

Madison lifted an eyebrow at her. No one close to her had betrayed her.

"Watch for a snake in the grass."

"Like an actual snake or a figurative snake?" Adam asked, seeming to think this hack was legit.

"Both," the woman said, gazing into her ball.

"Both?" Madison laughed.

The woman lifted her eyes from her window to the future and pinned her with a hard stare. "Warnings are no laughing matter, love," she said.

"That doesn't sound good," Adam said, rubbing his jaw reflectively.

Oh, please.

"Be wary of a stranger."

Excellent advice. Her mother had drilled it into her head before kindergarten. Next!

"Anything else?" Madison asked.

"Think about what you really want before you answer him."

"Who?"

She nodded at Adam. "Him."

"Okay . . . Do you have any concrete future plans in that crystal ball? Like what I should do about losing my job?"

"I already said someone close to you betrayed you."

Yeah, that was hella helpful.

"Okay," Madison said. "And what should I do about that?"

"Avoid snakes."

Since the woman was on repeat, Madison's session of enlightenment was apparently over.

"Um . . . *Thanks?*"

Madison stood, more than a little bewildered, and waited for Adam to pay the old woman.

"That was unsettling," Adam said as they strolled away.

"Why? She didn't tell me anything."

"She knew someone close to you betrayed you and that resulted in your job loss."

Madison shook her head. "She knew no such thing. *I* asked her about my job—which she never mentioned—and then she just reiterated exactly what she said the first time. And then she told me to beware of snakes. What in hell could that possibly have to do with being a counselor?"

"Maybe you'll be working at a reptile house in your next job," Adam said, looking pensive. "Do you live near the zoo?"

"No," she said, ready to smack him. "Can we go look at the cathedral now?" The tall white spires were calling to her.

"Whatever makes you happy," he said. He cuddled her up against his side as they walked toward the square.

When they rounded a corner, she thought she saw a figure watching them slink behind a bush. Or maybe she was imagining things. It had probably just been some tourist minding his own business. No matter. As long as Adam was beside her, she had nothing to fear.

"You make me happy," she told him.

"Likewise. As much as I'm looking forward to tonight, I'm having a great time with you today."

"Likewise," she said. "On both counts."

She enjoyed ambling through the perfectly tended garden, admiring the statue of Jackson, and studying the architecture of the Saint Louis Cathedral. As they wandered the French Quarter, the brick buildings with their ornate iron railings and flower boxes charmed her. And the food at the jazz club where they ate lunch was some of the best she'd ever tasted, with a flavorful kick that pleased rather than overwhelmed. But it was the company that was truly grand. Each stolen kiss, each longing glance, each heated touch served to remind her that she was the luckiest woman in the world.

"Are you ready to go back to the hotel?" Adam asked after their romantic stroll along the waterfront. "Have you seen everything you wanted to see?"

"I would like to see a real-life bayou," she said with a teasing grin. She'd much rather go back to the hotel for a bit of alone time before they ventured to the club. And she definitely needed to shower after sweating her ass off in the humidity all day.

"This entire place is a bayou."

"I guess. But I was thinking more along the lines of a natural bayou. Without buildings and people."

"Are there snakes in a bayou?" he asked.

She chuckled. "Probably. You aren't still thinking about what that hack of a fortune-teller said, are you?"

"No. I'll take you to a real bayou tomorrow," he promised. "But right now I need to see you naked."

She laughed. "I think you have my naked form memorized," she said, lifting the clipboard with his drawing. She'd been carrying it around for hours.

"Don't get me wrong, you *look* great," he said. "But you

feel even better."

"Taxi!" she yelled hoarsely, sticking her arm in the air to gain a driver's attention.

Adam had the audacity to laugh at her desperation.

If he thought her horniness was hilarious now, just wait until he got her alone. He'd die laughing.

As she stepped into the cab, she thought she spotted Chris observing them across the street, but when she paused for a closer look, there wasn't anyone there.

Seeing things. Perhaps she'd gotten a bit too much sun.

CHAPTER EIGHT

MADISON'S BELLY QUIVERED with nerves as Adam led her down a set of narrow steps to a basement situated beneath an old warehouse. She stared at the worn bricks along the corridor as Adam knocked a rhythm on the small wooden peep door built into the center of a heavy metal door. The impressive black barrier had rivets and everything. She wouldn't be surprised if it were grenade proof. Were they anxious to keep people out or keep them in? A shiver ran up her back. This place was far shadier than she'd imagined it would be. What was Adam thinking?

"Adam . . ." she said, her nerve suddenly fleeing back up the stairs in the direction she wanted to go.

He squeezed her hand, and the peep door opened.

"Tangerines go well with mangos," Adam said to the set of eyes observing them from within the club. Assuming the place really was a club. She could hear the sultry beat of music, voices, and even a few moans. A red glow escaped the now open peep door, but so far it wasn't like any club she'd ever been to.

"How cold is Siberia in December?" the doorman asked, his voice so low it made the hairs on the back of Madison's neck stand on end.

"Too cold for vodka."

The man stepped away from the door and Madison heard him say, "The other VIP has arrived," before he closed the peep door and opened the massive structure barring their way.

Adam entered first and tugged Madison in behind him with the hand he still held. Before she could see more than a naked woman on the bar, who as far as Madison could tell was pouring someone's beer with a bottle that was rammed up her vagina, she was ushered into a pitch-black room.

She'd lost her hold on Adam's hand at some point, and she couldn't see a damned thing. Her hands shot out in front of her, and she hit something solid and warm.

"Easy," Adam said, somehow finding her arms in the darkness. He stroked them soothingly, but she didn't let out the breath she was holding until an overhead light switched on.

Even though the lighting was dim, she blinked her eyes to adjust them after the absolute darkness of a moment before.

"Did I see that right?" Madison asked. "Was there a woman out there serving beer from a bottle in her *thing*?"

Adam chuckled. "Yeah, she's known for that. And the night's still young," he said. "She'll be serving wine by midnight."

"Shut the fuck up!" she said, her jaw about to unhinge itself as it dropped. "You aren't going to do that to me, are you?"

"Of course not," he said. "I don't like warm beer."

He crossed the room and picked up an ornately decorated white mask from a table. He slipped it over his face to cover his forehead, cheeks, and nose. But not his mouth. His mouth was free for kissing. And she definitely wanted to kiss him all of a sudden. He returned to her side carrying a second mask and helped her put it on. "Don't take it off, okay? Everything we do here remains anonymous. Anything you see or do here does not leave the premises. You can never share with anyone what goes on at one of Tony's clubs. Got it?"

She nodded. As if she would ever admit to anyone besides her sister that she went to a sex club in the first place. She checked out her reflection in the huge mirror that completely covered one wall of the small room. She had to admit she looked pretty sexy in the mask. Adam must have felt the same because he moved to stand behind her and she could feel his arousal against her ass. She rubbed against him and shuddered with longing. She didn't know how much longer she could endure his teasing. He'd spent their hours together in their hotel room feeling every inch of her, just as he'd suggested he would. But he refused to let her come. The pleasure he gave her had bordered on torture—sweet, sensual torture—but she was desperate for release.

"Tonight you are not Madison Fairbanks. You are a

queen." His fingers moved to the buttons of her top, and he slowly unfastened them. They both watched him reveal her lacy bra to the mirror. "*My* queen," he added.

So he'd brought her here so they could wear masks and have "anonymous" sex alone in some storage closet with a mirror? Not exactly the wild time she'd been anticipating. Heck, she could have been this brazen in Walmart.

Her shirt fluttered to the floor, and he cupped her breasts in both hands, rubbing the sensitive tips through the fabric. "You make me so hot," he said, his breath sultry against her ear.

"You have no idea how hot I am for you right now," she said. Her pussy was likely to catch fire if it produced any more heat. Good thing it was so wet.

A knock sounded on the door, and Madison turned. Then turned again. Actually the sound had come from in front of them. From the mirror. Madison squinted at the glass, wondering if they were being observed from the other side.

"Your ladies in waiting will now prepare you for court," Adam said.

"Court?"

Adam didn't answer, just snapped his fingers at the large mirror. The mirrored wall opened at once and two naked women with skin the color of the café au lait she'd enjoyed earlier entered the room. Each woman took one of Madison's hands and led her into a large room beyond the tiny closet-sized one she and Adam had been in.

Madison glanced around nervously, still not sure what to expect. In the center of the room was a large platform with giant black and white tiles decorating the surface in a checkerboard pattern. A bed stood against a wall along the far side of the room. A canopy of red satin decorated the headboard and red satin draped the mattress. Her gaze darted around the room as she searched for Adam. Beside the room they'd just exited, he was perched on a wide wooden chair that reminded Madison of a throne. He was taking this king thing seriously and if she hadn't been simultaneously nervous and intrigued, she might have laughed at his solemn expression as he watched her "ladies in waiting" direct her to the platform.

She stumbled up a set of steps and almost tripped when she was turned to face her king.

"What does his majesty command?" the shorter of the two naked women asked.

"Strip her."

Huh?

Her unbuttoned shirt slid from her shoulders before she could make a grab for it. Her bra followed and while she was crossing her arms over her naked breasts, the women removed her skirt.

Standing in nothing but her cowboy boots, Madison didn't know whether she should be afraid or embarrassed or annoyed. She was pretty sure she was not supposed to be aroused, but she definitely was.

"She looks tense," Adam said. "Perhaps a massage will soothe her."

Yes, the two naked chicks needed to vamoose and then she would gladly accept a massage from the still fully clothed but always virile Adam Taylor.

The taller woman coaxed Madison to sit on the bed so she could remove her boots and socks. The other woman approached Adam, which had Madison craning her neck so she could see what was going on. Madison trusted Adam, but she wasn't sure she trusted either of these women. The woman near Adam offered several bottles of golden oils for him to smell. When he selected one to his liking, the woman curtseyed and returned to Madison's side.

"Wait . . ."

But they didn't wait. Within seconds she was spread out on her belly atop the red satin and having sweet-smelling oil massaged into her flesh until her muscles were like warm butter. She rested her head so she could see Adam; he looked rather bored as he watched the women knead and stroke Madison's body.

She never expected to like being touched by a woman, but wow, it felt good. Soft moans of contentment seeped from between her parted lips.

"She seems a bit too relaxed," Adam said, and he nodded at one of the women. "You continue to massage her calves." He

nodded toward the other. "You spank her until I tell you to stop."

"What!"

Madison's protest was met with a swat to her exposed buttocks. She did love it when Adam spanked her, but this was different. This was . . . Oh. The woman's swats stung her tender cheeks, but weren't nearly as hard as the smacks Adam delivered when she begged him to spank her. Madison's pussy was soaked within several blows, and she was writhing on the mattress with excitement before any pain even registered.

Adam's low chuckle seemed to race up her spine, and she shuddered.

"Stop," he commanded.

"Wait," Madison whispered. She wasn't ready for her to stop yet.

"Now rub the rosiness out of her cheeks," Adam said.

Well, that didn't sound so bad. And it wasn't. She sighed with delight as practiced fingers massaged her ass, and then tensed whenever they got close to her throbbing back door. God, she wanted Adam's cock inside her. Front door, back door, side door. Did she have a side door? She didn't care where he penetrated her. She just wanted him.

"Adam?" she said, prepared to beg if necessary.

"I don't know any Adam," Adam said.

She supposed she wasn't supposed to use his name while playing their game.

"My king?"

"Yes?" His voice was calm and collected. A sensual caress to her ears.

"Take me. Please."

"Not yet. Turn her over," he instructed.

If possible, the massaging of her front side was even more erotic than the one on her back. Her arms, her collarbones, her breasts, and abdomen were tended to by one woman, her feet and shins, her knees and thighs by the other. The persistent stroking of her inner thighs and lower belly had Madison mad with need.

"Your majesty?" the woman now rubbing her hips said.

"Yes?"

"Her pussy is positively dripping. Might I have a taste?"

Madison's entire body shuddered at the thought of the woman's mouth on her.

"No," Adam said. "Her pussy is mine and mine alone. Is she ready?"

"I'd say so." The woman chuckled at the writhing, moaning spectacle Madison was making of herself.

"Yes!" Madison cried. "I'm ready."

The two women moved aside, backing away, and Adam rose from the chair. He stripped off his clothes and strode forward, so confident in nothing but his bare skin that Madison's thighs quaked. He was so beautifully masculine. So hard and huge, and oh, how she wanted him. He stopped on the platform, just short of the bed, and stood as if waiting for some cue.

Her legs snapped open, and she didn't care if the two masseuses watched them have sex. She actually wanted them to see how well she and Adam worked together.

"Court is in session," a voice said over an intercom somewhere above her.

A door on one side of the room opened and a line of naked men, each wearing a white mask, entered in single file. They formed a row on the edge of the platform just behind where Adam stood, each man standing in either a black or a white square on the floor.

Madison was too confused to think about covering herself.

"Your entourage may engage, encourage, or merely observe," the intercom voice instructed. "The choice is yours, my queen."

Madison's eyes traveled over the group of men assembled along the edge of the platform. Each man was stark naked save for their matching white facemasks and a thick white collar with a large metal charm dangling from the center. It took her a moment to recognize that the charms were chess pieces—two rooks, two bishops, two knights, and two pawns. Though the size and shape and skin tones of the men in her entourage varied, they were all very fuckable. Even if she couldn't see their faces, she could see their cocks and every last one of them was hard. Had they been watching her ladies in waiting prepare

her for their meeting? Or had they experienced erotic preparations of their own? No matter, they would observe her make love to their king, nothing more. She would not be *engaging* with her entourage.

She wanted only Adam. She always wanted only Adam.

"The first move is yours, my queen," the anonymous voice said.

"I want my king to lick my pussy until I come," she said, surprised by how confident she felt. How bold she sounded. Maybe her daring came from wearing a mask; none of the men in the room knew who she was, so she could be anyone, do anything. She could play a part. Or maybe she was strong because the power had been handed to her. Or maybe she was willing to ask for what she wanted simply because Adam had teased her until she was out of her fucking mind. Whatever the reason, she didn't even tense when Adam stretched out on his belly, spread her legs wide, and claimed her with his tongue.

As turned on as she'd been all day, she came far too quickly, but because her core was empty, her orgasm didn't satisfy her, not by a long shot.

"Your move, my king," the voice said.

Adam planted a sucking kiss on her clit and lifted his head.

He met her eyes and gave her a smile that would have seduced the panties right off her, had she been wearing any. "My queen will ride my cock until I am satisfied."

Oh, how she loved this man. That was exactly what she would have chosen had the move been hers.

Eager to be filled with him at long last, she toppled him onto his back and straddled his hips. He was hot and thick and hard, but she was beyond excited, so he slipped into her easily.

She moaned in bliss as he sank deep. Finally. God yes, finally.

He cupped her breasts and watched her as she rose and fell over him. A half groan escaped him, and he bit his lip to keep the rest locked inside.

Madison rode him harder, taking him deep and slow. Every pleasure sensor in her body tingled with excitement. Something about knowing over half-a-dozen men were watching her fuck Adam, her king, turned her on like nothing in her experience,

yet no matter how hard she took him, her ass felt underappreciated. Empty. She slid a finger into her mouth and reached behind her body to massage her back entrance. A moan escaped her as her ass tightened with need. Was this why Adam had refused to fulfill that need? So she'd want it desperately here at the club?

She knew what her next move would be. But first she had to fulfill Adam's request and ride him until he was satisfied.

"Your queen seems to enjoy anal play," the voice said over the intercom.

Madison jumped. She'd been lost in sensation and had forgotten he was there.

"She loves it," Adam said breathlessly from below her.

"Knight's move," the voice said.

Wait. *What?* The others got moves too? She had assumed this would all be about her and Adam.

"Knight requests the privilege of pleasing the queen's ass," a voice said from among the spectators. Madison looked over her shoulder. There'd been something familiar about that voice, as if she'd heard it before. Did it belong to a client of hers? A colleague? How embarrassing would that be? Was she really completely anonymous in this mask? She searched her memory for a match to the voice, but came up lacking.

"Does the queen grant her permission?" the announcer asked.

Madison paused in her motions. She wasn't sure what she was supposed to say to that.

"My queen?" the voice prompted.

Would Adam be okay with it? She stared down at him, but found his expression unreadable beneath his mask. He'd stop her from doing anything uncalled for, wouldn't he?

"Y-yes?"

"You may proceed, Knight."

Madison went completely still when a hand circled her wrist and drew her hand away from her backside.

"Concentrate on pleasing your king," a voice said from behind her. "I've got you covered."

When a pair of unfamiliar fingers first touched her ass, she tensed. How weird was it that some stranger was playing with

her butt? Pretty bizarre. But as her body responded to his persistent and arousing touch, she relaxed and forgot what was causing her pleasure, just that the pleasure existed. Her mask helped her maintain anonymity. Allowed her to experience what was happening to her body without connecting it to her real self. Allowed her to become a queen without fear or guilt, able to enjoy excitement and ecstasy with reckless abandon.

Adam shifted into a seated position and wrapped an arm around her lower back. He brushed her hair aside so he could whisper into her ear. "You're in charge here," he said. "If you're not okay with him touching you—"

"I'm okay with it," she blurted out.

He kissed her tenderly and then lay back again, lifting his hips off the mattress to drive himself deep before relaxing beneath her. His eyes never left her face as she began to work his cock inside her, rising and falling over the thick shaft. Her moans of bliss became more pronounced as the fingers stroking her from behind shot her into a frenzy.

A seeking finger pressed just inside her back entrance.

"Yes!" she cried, shifting her hips to give her daring knight free access. She was rewarded for her brazenness with pleasure as first one finger and then two fully claimed her ass, thrusting twice as fast as she could rise and fall over the cock in her pussy.

"Oh, oh, oh," she moaned as her body convulsed with an unexpected orgasm.

"Knight requests the privilege of *fucking* the queen's ass."

"What?" she heard Adam say, but she was already responding to the request. "Permission granted!"

A muttering of approval passed among her subjects. Over the blood rushing through her ears, she could hear the sounds of a condom being opened and lube being applied. What was she doing? She couldn't possibly let another man enter her body. She felt him against her back and instead of tensing when his cockhead brushed her back entrance, she relaxed the way Adam had taught her. Heat shot up inside her as a hard, thick cock filled her from behind.

"Oh God."

She did her best to fuck the two cocks stuffing her, but she

couldn't find the leverage to make it work. A pair of hands gripped her hips and assisted her in taking them deep. Pulling out. Taking them deep. And . . . and, oh God, she'd died and gone to heaven. Never in her life had she felt so complete. So full.

"Bishop's move," the voice said.

"Bishop requests the privilege of pleasing the queen's clit to ensure she comes."

Yes, she thought. "Yes!" she commanded. "Make me come, you, you . . . guy." Whoever or whatever the hell he was. She didn't much care. "Bishop."

A moment later something buzzed against her clit in powerful, vibrating bursts, and she screamed as she came. Her body squeezed the two cocks inside her in rhythmic spasms. When she calmed, she found her pussy suddenly empty, but that didn't last long. Soon someone was fucking her with a huge dildo. She didn't even know what she was agreeing to any longer. There were mouths sucking her nipples, her fingers, her clit. Teeth sinking into her breasts and ass. Dicks in her mouth. In her hands. Fucking her in the ass. Between her tits. She was spanked and pinched. Caressed and massaged.

She'd been so thoroughly taken by the time her reign as queen was over, she couldn't move. Every inch of her body throbbed with pleasure and pain. Trembled with exhaustion. She wasn't sure when she fell asleep, but eventually the sound of a door slamming jerked her awake.

Something landed in the center of her back.

"Put your clothes on," Adam growled at her.

"Adam?" she murmured. She lifted a trembling hand to pull off her mask. God, her arm wouldn't stop shaking.

"Well, you definitely got into the game, my queen," Adam said. "You didn't refuse anything."

He didn't sound too happy about it.

She turned her head. It took a moment for her eyes to adjust, but soon she could see that they were alone. Unless the man behind the voice on the intercom was still observing them.

"Put your fucking clothes on, Madison!"

She attempted to roll onto her side, but she didn't have

enough energy to move, much less dress. And why was he yelling at her?

"What's going on? Are the cops busting the club or what?" Right before they'd arrived, he had warned her that a raid might happen.

"I can't believe you let them do that to you."

"Huh?" She lifted her head with considerable effort. "Let them do what?"

Her mind was as numb as her body was. She couldn't feel anything. Except her ass. God, she was sore back there. Someone had done a number on her. Not taken her the way she liked it. Not the way Adam did it. She doubted if she'd ever be able to sit on her butt again.

"Anything they wanted," he said.

"Why are you so upset?" she said, her voice slurring as if she were drunk.

"I don't know, Madison. Maybe because I just watched my girlfriend get gangbanged and she loved every minute of it."

"You're the one who brought me here," she said, finding a reserve store of energy as her anger sparked to life. "You're the one who always tells me I need to loosen up. Experience life. Live a little."

"You are unquestionably loose, and I think you've done quite enough living for one night," he said. "We're leaving now. Get dressed."

"I would love to," she yelled, "but I can't move my arms and legs!"

His scowl was replaced with a look of concern. "Did one of them hurt you?"

She shook her head as much as she was able, knowing that he didn't want to hear her whine about how raw her ass felt. "Just exhaustion. I'll recover."

"I'm sorry I brought you here," he said, the temporary look of concern already gone, replaced by a scowl. He scraped the clothing from her back and slipped her panties over one of her trembling feet. She was uncomfortably wet between her legs, but she was suddenly too ashamed to draw attention to her discomfort.

Her body would recover, but she wondered if her

relationship with Adam would. Something had changed between them. She could feel it in the brusque way he shoved her into her clothes. The tenderness he usually showed her was lacking. His gaze was hard. And cold. He refused to look at her, to see her. He was back to shutting her out, the way he had when they'd first met. She couldn't stand it.

She lifted a weary arm to touch his face, but he jerked away, stumbling from the platform in his haste to find the exit. To escape her touch. Escape from *her*.

"I'll wait outside," he said and before she could tell him not to bother, he was gone.

CHAPTER NINE

ADAM TOOK A DEEP BREATH and slammed his fist into a brick wall. He needed to get his shit together before Madison came out of the club, because he was seconds from losing everything he'd worked so hard to accomplish and he knew it.

Would he ever be able to look at her again without remembering the hands of other men on her body? Would he ever scrub away the feel of her pussy tightening around his cock as two other men brought her to orgasm? Would he ever hear those sexy sounds she made without recalling that she made them even louder when some stranger had his dick up her ass?

There was only one thing that ever made him forget how to feel. Forget how to care. Forget the pain of living and the fear of dying. One thing made it all go away.

But he didn't do that shit anymore. He knew if he slipped up—if he joined the guys snorting lines of coke off some woman's bare ass on the bar or shot up heroin in the bathroom—it wouldn't fix anything. Not really. For a few hours it might seem that his cares were gone and that bringing Madison to the club hadn't been a huge mistake, but he knew the drugs' effects would wear off and he'd need more of them to make those cares go away again. And then he'd need more and still more just to hold on to the illusion of that pain being chased away. And then he'd be back where he started, and he hated that place. Hated it even more than feeling this broken inside.

So he had to get his shit together and fast. For her sake. But mostly for his own.

He took a moment to count his blessings. Sometimes he felt as if he didn't have many, but if he reflected on the positive things in his life, it made dealing with the negative a lot easier.

He had his music and his bandmates who'd stuck with him through all the shit he'd put them through, and he had his drawing. And . . . and he had Madison.

Madison. What the fuck was wrong with him? He couldn't ruin one of the few good things going for him in a fit of jealous rage. How could he have been so stupid? How could he have said those things to her? How could he have left her there in the club, alone? He'd lost it because he hadn't been able to handle her behaving the way he'd expected her to behave. The way he wanted her to behave. Or so he'd thought. Hell, he'd been planning and fantasizing about this scenario all week, prepping her for it for two days. Shit, he couldn't take it out on her, because his expectations and the reality had been exactly what he *thought* he'd wanted. But his reaction to her brazenness was completely at odds with what he'd expected. If he'd been watching some other woman get that thoroughly fucked, he'd have thought it was the sexiest sight he'd ever seen. But it hadn't been some other woman, it had been *his* woman. Why hadn't he realized he wouldn't be able to stand another man's hands on her until it was too late? Maybe because he had expected her to draw a line. But she hadn't. She'd crossed it without a shred of hesitation.

Shit.

And who did he have to blame for that? Himself.

It was no wonder that everyone thought he was such a fuck-up. He kept proving them right over and over again, living up to their poor expectations of him. Everyone's except Madison's. She believed in him. She trusted him, trusted him to keep her safe. And he'd failed her. There was no telling what those men could have done to her when he'd fled.

He went back inside and found her where he'd left her. She was lying on her back staring up at the ceiling, her expression completely blank. It was as if she were in some sort of trance.

He sat beside her on the firm mattress—forcing himself not to think about everything that had happened in this very room not even half an hour ago—and touched her shoulder.

She didn't look at him, but she spoke. "What's wrong with me? How could I have done that? How could I have *liked* it?"

"There's nothing wrong with you," he said. "You were

supposed to like it. The scenario was designed specifically to give you pleasure."

"Then why do you hate me?" She closed her eyes, and her body began to tremble uncontrollably.

"I don't hate you," he said. "I love you, and that's why I reacted the way I did. Why I had to leave. I've done this sort of thing with dozens of other women. Not the chess board, but other games."

"Lovely to hear that," she said dully.

"And I enjoyed every minute of it," he made himself continue. "But with you—"

"You realized what an insatiable tramp you have for a girlfriend."

"That isn't even close to the truth," he said. "I couldn't stand them touching you. Couldn't stand knowing you could enjoy sex with someone besides me. Because . . ."

She opened her eyes and shifted her gaze to his. "Because?"

He took a deep breath. "Because you're mine." He stared at her, challenging her to deny his claim. Unquestionably relieved when she didn't.

"I am yours, Adam," she said. "When they were touching me and—and doing stuff to me, I wasn't really myself. I was playing the role of the queen."

"I think I knew that," he said, "but it didn't offer me any peace of mind. It made me sick to watch what they were doing. And even sicker that I didn't stop them."

He hadn't stopped them because she'd seemed to be enjoying it so much, and her mindless enjoyment *that didn't require his participation* had pissed him off. *Let them fuck her,* he'd thought when he'd lost his erection and had to leave the game. *I don't care.* He'd behaved like a petulant toddler and had left her alone with them. With all of them. They could have really hurt her. He wasn't even sure what did happen because he didn't watch, couldn't, though Tony—who'd played the announcer—had assured him that no one had broken his one rule. No one besides him had claimed her pussy. Taken every other inch of her, maybe, but not that. Now he knew what a ridiculous stipulation that had been. Her pussy wasn't the only part of her that was sacred to him. All of her was. And he'd

brought her here, knowing what was going to happen. What the hell was wrong with him?

"Does this mean we're over?" she asked.

He wondered why she thought she should take any of the blame for this. He forced a smile, hoping that by making light of the situation, that look of misery would be wiped from her beautiful face.

"No, it doesn't mean we're over. It means we aren't ever participating in another sex club orgy. I don't care how desperate you get for cock."

"But we can participate in a *regular* orgy, right?" He could hear the laughter in her tone, or he might have gotten upset. "I mean, you know how desperate I get for cock. I need it twenty-four hours a day."

"I'll do my best to satisfy your desperation," he said, stroking her cheek.

She laughed. And then she bit her lip. Her eyes welled up with tears, and he had to look away or the knot in his throat would strangle him.

"I'm sorry," she said. "I'm so sorry, Adam."

"Don't be sorry—we all have our weaknesses. Mine are of a chemical nature. You just crave butt sex."

He couldn't stand that she was hurting, that he was the cause of her trouble. He was pretty much always the cause of her trouble. But knowing that did not make him willing to give her up for her own good. She was stuck with him through thick and thin. He was selfish that way.

"I don't need the butt sex, Adam," she said. "I just need you."

Did she mean that? She looked sincere, and he knew she was a terrible liar, so he let himself believe her. Because he needed to believe her. He pulled her into his arms, pretending he didn't know why she flinched when her naked rear settled on his lap.

"You have me," he assured her as he stroked her soft hair and she nestled her face in the crook of his neck.

"And you have me," she said.

He was counting on that. Because without her, his only happiness came in chemical form. And realizing how easily he

could go back to his old ways scared the shit out of him.

CHAPTER TEN

ADAM HELPED MADISON out of the shower and wrapped her in a thick white towel before carrying her to the bed. The ride back to the hotel had been cursed with tortured silence. Neither of them would say something was wrong, but he was sure she felt the tension as much as he did.

He dried her carefully and stared down at her in the dim light coming from the bathroom. Did she really love him? If she did, he could get through this. *They* could get through this together. But if she was just saying the words and going through the motions . . .

He closed his eyes and spread kisses over her throat and collarbones. She didn't protest as he sucked marks on her chest. Normally she didn't let him do that, not where the hickeys might be visible. But maybe she let him do it tonight because she no longer had a job, so it didn't matter if she had his marks all over her. Or maybe she realized how much he needed to claim every inch of her as his. To let people see it as much as he felt it.

He wanted to erase all memories of those other men from her mind and from her body. He used his hand to guide himself into her warm, slick pussy and then tangled both hands in her hair, staring deeply into her eyes as he claimed her with slow, sensual strokes. Her lips parted, and her breathing quickened. Face flushed, she arched into him, her hands gripping his ass to encourage him to take her deeper. As her pleasure intensified, her eyes drifted closed, but he would have none of that. He tugged at her hair, pausing in his strokes to wait for her eyes to open again. When her gaze focused on him once more, he thrust into her, driving his length deep and churning his hips.

As their bodies connected and their souls mingled, his

pleasure raced toward its peak. Just before he lost himself, he pulled out. He needed more time to drive those other men away. Could she still feel their hands on her? Their mouths? Their dicks? He didn't know if she could or not. But he could still see them. Every time he looked at her he saw them. And he had no one to blame for this particular stint in Hell but himself.

"Adam?"

His name on her sweet lips made his heart ache. He kissed a trail down her body, between her perfect breasts, down her quivering belly, and lower until his face was buried between her thighs. He teased her clit with his lips and tongue and the occasional sucking kiss until she cried out and her body quaked with release. He surged upward, claiming the remnants of her orgasm by fucking her clenching pussy until she was spent.

"Oh God, Adam," she said between gasps for breath. "That was amazing."

But he was far from finished. He pulled out again and shifted to pleasure her with his mouth once more. Each time he brought her to climax with his mouth, he rode out her storm, but he dared not stay inside her for long. He wasn't ready to let her rest. Not until she came as hard as she'd come when that knight had settled up against her back and shoved his cock up her ass. He needed to make her come that hard all on his own. He had some strange personal vendetta against her orgasm. He needed to prove to her—or maybe to himself—that he was good enough to truly satisfy her. After several failed attempts to bring her to the peak he knew her body was capable of, he feared that she really did need double penetration to find true bliss.

"Adam, you have to stop. I can't take any more," she said, clinging to his hair as he worked her clit with his mouth.

Maybe she'd come so hard because he'd teased her mercilessly before they'd arrived at the club. Maybe that had been the difference. He slid a finger into her ass, knowing she was tender back there, but rather than protest, she begged for more.

"Oh yes," she groaned. "Deeper. Please."

He turned her on her side, with one of her legs around his

waist, so he could more easily fill her with cock and fingers simultaneously. It wasn't quite double penetration, but it was the best he could do without the assistance of sex toys. Or other men . . .

Fuck.

Madison screamed when a particularly strong orgasm ripped through her. He didn't think it had been quite as all-encompassing as the one she'd had at the sex club, but it was close. As he sought his own release, he promised himself he'd get her there next time. His climax built quickly, tearing a deep groan from him as he let go. He filled her with his body's offering, fixed on the knowledge that none of those other men had experienced the bliss of her pussy or found release inside her. No other man's cum had ever entered her body in her entire life. Only his.

And when he could get hard again, he would forgo his usual condom to fuck her ass raw so he could fill her back passage with his cum as well.

He sucked another mark on her shoulder. His possessiveness was confusing and completely overwhelming, but he couldn't deny it existed. Madison was his, goddammit. He was not good at sharing. He rested his head on her shoulder and closed his eyes. His. She had to be his. Had to be.

The ring of his cellphone jerked him awake. He wasn't sure when he'd fallen asleep, but the familiar ring tone—*Bad to the Bone*—was one he didn't particularly want to hear. He leaned over the edge of the bed and pulled his phone out of his jeans pocket.

"What happened?" Adam answered, his heart hammering anxiously in his chest. He knew he was supposed to hate his father. He had every reason to hate his father. But the stupid bastard was the only family he had and rushing him to the hospital last week had reminded Adam of how truly alone he'd be if the son of a bitch died on him.

"I need more money," Dad said in that naturally loud and gravelly voice of his.

"I asked you not to call unless it was an emergency." Adam's initial panic was instantly replaced with annoyance.

"Being out of gas three hundred miles from El Paso in the

middle of a nowhere Texas desert *is* an emergency."

"Just use some of the extra money I already gave you."

Madison touched his shoulder and lifted her head to mouth, "Who is it?"

"My dad," Adam whispered.

"I'm out of that money," his dad said.

"How can you be out of that money?" Sheezus. Adam had given him five thousand dollars to set up a shared house with his buddy Jose who lived in El Paso. He'd also given his father the use of one of the cars he owned but never drove.

"I took Honey shopping."

Adam groaned inwardly. What was he doing with her again? "You took your ex shopping on my dime?"

His dad laughed gleefully. "She ain't my ex no more thanks to your dime. She's gonna come down and see me in El Paso in a couple weeks."

Adam was sure she would. As long as his idiot father had some of Adam's spare cash to blow on her.

"Well, are you going to help me out, or what?"

Or what, Adam wanted to say, but instead he said, "I'll wire you enough cash for some gas—"

"And supper?" Dad interrupted. "I ain't ate nothing all day, and you know I need to have something in my gullet when I take my pills."

Adam's stomach sank at the mention of the pills. His father's most current overdose had done even more injury to his aging heart. They'd discovered the damage after the overdose. The doctor had said he'd probably had a heart attack over a year ago, but hadn't had the sense to go to the hospital with his chest pains. Fucking idiot. Someone had to look after him. Adam hoped Jose could keep him under control better than Adam could. Jose was an okay guy. He had a criminal record, sure, but he'd served his time and was walking a straight and narrow path now. At least he was according to Adam's father.

"And supper," Adam conceded. "But that's it. I'll send Jose money for your half of the rent and utilities directly." Since the old man was entirely untrustworthy with a stack of cash.

"Yeah, yeah. I fucked up again. You knew I would. Why do

you sound disappointed?"

"Can I talk to him?" Madison asked.

Adam turned his head to gawk at her. Why in the hell would she want to talk to his father? She'd taken the phone from Adam's hand before he could refuse.

"Mr. Taylor?"

"Who the hell is this?"

Adam was close enough that he could hear his father's boisterously loud voice.

"I'm Madison Fairbanks. I've been wanting to meet you."

"Why?"

"I've been treating your son."

"Treating him?" The old man chortled. "You mean *banging* him. He told me about you."

Madison glanced at Adam, her blue eyes wide with curiosity.

Adam looked away. Yeah, he'd discussed her with his father last weekend and had explicitly forbidden Dad from fucking things up for him by being himself around Madison.

"Our relationship has progressed with time," Madison said, a hint of amusement in her tone, "but initially I was his rehab counselor."

"You can lead a junkie to rehab, but you can't scrub him clean." The old man apparently thought he was hilarious as he cackled with glee.

"That's true," Madison said. "Getting clean is a lot of hard work. A person has to want to be clean to stay that way. Do you want to get clean, Mr. Taylor?"

Adam scowled at the floor. He still wasn't one hundred percent sure he *wanted* to be clean. He did know he never wanted to disappoint Madison. She'd worked so hard to get him clean. He planned to stay that way. For her. He could do anything—no matter how challenging—as long as it was for her.

And soon—very soon—she would be his legally.

CHAPTER ELEVEN

ADAM DIRECTED THE BIKE onto a desolate road in some long-forgotten bayou. He parked on the shoulder and turned to Madison, who was holding his waist.

He took his helmet off and accepted hers as well, watching her run her fingers through her curls and loving the way the sunlight dappled her body through the scattered leaves overhead. Near the road, the trees weren't so dense, but the canopy thickened over the green-tinged water that rocked in gentle waves beneath the strange twisted roots of the mangrove trees.

He slapped at a mosquito buzzing near his ear and offered Madison an arm so she could climb from the back of the bike.

"Well, you wanted to see a real bayou while you were here," he said. "What do you think?"

"It smells funny," she said with a laugh.

Adam covered his nose against the offending odors of wet decay and funk. "Is funny another word for bad?"

"In this case?" She pursed her lips and then crinkled her pert, freckled nose. "Yes."

He laughed and climbed from the bike to stand beside her. He wrapped an arm around her shoulders, so glad that the discomfort between them the night before had been chased away by the morning sun. As far as he could tell, they were back to their normal, easy camaraderie. The woman, and her ability to forgive, amazed him. He'd already forgiven her for her wild times at the club the night before, and he was working very hard on forgetting. The forgetting was a little more of a challenge. Especially when she flinched every time she sat down.

He drew her closer to his side. It was the simple moments when they were alone and silent—touching but not overly

physical—that he relished with her. But he felt sort of stupid for feeling that way. Sex with Madison was always spectacular, and he knew he should cherish that intimacy most, but he'd never been with a woman long enough to feel completely comfortable with her—not necessarily inside her, just *with* her. The emotional part of being with a woman was entirely new to him, and damned if she didn't have the power to destroy him.

He held her against him, fingertips toying with her now frizzy curls, as they stared out into the murky, smelly waters and tried to decide if the large, elongated object floating near a particularly gnarly mangrove root was a log or an alligator. They slapped at mosquitoes and watched a heron wade near the shore hunting for fish, laughing when the bird noticed them and flapped its expansive white wings.

Content and happy. Adam rarely had moments when he felt either. This was one of those rare times.

Adam slipped the tip of his little finger into the warm ring nestled deep in the pocket of his jeans. He stroked the smooth and warm metal, wondering if he should go through with this crazy idea of his or wait until he was sure she wanted to marry him. They'd never actually talked about marriage, but he knew that family was important to her, and if he married her, he'd not only be her friend and her lover, he'd be her family. If their relationship was strong enough to get through last night without irreparable harm, then marriage would be a snap. Wouldn't it? Of course it would.

He supposed there was no use in putting off the inevitable. He wanted her as his wife, so why wait?

Adam wasn't one to get down on one knee and ask for anything, but he'd make the concession for Madison. She'd given him his life back; he loved her; she deserved the best. The best ring. The best proposal. The best husband.

Well, at least he knew the ring was good.

Adam took a deep breath, pulled the ring from his pocket, and sank to one knee in the soft moss at Madison's feet.

Her eyebrows drew together in confusion as she stared down at him. Her lovely heart-shaped face made his heart thud just from looking up at her.

"Are you okay?" she asked, tilting her head to look behind

him to see why his leg had suddenly given out.

He couldn't help but chuckle around the nerves churning in his belly. "I'm perfect," he said. Perfectly insane.

He took her right hand in his before remembering he was supposed to put the ring on her left ring finger. He kissed her knuckles before reaching for her other hand. Apparently the gesture made her realize what he was about to do. Her eyes widened, and her face went pale. She swayed slightly, and he wondered if she was about to faint.

"Adam!"

"Madison," he began, searching for words and finding few. Perhaps he should have thought this through a little more. Not asking her to marry him—he knew without a doubt he wanted her to be his wife—but the actual proposal. He probably should have come up with something a little more romantic than a spur of the moment proposal in a bayou loaded with mosquitoes, a heron and *maybe* an alligator as their only witnesses. "I saw this ring and could think of nothing but how much I want to see it on your finger. How much I want you to be my wife. I love you, Madison. Will you marry me?"

He held the ring suspended over the tip of her ring finger, waiting for one three-letter word to leave her lips and greet his ears.

Her hand closed unexpectedly, preventing him from slipping the engagement ring on, and she took a step back.

"Adam," she said in that calm, rational voice she used with her clients. The same voice she'd used on him so many times when he'd been going through treatment.

His breath caught, and the feminine fist he held clutched desperately in his hand seemed to punch straight through his breastbone and rip his heart free of his impossibly constrictive chest. Why wasn't she squealing with excitement? Why wasn't she wrapped in his arms and kissing his lips, pressing her body against him? Why wasn't she wearing his ring? Why hadn't she said yes?

"Madison," he said, her name a whispered breath of anguish.

"This is rather sudden," she said. "I—I don't know what to say."

"Say you love me," he said, not sure why her face was so blurry all of a sudden. "Say you want me. Say yes."

"Adam, I do love you," she said calmly.

He didn't believe her. Not when she said it like that.

"We need to talk about this."

He didn't want to fucking talk about it. He wanted her to accept him. All of him. He shot to his feet and crammed the ring back into his pocket. She reached for his arm, but he shrugged off her piteous touch. Had she ever truly loved him, or had it always just been pity?

God-fucking-damn it. Why had he ever trusted her with his heart? Why had he ever thought she'd want it?

He stalked to the Harley and climbed on. Whenever he wanted to escape what was currently eating him alive—it seemed to change on a daily basis—he took his bike for a long ride. But even as he started the engine, he knew running off wouldn't work this time. He couldn't escape Madison. She was under his skin. Lodged deep in his heart. And he couldn't leave her here among snakes and other dangerous creatures.

"Get on the bike," he said.

"Adam . . ."

"Get on the goddamned bike, Madison!"

Hands knotted in the hem of her T-shirt, she just stood there staring at him. "You aren't leaving me here?"

That stung almost more than her rejection. "I love you enough to ask you to marry me, but you don't think I love you enough to give you a ride?"

"But you're mad."

"I'm not mad," he said. Hurt. Broken. Gutted. Worthless, hopeless, and devastated. Yes, all those things. But not mad.

"I'm sorry." She blinked back tears, and if she started crying then he *was* going to be mad. She didn't have the right to cry over this. He was the one who should be crying.

He ripped his gaze from her, stared straight ahead, and revved the engine. "Get on."

"Adam, I—"

He clenched his teeth. "Get. On."

"I think . . . I should go . . . home," she said.

"Then I'll take you to the airport," he said, forcing his voice

to remain calm. "But I'm not leaving you here."

"Adam, I just need some time to think things over. This would be a big step for me. For us. I'm not sure we're ready. Maybe if we talk about it—"

"I don't want to talk about this now," he said, revving the engine again.

"Then when?" she said.

"Maybe after I get my guts shoved back inside where they belong." He released a small huff of breath and shook his head. This was why he pushed people away. Exactly this. He had a low tolerance for pain. Not physical pain—he could take his fair share of that. But every time he let someone in, they hurt him. This emotional bullshit had always ripped him apart. He couldn't stand it. He had to escape somehow. On his bike. In his music or his art. With drugs or sex or some other vice. And since the only route available to him at the moment was the Harley, he revved the engine again.

Madison touched his sleeve, but he couldn't bring himself to look at her. He knew she'd be staring at him with pity, and that was the last fucking thing he wanted at the moment. And if she understood him, she'd know that.

CHAPTER TWELVE

MADISON CLUNG TO ADAM'S HIPS and pressed her face against his back, fighting tears and trying to breathe through the tight knot in her throat. She didn't want to hurt him, but knew it was too late for that.

How could he just ask her to marry him out of the blue like that? And why had it shocked her so much? She was still trembling.

They just needed to talk through this. Marriage was a huge step and while she wanted to settle down someday, she wasn't sure now was the right time. She didn't want to rush into something so monumental. She'd had no idea Adam had even considered marriage as an option. And while her heart was vying for the chance to call Adam her husband, she couldn't seem to ignore the doubts placed there by everyone who didn't think they stood a fighting chance to maintain any relationship, much less one as important as husband and wife.

And then there was the fact that he didn't want kids. And had never discussed the topic with her. He never discussed anything with her. How could they make a marriage work if he kept things from her? Important things. At least they were important to her. He blew them off as if they were frivolous.

By the time they reached the hotel, she had almost calmed down enough to think. She still wasn't sure what to say to him to make things right. She wanted to be his friend, his lover, his woman. But did she want to be his wife? The reckless part of her that Adam had awakened wanted to forge headlong into the future and accept his proposal right there, but the ingrained part that always held her back with fear wanted to retreat.

Adam parked the bike and just sat there.

"Adam?" she said after an unbearably long minute of silence.

"Get off."

She scrambled from the back of the bike, using his arm for stability. She removed her helmet and waited. The sinking feeling in her stomach and her heart was almost too much to bear.

"We can talk about this," she said. She *wanted* to talk about it. So she could figure out what was in his head before attempting to tackle what was going on in hers.

"Can you go up to the room alone?" he said quietly. "I need a minute."

"Adam, it's not that I—"

"Please." His voice sounded thready. Desperate. She'd never heard him sound like that before.

"Okay," she said. "But we need to talk."

She tried to hand him her helmet, but his hands tightened around the handlebar grips, so she set it on the ground near his heavy leather boot.

"Soon," she added, before turning away. "We need to talk soon."

She headed through the parking garage toward the elevator, hoping he'd call after her saying he was ready to talk now. Praying she hadn't destroyed the bond between them.

She stepped onto the elevator and pressed the button for the lobby. Just before the door slid shut, she saw him remove his helmet and wipe at his eyes with the heel of his hand. Her heart shattered as the doors slid shut.

She had to make this right. Or at least make him feel confident in her feelings for him until she could make a sound decision about their future. She knew he wasn't ready to talk. It would take time for him to open up. She knew that about him. And she could be patient. But how could she keep him from pushing her away when she'd hurt him so profoundly? First last night and again today.

She needed time to sort through it all, but Adam had never been a patient man. He was used to taking what he wanted, and if he couldn't attain it, he moved on to the next thing. She didn't want him to move on to the next thing. She loved him too much to let him get away.

She let herself into the empty hotel room, checking the

hallway in both directions in hopes that he'd caught up with her before she closed the door.

They always connected best on an emotional level when they were connected on a physical level. So maybe if she could get him into bed, he'd realize that she still loved him, still wanted him, still needed him, and that maybe after she reflected on the idea of being his wife for longer than five seconds or even an hour, she'd want to marry him. But she wasn't going to make any promises she didn't intend to keep, no matter how much she wanted to spare his feelings.

She shed her clothes and climbed into bed, curling her body around the tangle of sheets. Her mind raced through a thousand possibilities of what her life would be like as Adam's wife. Where would they live? Would her family accept him? Would the world accept her—a nobody—as the wife of a guitar legend? How often would she get to see him? Could she tag along with him on the road? Would she even want to? It seemed such an unsettled life, if fun. At least for a while. Would he change his mind about wanting children? Having kids was important to her. Having stability was important to her. As much as she loved him, could they forge a future together that satisfied them both? And how would she know the answer to any of these questions if she couldn't get him to fucking talk to her?

Patience, understanding, and listening when he was finally ready to talk had worked with him before, but this situation wasn't only about him. It was about her as well.

She growled in frustration and threw a pillow across the room. Her breath caught when she heard the door open.

He stood on the threshold for a long moment with the door wide open. Madison tucked the sheet around her bare hips and watched him, afraid to say anything because she was sure if she did, he'd leave.

"Can I come in?" he asked.

Odd that he'd ask. It was his hotel room.

"Of course."

He approached the bed and stood at its edge. His gaze moved over her face, her bare shoulder, the curve of her hip beneath the sheet. He sucked in a breath and lifted his eyes to

stare toward the window on the far side of the room.

After a moment of watching him and finding his expression entirely unreadable, she asked, "Are you ready to talk?"

He shook his head. "Still too . . . raw."

"You might like what I have to say."

"But I might not."

He was such an unusual mix of strong and sensitive. She hadn't realized that she had such power to hurt him. Since his mother had left, he hadn't given anyone that amount of power over him. He'd trusted her with his heart, and she hadn't been careful enough with it.

"Can I touch you?" she asked.

"If you don't, I might very well die."

Madison rose to kneel on the bed, the sheet falling to pool around her legs. She slid both hands up his T-shirt, drawing the soft fabric upward as her palms bumped over the hard contours of his muscular belly and chest. Impatient, he yanked the shirt off over his head and tossed it aside. She planted a row of gentle kisses down his belly, her fingers working at his fly as she made her way toward her final destination.

He groaned in pleasure as she took him into her mouth, sucking and kissing and licking his length until he was hard with excitement.

"Madison," he whispered, his fingers threading through her hair and tilting her head back.

Lips pressed against his tip, she lifted her gaze to his.

"Tell me what I need to hear," he said.

She wasn't sure what he wanted her to say. She wanted to say she loved him, but was afraid he'd throw it back in her face, the way he had earlier.

"I want you," she said.

He eased away and then tumbled her back onto the bed, covering her with his body, sinking his hips between her thighs.

"Close enough," he said, claiming her with a solid thrust.

CHAPTER THIRTEEN

ADAM KNEW that Madison needed time to think about his proposal, but he had never been a patient man.

"I know you're against marrying me," Adam said, idly trailing his fingertips back and forth over her bare shoulder. "But we could just move in together. Would that be a more reasonable next step?"

She was silent for so long, he lifted his head to see if she'd fallen asleep on him. He *had* taken her rather enthusiastically, glad that she still wanted to be with him on a physical level, even if she wasn't sure about marriage. He found she wasn't asleep though. She was staring wide-eyed at the wall.

"Madison?"

Her gaze met his.

"I don't think I'm ready to take the next step," she said. "*Any* next step."

"Ever?"

She bit her lip and looked away. "I don't know when I'll be ready. I just lost my job and my life got complicated all of a sudden."

Less complicated, he'd say, but apparently they saw eye to eye on little.

"I don't think now is the right time to add more complications."

So that was what he was to her, a complication? Did she seriously see him that way?

"Maybe we can go back to how it used to be," she said. "You know, before we got serious."

Realization hit him like a steel beam through the chest. "You don't love me." Even when he'd prompted her to say it earlier, she'd said she *wanted* him, not that she loved him. Had she ever loved him?

"Of course I do, Adam. I just think we were hasty in taking our relationship to the next level so quickly."

A year was too quickly? He knew he'd reacted badly to her rejection of his out-of-the-blue proposal, but he hadn't thought that it would make her fall out of love with him. The thought made his chest ache so badly that he rejected the idea immediately.

Maybe all she needed was time to sort things out. He shouldn't have tried to sway her in his direction. He should have been patient. He should have behaved like a loving, understanding boyfriend instead of a selfish prick. This being good was really a challenge for him. It was so much easier to take what he wanted or find a new means of excitement to distract himself. But he didn't want to give up on Madison. He loved her too much. So he was going to try to compromise even if it killed him. And it just might.

"I didn't mean to blow up on you like that," he said. "I know things are rocky for you right now, especially since you just lost your job. Take as much time as you need to sort things out, find a job, get your head on straight, and then we'll go from there. Do what you need to do. I'll wait."

She shook her head vehemently. "Adam, I don't want you to wait."

Ouch. He winced as his heart panged.

"I want to be with you now," she said. "I'm just not sure I'm ready for what comes next. Can't we just have fun, make love, no pressure?"

He had to laugh at the irony. Less than two weeks ago, he hadn't been ready to call her his girlfriend, and now he was set on her being his wife. He couldn't go back to where they'd been. He'd leapt over the hurdle of fearing commitment and jumped straight into being all in. He wanted it all or he wanted nothing. He wouldn't be able to go back to having a frivolous relationship where they hooked up—shared great sex, a few laughs, and what she'd consider a grand adventure—but ultimately parted without any promises. He couldn't believe he'd actually liked that type of relationship, and he really couldn't believe that she wanted to go back to it.

"So let me get this straight," he said, hurt rapidly turning to

anger. "You want to meet up every so often, get fucked properly, and then go on your merry little way?"

"You make it sound so negative. It worked just fine for over a year."

"Just last week you were the one who said you had to have a commitment to stay in this relationship."

"I do want a commitment," she said. "I want to be your only hook-up. And you'll be my only hook-up. It's just that this . . . this is getting too serious too fast. I'm not ready."

Hook-up? Was that all she wanted from him? He couldn't believe what she was saying.

"You can't have it both ways, Madison. You can't have my utter devotion and treat me like I mean nothing to you."

She captured his face between her hands. "Baby, you mean everything to me."

He pushed her hands away and shook his head at her. "How can you say that?"

"It's true."

How could it be true? She didn't want to marry him. Didn't want to live with him. Hell, he wouldn't be surprised if she requested he stay in a separate room tonight as soon as she met her orgasm quota for the evening. He took a calming breath. He knew she wanted to reach a compromise. Or rather, she required that *he* relinquish everything he wanted just so he could keep her. But that wasn't a compromise. That was her getting her way with no promises of the future he wanted, a full-out retreat from the direction they'd been heading. He didn't like to be manipulated, but he definitely felt that he was a puppet and she was pulling his strings.

"You don't have to agree to marry me, Madison," he said, "but if you think I'm going to rush to Dallas every couple of weeks for the sole purpose of getting you off, it's not going to happen. There are any number of women I can fuck whenever and wherever I need it. I can't deny that our sex life is great, but it's great because of how I feel about you, not because you're especially good in bed."

Her jaw dropped. Perhaps he should have worded that differently, but it was true. What made her special to him had absolutely nothing to do with sex. And what made sex great

with Madison had absolutely everything to do with his emotional attachment to her. He'd assumed it was the same for her, but now he was almost positive that her so-called feelings had blossomed from sexual attraction and not the other way around. She liked him because he fucked her properly, not because they were compatible outside the bedroom. Why hadn't he recognized that before?

"You can be such an ass," she said indignantly and rolled out of bed.

"What are you doing?"

"Going back to Dallas."

"You're leaving." It wasn't a question; she was leaving. Without fighting for him. Just like his mother had done. But Madison wouldn't do that to him, would she? They just had to work together to build a stronger relationship—slowly if that's what she needed—but they could not take a step back. There was nothing but loneliness and bitterness behind him. Adam couldn't go back. He could only move forward. Fuck, she'd been the one who'd taught him that.

Adam sat up in the center of the bed, the bed sheets crumpled in his lap and tangled around his legs. He watched Madison dress. Watched her shove her belongings into her suitcase. Watched her rip his heart out. What little he had left.

When she was all packed, she turned and stood near the edge of the bed, refusing to meet his eyes.

"You gave me something I thought I'd never have and now you're going to take that away from me?" he said, surprised by how raw his voice sounded.

"I don't want to leave, Adam. Say the word, and I'm back in your bed."

In his *bed*. He didn't want her in his goddamned bed. He wanted her in his life, every fucking facet of it. He glowered at her.

"Honestly, Adam, I don't understand why you're so mad. We can still be lovers. I just want to slow down."

She didn't want to slow down. She wanted someone to fuck her, not someone to love her.

"I just need one person in my corner, Madison. One person who believes me without fail. One person who believes *in* me.

I thought that person was you."

"I *am* that person, Adam," she insisted.

He would have believed her yesterday, but now he wasn't so sure. She stared at him as if she had a thousand things to say, but either couldn't find the words or didn't want to.

"What do you want from me?" he asked. He probably didn't want the answer, but he'd rather know what he was dealing with and try to cope instead of being pulled in a dozen different directions. "Just tell me."

"I wish I knew," she said, shaking her head. "I thought I knew, but now I'm not sure. I need to figure this all out before I say something I'll later regret."

"Are you sure about anything?" he asked.

"I'm sure I'm happiest when I'm with you. We always have fun."

She trailed her fingertips over his bare shoulder, and he realized that if he let her go, that touch would become a memory rather than being part of his reality.

"I'm sure you know how to please my body like no one else," she said.

He waited for the words he longed to hear, but she didn't say them. She wasn't sure she loved him, that had to be what had her acting so emotionally closed off from him all of a sudden. Or maybe she was sure that she *didn't* love him and simply wasn't done using him for her amusement just yet.

"I see how this is," he said, brushing her hand aside. "Instead of making a clean break, which would be better for both of us, you want to keep me hanging until you decide you've had enough of me. Why put off the inevitable?"

She closed her eyes and tilted her head back, a strangled breath escaping her parted lips. He'd reduced her to tears, and he frankly didn't care.

"But I'll never have enough, Adam. Don't you know that I'm addicted to you?"

Addictions were never healthy. He was proof positive of that fact.

"And we both know the best way to break an addiction," he said.

She nodded, fresh tears spilling down her cheeks. "Quit

cold turkey."

Was she really leaving? Was he really telling her to go? What the fuck was wrong with him?

He wasn't going to let her use him as she liked just so she could leave him later. *That* was what the fuck was wrong with him.

"You're right," she said after he'd glowered at her for a long, tense moment. "It's best if I go now."

She wasn't going to fight for him? Not even a little? She'd given up on him that easily. Not that it surprised him— everyone in his life eventually gave up on him—but still it hurt. No, it fucking ached.

"Yeah," he said.

He wanted to take her into his arms and kiss some sense into her. Wanted to force her to see reason and to love her unconditionally—the way he so desperately needed her to love him. Part of him wanted to back down and let her have what she wanted just so he could be with her in any capacity.

But he let her leave. He had to. Because the other part of him couldn't back down. He needed to know that she would fight for him, would choose him. That she would push back against him and against all her doubts and simply say that she'd love him no matter what.

He was trying to be a better man and do the right thing, trying to be strong and stand up for what he believed in, trying to be rational and not driven by emotion or his libido.

God, acting like an adult fucking sucked.

"I'll call you when I get it sorted out," she said from the open door. "Please don't give up on us just yet."

Me? he thought. *You're the one who gave up.*

But he said, "I'll look forward to your call."

And he knew he would, because nothing had changed about the way he felt about her. If anything, he loved her more for having the strength to walk away. Which made absolutely no fucking sense to him.

The door closed behind her with a punishing click. Adam flopped back on the mattress and buried his face under a pillow.

Go after her. Go after her, his reckless side demanded. *Make her*

stay. If you have to steal her away and bind her to the fucking bed, make her stay.

Give her space, his rational side argued. *Trust that she knows what she needs. She'll end up hating you if you act like a stalker. If she really loves you, she'll be back.*

So he compromised. He'd give her a week to figure out her psychological bullshit and call him. If he didn't hear from her by then, he'd go after her and convince her by whatever means necessary that they belonged together.

A week? his reckless side protested.

"Three days," he said aloud and tossed the pillow aside so he could stare at the ceiling and figure out the words he'd need to say to win her over.

He wasn't sure how long he'd stared at the ceiling or how many times he went over in his head where he'd gone wrong. He probably would have continued in the same vein all night if his cellphone hadn't rung.

Having spent a lot of his evening staring at it and willing it to ring, he was surprised at the way he fumbled with the blasted thing in his haste to answer.

The name *Gabe* in the caller ID registered in his jumbled mind, and his heart sank with disappointment. So Madison hadn't come to her senses yet. At least he had someone to talk to.

"Yo," he answered, hoping Gabe didn't recognize the appalling emotional edge to his voice. He needed to get his shit together before the guys got back to New Orleans.

"Are you in the hotel?" Gabe asked.

"Yeah."

"Can you do me a favor?"

"I guess so." It wasn't as if he had better things to do.

"Can you go check on Melanie's friend Nikki? Mel hasn't heard from her all weekend and she's starting to worry."

"Uh." Adam thought the request exceedingly odd. "And how exactly do I go about checking on her?"

"Just knock on the door of the room next to yours and see if she answers."

Adam slipped out of bed and found a pair of shorts in his luggage. He held the phone between his ear and shoulder as he

slipped into them.

"Is there a reason to worry?" Adam asked, grabbing his room key and venturing into the hall.

"With Nikki there's always a reason to worry," Gabe said.

"Is she there?" Adam heard Melanie say in the background.

"He's checking."

"She's probably fine," Melanie said. "Probably not answering her phone because she's mad at me."

Adam knocked on the door next to his and waited. When there were no sounds of movement within, he knocked louder. "Nikki, are you in there?"

Still no response.

"Well?" Gabe asked.

"She isn't answering the door. I guess she could be asleep."

"Is she a heavy sleeper?" Gabe asked Melanie.

"No, she's an insomniac. Unless she sleeps with me or she took some pills."

"She's probably just out enjoying the city," Gabe tried to reason with his distraught girlfriend.

Adam stood outside the hotel room and nodded at the well-dressed woman who passed him in the hall. Her steps slowed as she walked by so her eyes could take in every inch of his exposed torso. If he was looking for company, he was certain he could have some, but he just wanted to return to his room and be alone with his turbulent thoughts. He turned his back to the woman and leaned one bare shoulder against the wall.

"Am I finished here?" Adam asked.

"Can you get the spare key and check to see if she's inside?" Gabe asked.

Adam sighed. "Is the woman capable of taking care of herself?"

"Not really. That's pretty much the issue."

"Fine," Adam said, before retrieving the extra keycards everyone had so thoughtfully left him in charge of when they'd scattered to various locations during their short break. After figuring out which one to use, he slipped it into the lock and was rewarded with a flashing green light. The security latch had not been bolted, so there was probably no one inside, but he

knew Gabe and Melanie wouldn't leave him alone until he checked to be sure. He opened the door a crack.

"Nikki, it's Adam. I'm coming in. Is that okay?"

He waited a tense moment, listening for sounds of movement.

"Is she in there?" Gabe asked again.

"Calm your tits, dude. I'm checking. I don't want to just barge in with guns blazing."

He eased the door open. The room was dark and deserted. There was an open suitcase on one bed and toiletries in the bathroom, but no other signs that anyone was staying there. No towels had been used, and the bed was still made.

"She's not here. Doesn't look like she's been here all day. Maybe not even last night."

"She's not there," Gabe said to Melanie.

"Where could she be?" Melanie said, sounding even more distraught than when Gabe had first called.

"I'm sure she's fine."

"I'll leave her a note to call you and if I hear her come in later, I'll call you myself and let you know," Adam said, as he searched the desk for something to write on.

"Thanks, dude. I really appreciate your help."

"I didn't do much." Adam scrawled a hasty message on hotel stationary and set it on the closed lid of the toilet. He figured Nikki would eventually see it there and be unable to overlook it.

"Hey, you tried. I'm sorry I had to bother you. Are you having a good weekend with your woman?"

Adam hesitated. Most of his time with Madison had been spectacular, and he didn't want to get into his problems with Gabe—or anyone—so he said, "Yeah. I gotta go."

"Okay. I'll check you later. Thanks again, bro." Gabe disconnected.

The kit of toiletries and makeup on the counter drew Adam's attention. He couldn't seem to stop himself from touching all the feminine items inside. There would be no such items in the bathroom of his hotel room. No tangible reminders of Madison except the hole she'd left in his chest.

Perhaps he should go out and bury his sorrows with a

bottle of whiskey. Or maybe he could find something a little more to his liking. His vessels hummed with the memory of the heroin he used to shoot into them. The craving that never really left him tied his stomach in knots. His mind reveled in thoughts of euphoria and his favorite part of being wasted—the not giving a fuck part. But he didn't try to solve his problems that way anymore. Only he couldn't remember how he was supposed to try to solve his problems now that he was clean. He usually called Madison and talked things over with her, but that safe haven was closed to him. She'd been gone mere hours, and he was already floundering without her.

"For fuck's sake, you can make it three days," he chastised himself. In the past, he'd gone a lot longer without seeing her.

But he'd never suffered this gut-clawing agony before, and he wasn't sure how to deal with it.

He didn't know what to do to ease the pain. Actually, he did know. What he didn't know was if he could resist the temptation.

CHAPTER FOURTEEN

MADISON STARED at the departure sign above the airport gate and clenched her hands together. Why hadn't she just said yes? Why had she left? And why was she so fucking stupid?

She loved Adam. She *wanted* to marry him. She wanted to spend her life with him. She should have jumped at the opportunity to be his wife. And her hesitation had hurt him. She knew it had. She saw his pain in the way he'd hunched his shoulders and shied from her touch and in his refusal to look her in the eye. Trying to hold him at arm's length so he didn't destroy her had ended badly. Very badly. She was sure she'd made him feel like he didn't mean any more to her than a very talented sex toy, but it couldn't have been farther from the truth. She'd thought that giving him what she assumed he wanted—awesome sex—while she sorted through her stupid emotions and her equally stupid life would keep him interested long enough for her to get her head on straight.

It hadn't. He'd basically told her to go fuck herself.

The worst part was, she deserved his animosity.

For someone who'd once been paid to help other people get their lives on track, she sure was terrible at keeping her own in order.

She slid her hand into the pocket of her jeans and pulled out her phone. She could call him. Apologize. Accept his proposal. Move in with him. Tell him that she didn't only want his body, she wanted his heart. His soul. She wanted all of him.

She ended up dialing Kennedy instead of Adam. She and Kennedy had been inseparable since birth—actually their bond had started before birth. No one knew her better than her twin. If anyone would be able to explain to Madison why she had behaved like such a raving idiot, Kennedy could. And Madison knew her sister wouldn't hold back to spare her

feelings.

Madison held her smart phone against her ear and massaged the tense spot between her eyebrows as she waited for the call to connect. She hoped her sister wasn't with a patient. She really needed to talk to someone who would talk back to her.

"Uh, how did you find a spare minute to call me?" Kennedy answered. "Aren't you too busy getting laid to have time for the likes of me?"

Just hearing Kennedy's teasing voice made Madison's eyes fill with tears.

"I messed up," Madison said, her voice catching. The huge knot in her throat made it difficult to breathe, much less speak.

"What's wrong? You sound upset, and when you're upset, *I'm* upset."

"Adam asked me to marry him."

There was silence on the other end for a long moment. "*And?*" Kennedy drew out the word.

"And I didn't say yes."

Another pause. "Did you say no?"

"I didn't say no either. Not exactly. I told him we needed to talk about it, and he freaked out. And then we made up and he asked me to move in with him, and I freaked out again. Then I think I broke up with him. I'm not sure. I'm not sure about anything right now. I left, but I'm not sure I meant to leave. I didn't want to leave, but it seemed like the only option at the time because I wasn't thinking clearly and he wasn't listening properly. What am I doing, Kennedy? I don't know what the fuck I'm doing." She dashed away her foolish tears. The airport was not the place to have an emotional breakdown. People were starting to stare.

"Where are you, honey?"

"I'm at the airport trying to get on an earlier flight." She hoped a standby seat became available soon so she wouldn't have to hang around the airport all day. Her ticketed flight wasn't until the next day, so the odds weren't looking good for her.

"Good. I'll help you sort things out when you get here. What time does your flight land? I'll make sure I'm home when

you arrive."

"Don't cancel appointments or anything; I'll be okay."

"What time, Madison?"

"Half past three, I think. They said my best chance is the two o'clock flight." She wiped at a few stray tears that insisted on falling. She could always count on her sister to be there for her. "I'm sure I made a huge mistake by leaving, Kennedy, but I didn't know what to do. I panicked."

"You did the right thing. He shouldn't have freaked out because you told him you needed to talk about something as monumental as marriage. I didn't even know marriage was on his agenda."

One of the main issues was that Adam didn't see marriage as monumental. He seemed to think it was something to do on a whim. Madison sniffed her nose, and dug through her purse for a tissue. "Neither did I. It was a complete shock. I still can't believe he asked. But I messed up with him so bad. I'm not sure he'll ever forgive me."

"You didn't mess up, he did. And he's obviously more serious about you than you are about him."

Madison closed her eyes and shook her head. "But he's not. I should have just said yes. I don't know why I didn't. He means everything to me. I love him. I want to marry him. I do. I just . . . I'm confused. Or . . . I don't know. Maybe I'm delirious. I did get bitten by a bunch of mosquitoes. Isn't delirium one of the symptoms of Ebola?"

"You don't have Ebola, Madison. It isn't even transmitted by mosquitoes."

"I know. That was a joke." Apparently not a very good one.

"In all seriousness, Madi, something held you back. Some kernel of reason prevented you from accepting his proposal."

"But I love him. I love him so much, Kennedy."

"Love isn't all there is to being this man's wife. You know marrying him is going to be a huge hairy deal. He's a celebrity. He's an addict."

"Recovering addict." Sometimes she hated how even kiltered her sister could be. She so rarely got worked up about anything. And Madison had once been the same way. She was glad Adam had shown her how to be passionate. She just

wished that embracing that part of herself didn't scare her so much.

Kennedy ignored her interruption. "Had you ever even discussed marriage with him before he popped the question?"

"No," Madison said. "That's why it completely threw me. We're standing in this bayou joking about fish and alligators and mosquitoes and the next thing I know he's on one knee proposing and . . ."

She could still picture him at her feet, staring up at her with absolute adoration, the ring he offered catching stray rays of sunshine. She took a deep breath.

"You should have seen the ring he tried to give me. It was gorgeous. And my heart wanted me to say yes, but I just froze up completely." She blew her nose and tossed the tissue into a nearby garbage can.

"And you tried to talk to him about it?"

"Of course I did, but he's hurt that I didn't accept immediately. He seems to think that because I act on logic instead of pure blind emotion that I don't love him."

"He said that to you?"

Madison toyed with the plastic armrest of her chair. "Well, not exactly, but I could tell he was thinking it."

"Maybe he needs a few days to think it over himself," Kennedy said.

"But I'm afraid he'll think I don't love him. That I left him. Actually left him. For good. I think I need to go back immediately and make him listen to me. Make him see reason."

"He's not a reasonable man, Madison. He is completely driven by emotion and desire. I honestly don't get what you see in him. He's your exact opposite."

Madison sighed. "That's what I love most about him, that we're so different. He brings things out in me I didn't know I held inside. You know?" Of course Kennedy didn't know. She only ever dated Mr. Safe and Dr. Secure. "I need that, Kennedy. I need him in my life. And he needs me in his."

"Dr. Fairbanks"—Madison heard Kennedy's receptionist—"your one o'clock appointment is here."

"Thanks, Cyndi. Just give me a minute," Kennedy answered her. "I'll be home when you arrive, honey, and we can discuss

this like *rational* adults," she said to Madison.

Like a psychiatrist and a counselor, she meant. Kennedy still didn't know that Madison had been fired. They didn't have time to add that bit of crazy to the discussion now. Kennedy disliked Adam enough as it was; she'd flip out when she learned that he was responsible—at least in part—for Madison losing her job.

"Okay," Madison said. "I'll see you in a few hours."

"Love you, sis."

"Love you too."

When the call disconnected, Madison felt that a lifeline had been yanked from her hand. She always felt a bit disconnected when she didn't see her twin for a couple of days, but the sudden feeling of panic was extra strong. And ridiculous. She'd never quite understood what her patients who suffered from anxiety attacks went through. She completely understood now and was sorry she hadn't been more sympathetic to their need for Valium.

Madison took several calming breaths and tucked her phone into her purse.

"Passenger Madison Fairbanks, please report to the counter at Gate C10. Passenger Madison Fairbanks."

Madison hesitated at hearing the announcement, but she wasn't sure why. She needed to go home where she felt safe and secure so she could determine her next move. Adam said he would wait. But for how long? He's said it himself. He wasn't a patient man. The faster she figured out why her head and her heart were at odds, the faster she could return to him. Because she was pretty sure the heart was going to win this particular battle. She rose from her uncomfortable airport chair and headed to the counter.

"I'm Madison Fairbanks," she told the attendant.

"There's a seat available on the next flight to Dallas."

The woman glanced up from her monitor when Madison didn't say anything.

"If you changed your mind, there's another passenger—"

"I'll take it," she said, not sure why her stomach sank as the words left her mouth. If Adam had just talked to her when she needed to talk and acted as *her* sounding board for a change,

then she wouldn't have had to leave. Or maybe if she wasn't such a coward when it came to huge life decisions . . . But she should be allowed to think such things through, shouldn't she? Just because he was impulsive and reckless and bold didn't mean she had to be, did it?

She scrubbed her face with both hands. Kennedy would help her sort through her jumble of thoughts. Suddenly she couldn't wait to be home.

"Photo ID please."

"Huh?" Madison said, hearing what the woman was saying, but not comprehending her words.

"Driver's license? Passport?"

"Oh, sorry," Madison said. "I'm a little distracted."

She showed her ID and was handed a boarding pass. She wandered toward the enormous windows, where she watched handlers fling bags on the conveyor belt that carried luggage to the cargo hold beneath the plane. She didn't know if her own pink bag would actually make it on the same plane. They'd checked it when she'd inquired about a standby, but she wasn't sure how they would know which plane to put it on. The airline seemed to know how to handle her situation, so she supposed she'd worry about it when she arrived in Dallas.

It wouldn't be long before they boarded. And the weekend she'd been so looking forward to would be over. A complete disaster. Could her life get any worse? Staring at the plane that would soon carry her tens of thousands of feet into the sky, she decided she shouldn't tempt fate.

A presence close behind her made her body stiffen.

"So we meet again," a vaguely familiar voice said close to her ear. "Meeting once would be chance, twice coincidence, three times a miracle, but four times? It has to be destiny."

She'd heard the voice before—a knight asking quite plainly to please his queen's ass.

She jerked her head around, and her stomach sank. She knew the face as well. The guy who'd sat beside her on the plane on the way to New Orleans and tailed her through the airport to baggage claim. He'd been the one who'd started her down a path to no return at the club? Well, that fucking figured.

Destiny, my ass, she thought. He had to be following her. But why?

"You're not too good for me *now*, are you, little queen?" he said. He caught his bottom lip between his teeth as he gave her the twice-over. *Again.* Yet it wasn't as if he had to imagine her naked. He'd seen her at her most vulnerable.

Or perhaps she'd been at her most powerful in those moments of utter abandon.

"I'm sorry," she said, playing dumb. "Do I know you?"

"Your ass is well acquainted with my lips. My fingers. My cock."

She lifted an eyebrow at him and shook her head. "I'm afraid you have me confused with someone else."

"I could tell by the look on your lover's face that he'd never made you come as hard as I did when I fucked your ass."

"You don't know anything about how hard my lover makes me come. And as I recall, he was inside me at the time."

Chris chuckled. "And not for much longer. As *I* recall, as soon as you came, his dick went soft and he left the room. And where is he now? For someone you claim to be your boyfriend, he sure leaves you alone a lot."

Her heart twisted. Adam would really be leaving her alone a lot now. "My relationship with my lover is none of your business. Now go away. We aren't supposed to talk about the club beyond its walls. Remember?"

"I remember well." He ran a finger down her cheek, and she slapped his hand away. "Every time you came that night, it was my dick in your ass. You couldn't get enough. You aren't as sweet and innocent as you pretend to be."

She snorted. "You're right, I'm not. I like it rough and dirty. Being fucked up the ass gets me off like nothing else. But that doesn't mean you're free to talk to me outside the club. Go away."

His face fell. "You can't dismiss me."

"I think I just did."

Chris scowled at her. "All you bitches are alike."

"Yeah, none of us want you."

Chris stepped back, and Madison clung to the window ledge behind her—standing her ground even though she

wanted to run. When it came to the fight or flight reaction, she typically ran, but she wasn't going to run this time. She wasn't a meek little kitten. She was a tigress—a *lion*—and she would no longer repress her roar. A new-found strength had blossomed within her. She wasn't sure when or even why, but she was no longer afraid to say what she wanted. And what she wanted at the current moment was for this jackass to get lost. Was she afraid that he might physically harm her? Hell yes, she was. Was she creeped the fuck out that they kept running into each other? Of course. But she was finished being a doormat. From now on she was going to stand up for herself and go after whatever she wanted. Now if she could only figure out exactly what she wanted.

"Fuck you," Chris said.

"You already have. And believe me, I've had better." She made a shooing motion with her hand.

He offered her one last look of disgust—his lip curled and brows drawn together in a harsh scowl—before he turned and stalked away.

"And if I see you again, I'm calling the cops!" she yelled after him.

She wasn't sure if he'd heard her threat. He kept right on walking.

When he was out of sight, Madison sucked in a deep breath, her entire body trembling from the adrenaline coursing through her veins. She rubbed both hands over her face and then sank into a nearby chair.

She felt less like a lion and more like a disgruntled house cat as she regained her breath. Why did she keep running into that guy? It was as if he was following her. And how had he gotten into the club? She knew the place was invitation only. Had he gotten in to be with her, or was it a coincidence? Both options seemed far-fetched. And running into him again here at the airport? That was just too bizarre. She wondered if she had a reason to worry about his reappearance or if telling him off had gotten rid of him for good. It had felt great to tell him off. She was tired of compromising, of folding. She probably had Adam to blame for her dissatisfaction with taking the high road, turning the other cheek, and all other means of

conceding defeat.

Adam.

He hadn't changed her. He'd just helped her discover who she was.

She had to find a way to make it work with him. Her first instinct was to leave the airport immediately, do anything and everything to win him back. But she had a lot of thinking to do—that hadn't changed. She needed to know exactly what she wanted before she could go after him.

Shit. She hoped her heart and soul and head came to a consensus soon, because this indecisiveness was driving her crazy. She could only imagine how her over-analysis of every situation, made Adam feel.

But she was willing, had always been willing, to be patient with his needs. Shouldn't he at least try to understand hers?

Hours later Madison dropped her bag—it had made it onto the plane just fine and was actually the first unloaded—inside the back door of the creaky old farmhouse she shared with her sister. The flight had done little to help her sort through her jumble of feelings. She was just glad that Chris had not been on her plane. That guy was gone for good, thank God. She didn't need the added stress. She mentally high-fived herself for standing up to him when he'd approached her in the terminal. She was sure she'd never see him again even if she would be reminded of him for a few more days—her ass was *still* tender from his lack of skill. After the events at the club, she was now pretty sure the reason she loved anal sex was because Adam was so good at it. She hadn't realized how lucky she'd been in that regard.

The heavenly scents of cinnamon and vanilla and baking yeast drew her through the mudroom and into the kitchen. She paused in the doorway to inhale deeply as she watched Kennedy drizzle icing over the tops of the steaming cinnamon rolls she'd just pulled from the oven.

"I love you," Madison said wearily. She couldn't remember the last time Kennedy had made cinnamon rolls. Her sister had been so busy with medical school and her psychiatric residency that the poor woman scarcely had time to eat, much less bake.

Kennedy turned to smile at her. A smudge of flour was

smeared across one suntanned cheek, and for a moment Madison was transported back in time to when their grandma was standing at that same stove with flour on her cheek, smiling as she watched her twin granddaughters giggle while they kneaded dough for the same recipe Kennedy had just used. God, how Madison missed that marvelous woman. But at least she still had the house and the memories. And most importantly at the moment, her delicious cinnamon roll recipe.

"You love me or you love my baking?" Kennedy teased.

"Both." Madison settled onto a stool at the center island and hooked her heels into the rung beneath her.

"I figured you could use a little sweet-tooth therapy."

"Smart lady," Madison said.

Kennedy shoveled a gooey, sticky roll onto a dessert plate and slid it across the counter to Madison before serving herself and perching on the stool beside her.

"How was your flight?" Kennedy asked as Madison pulled off the outermost ring of her roll and stuffed it into her mouth. It wasn't lost on her that Kennedy had given her the prized center roll, the softest and gooiest of them all. The two of them usually fought over who was privileged enough to eat it.

"Okay," Madison said, licking icing from her fingers. "I was a little worried about my bag, but it made it onto the flight and was waiting for me when I arrived at DFW."

"Talk," Kennedy said. "Or do you need the prying questions?"

She didn't, not with Kennedy. She could tell Kennedy anything. So she did. She started with the leather shop and how Adam had asked her to wait outside while he argued with Phaedra.

"He's always hiding things from you," Kennedy said.

"I don't think he trusts that anyone could love all of him."

Kennedy shook her head. "He's *so* not ready for marriage."

Madison hadn't looked at it that way, not consciously. But maybe that's why she'd hesitated. Not because *she* wasn't ready to settle down and marry Adam, but because she knew that *he* wasn't ready for that step.

"I think you might be right," Madison said.

"You know I always am."

"I love you."

"You love me or my psychiatric evaluation?"

Madison chuckled. "Both."

Next Madison told her about their early dinner with Shade and Owen.

At the mention of Owen, Kennedy perked up. "I still want to ask that guy why he got his junk pierced."

Madison shook her head. "One. Track. Mind."

"You could ask him for me," Kennedy said.

"He has other things to worry about," Madison said.

When she told Kennedy about Lindsey's pregnancy, her sister's jaw dropped.

"Oh God, you're all going to end up on the Maury Povich show, aren't you?"

"Shut up. We are not."

"And did you meet this chick? Is she the biggest slut you've ever seen?"

"Yeah, I met her. And she's just a normal girl. Very pretty. Completely fixated on Owen."

"How can a woman not know who the father of her baby is? I mean, come on, Madison, how could any woman enjoy getting screwed by a bunch of strangers? That's pretty fucked up by anyone's standards."

Madison's face went hot, and she concentrated on her cinnamon roll, as if trying to move it with the power of her mind.

"You're not telling me something," Kennedy said. She elbowed her in the ribs when Madison continued to stare at her plate. "Madison?"

"Adam took me to this club," she said, "And, well . . ." She shrugged.

"The sex club? I thought you were just going to observe."

Madison bit her lip. "Well, that's what I had planned to do, but I kind of got caught up in the moment. Anyway, I can totally identify with getting off with a bunch of strangers. I can't really judge Lindsey for it, now can I?"

Madison peeked at her sister, who appeared to be trying to catch flies with her gaping mouth.

When Kennedy finally decided to inhale, she blurted out, "I

can't believe Adam would force y—"

"He didn't force me. Actually, he was very disturbed by my behavior."

"If he hadn't taken you there—"

"Stop trying to blame him for everything, Kennedy. He's not a villain."

"You're not the same person since you met him."

"You're right, I'm not. I'm much more true to myself. Much less afraid of being who I was meant to be. I don't even know why I came home," Madison said, slipping from her stool. "I have to go back and make it right."

"What? Tonight?" Kennedy hopped from her stool and wrapped Madison in a bear hug. "You are not going to talk to him until you sleep on this. Besides, you don't have time to drop everything and chase after him again. You have to work on Monday."

Madison stopped trying to force her way to the door and went limp.

"About that . . ."

And just that quickly it was all too much. She couldn't hold it together any longer. Her life had completely come apart over the last forty-eight hours, and the enormity of it all crashed down on her like a landslide. A strangled sob escaped her, and her vision blurred with tears.

Kennedy took her by both arms and gave her a shake. "What is it, Madison?"

"I got f-f-fired."

"What? How the hell did you get fired?"

"Somehow Joanna found out about my relationship with Adam and—"

"Oh God," Kennedy said, covering her mouth with a trembling hand. "Oh God. Oh God. I'm so sorry, honey. I'm so sorry." She hugged a very bewildered Madison tightly. "You have no idea how sorry I am. Oh God."

Madison let Kennedy hug her and stroke her hair and cry with her until her brain started to ponder why Kennedy was so freaking sorry.

"*You* told her!" Madison accused, pushing her comforting sister away.

Kennedy didn't have to validate Madison's suspicions; her look of guilt was unmistakable.

"I didn't know," Kennedy said, avoiding Madison's accusatory glare.

"You didn't know? You didn't know what, Kennedy? That sleeping with one of my clients is unethical?"

"Well, yeah, of course I knew that," she said. "I didn't know she'd fire you over it. I hoped she'd just talk to you about getting that poison out of your life."

"*Poison?* Do you really think of Adam that way?"

"You know I do, Madi. I've told you so many times that he isn't right for you, but my words go in one ear and out the other. I thought maybe if reason came from someone you respect, it might stick somewhere in that gray matter between your deaf-to-reason ears."

"I can't believe you would get my boss involved. What the hell were you thinking?"

"You know I only want what's best for you."

"What's best for me! How is this what's best for me? I've lost my job and maybe the love of my life. Why would you risk something like this? Just to prove you're right? Don't you want me to be happy?"

Her own sister had gotten her fired. Madison was so stunned she couldn't wrap her head around the betrayal. Madison knew that Kennedy didn't like Adam—even though she'd never actually met him—but to get her fired over the relationship? Why would she do something so damaging to Madison's career? The longer she thought about her sister's treachery, the angrier she became. And beneath the anger was plenty of hurt.

Kennedy cupped Madison's face between her hands and tried to get her to look at her. "Of course I want you to be happy. That's why I intervened. It just didn't go the way I'd planned. That man operates as blinders in your life, Madi. All you see is him."

Madison's angry glare burned from her aching heart and seared into her sister's troubled gaze. "That's because I love him!"

And now with the puppy dog eyes. "I said I was sorry,

Madi—"

"And that's supposed to make it all better? Ugh! I can't even look at you, at your treasonous, backstabbing, cruel, selfish jerk face." Heat rushed through Madison and she shouted, "Stop touching me!" She shoved Kennedy out of the way and fled toward the back porch, the only direction open to her with her betraying, sorry-excuse-for-a-sister blocking her path to the rest of the house.

How could Kennedy have done this? Did she really hate Madison's relationship with Adam that much? Her sister was usually an intelligent person. A caring sister. This was undoubtedly the stupidest and cruelest thing she'd ever done. And Madison didn't care how many times Kennedy apologized, she was not going to forgive her easily for this.

The screen door banged shut behind Madison as she marched down the creaky porch steps. She crossed the yard, the carpet of grass drought-brittle beneath her boots. She paused beneath the large oak tree where a long-abandoned tire swing still hung and leaned a hand on the rough bark for support. Her knees were shaking. Hell, her entire body was shaking.

Madison rubbed the center of her chest and sucked calming breaths into her lungs. She had no one to turn to. Not Adam—he wouldn't want to hear her sob story after she'd left him. Not her best friend—that had been Kennedy. Most of her other friends were from work, so she'd hidden her relationship with Adam from them. How scandalized would they be that she'd had an affair with a client? Her parents? They always took Kennedy's side. She doubted they'd celebrate her role in getting Madison fired, but she knew they'd be upset that she'd been hiding Adam from them as well. And grandma was gone.

She was going to have to sort out this mess on her own.

"Madison!" Kennedy called across the yard. "We need to talk this out."

"Fuck you," Madison shouted and pushed off the tree. She could just make out the roofline of her parents' house up the road. Her parents might be there, but that wasn't why she started walking in that direction. Ginger was there. Sometimes

a girl just needed to ride.

"What did you say?" Kennedy said incredulously.

"*Fuck* you!" she said louder, sending a one-finger salute over her shoulder in case her sister had lost her hearing. They both knew sign language.

She could hear Kennedy's gasp of disbelief all the way across the yard. "Really? That's how you talk to your own sister?"

"You're not my sister. My sister isn't such a raging bitch!"

Madison kept walking, the heat of the late afternoon bringing a sheen of sweat to her skin.

"I want to help you make things right." Kennedy called after her. "I said I was sorry!"

"And I did not accept your apology!" Madison yelled back. She would probably forgive her sister eventually, but it would not happen today.

As soon as Madison came in sight of the pasture, her gorgeous sorrel mare released an exuberant whinny and raced for the split rail fence as fast as her hooves could carry her.

People often confused the Fairbanks twins, but their respective horses never did. Kennedy's silver gelding, Bullet, lifted his head to see what all the fuss was about, but immediately turned his attention back to dining on blades of grass. Ginger was already dancing sideways along the fence, nodding her big head in greeting.

Smiling, Madison cut across the ditch beside the gravel road and stretched both arms over the fence to rub Ginger's neck. The massive animal nuzzled Madison's shoulder, the horse's hot breath stirring her hair, and she giggled as it tickled her neck.

"Do you want to go for a ride, girl?"

Madison jerked in surprise when Ginger nickered loudly in her ear. She laughed and hugged the horse's broad neck.

"Me too," she said.

She never felt freer than when she was astride a galloping horse with the ground racing beneath her in a blur and the wind catching her hair. Was that why Adam liked to ride motorcycles?

She pulled several twigs from Ginger's mane as she mused

about Adam.

Maybe they really weren't such different people. Maybe they sought the same comforts but in different ways. She'd love to introduce Adam to her horse. She didn't know if he'd ever ridden one. Being from a small town outside of Austin, he probably had, but he'd never mentioned it. When she talked about her happy past of barrel racing in rodeos and raising horses on the family farm, he'd always looked so sad. She'd felt he resented her for having a close-knit and loving family, so she tried not to mention them much. She knew his lack of a caring family had damaged him. And, God, if it hurt this much to be betrayed by her sister *once*, it must have been a living hell for him to be betrayed by both his parents again and again.

Families were supposed to love and support each other. Parents were supposed to protect their children. Sisters weren't supposed to rat each other out.

In retrospect, maybe not talking about her family had done more harm than good. He needed to know all of her just as she needed to know all him. She *had* been shutting him out—only showing him the pieces of herself that she thought fit him best. Why had it taken a broken heart for her to see that?

She and Ginger walked the length of the fence, which served as a barrier between horse and rider until they reached the barn. Ginger was waiting in the paddock by the time Madison entered the barn from the opposite side. The half of the massive structure that faced the pasture was open so that the horses could find shelter from storms or the brutal Texas sun. Ginger took a long draw from the water trough while Madison collected her tack.

Without protest, the horse accepted the bit into her mouth. Madison then pulled the leather over Ginger's velvety ears and carefully arranged her long reddish forelock so the leather didn't pull her mane. The horse worried the bar of metal with her tongue. Interesting. Madison wondered what it would taste like and feel like to have a human-sized bit in her mouth. She was sure Adam would be willing to show her if she asked him nicely.

No, he probably wouldn't. Not after she had walked out on him. She wouldn't be surprised if he never wanted to see her

again. And she couldn't blame him. She was the one too cautious or stupid or scared to accept what he offered. What she wanted.

Fuck.

She dashed a tear aside and reached for the saddle pad resting on the top bar of the orange metal gate. As she turned, she caught sight of her father coming through the barn door. Her first instinct was to run to him and have him make everything all right, the way he had when she'd been a child. But if she did that, he'd want to know why she was upset. And that would lead to lots of questions, and she just didn't have it in her to answer them at the moment. She needed to clear her head. When she got back from her ride, she'd sit down with her parents and explain what had been going on in her life for the past year.

Abandoning the remainder of Ginger's tack, she clicked her tongue at the horse and gently tugged the reins to draw the animal alongside the gate.

Her dad waved eagerly and called, "Going for a ride?"

"Yeah," she called back, not looking at him. Knowing she'd break if she did. Just seeing his strong profile in that familiar Stetson had her feeling all sorts of little-girly weaknesses. "We won't be gone long." To keep him from trying to delay her, she added, "I'll stop by the house when I get back."

She scrambled up the gate and slid her leg up and over Ginger's bare back before turning the horse toward the pasture.

"Be careful out there," her father said.

"Don't worry!"

Ginger trotted out of the barn and sprinted through the pasture with her head and tail held high, as if to brag to the other horses that *she* was going out with her human and they weren't invited.

Madison's knees clamped into Ginger's sides as the horse took a sudden turn around Bullet and almost unseated her. Perhaps darting off without a saddle hadn't been the best idea. It had been months since Madison had ridden a horse, and she couldn't recall the last time she'd ridden bareback.

Ginger automatically headed for the gate that led to the

back eighty acres of the Fairbanks' property. The extra pastures were not often used now that her parents had stopped raising cattle and only kept half a dozen horses for recreational use. The expanse of land was now more wilderness than ranch, but she preferred to ride the trails there. The terrain was familiar, and she didn't have to worry about trespassing on some trigger-happy rancher's land or worry that any motorized vehicles would make Ginger nervous.

As Ginger's steady gait allowed her mind to wander, her thoughts kept returning to one person: Adam. The only thing that was clear to Madison was that she loved him. She couldn't let him go.

It boggled her mind how easily he could throw caution aside and fall headlong into forever. She wasn't half as impulsive as he was. She never would be. She admired him for it and appreciated that quality in him, but when his tendency to jump over barriers before checking if there was a cliff on the other side confronted her head on, she panicked. That was what had happened when he'd asked her to marry him. And happened again when he'd asked her to move in with him. She'd panicked. He encouraged her to be more spontaneous— more reckless—but when it came down to action, she was intrinsically cautious. She'd always been that way. She wished he could be more understanding of her hang-ups and not assume that because she didn't immediately jump aboard his crazy train that it didn't mean she never wanted to ride his rails. She just needed time to think and since her brain seemed nonfunctional when his sexy self was in her vicinity, that meant she had to do her thinking when she wasn't around him.

She spent the entire ride thinking. About her life. Her job situation. Her *living* situation. She thought about her parents and her sister. But most of the time she thought about Adam. She missed him like crazy already. And she wanted him in her life. She was going to get him back, and she would never let him go. If she'd had her cellphone with her, she'd have called him right then and shared all her thoughts with him. Unfortunately, she'd left it in her purse, which was in the kitchen next to more of those cinnamon rolls.

That wasn't so difficult, was it? For once, the voice of reason in

her head was her own, and not her sister's.

Not difficult exactly, but definitely not easy.

She turned Ginger and headed back for the barn. Now that she had that bit of crazy sorted out, she could go back to Adam and explain where her heart was. Hopefully, she could fix things between them. He had to take her back, he just had to. She laughed, hearing herself sound like a teenager with her first crush.

But she was no teenager and Adam was no crush.

After she called him she would hop on the next flight to New Orleans and see him again before the evening was out. And if she couldn't get on a plane, she'd drive all night—whatever it took to get back to him as soon as she could. Why had she left him in the first place? Oh yeah, because he loved her enough to marry her.

"Ginger," she said, patting the horse's shoulder, "sometimes I can be completely daft."

Ginger bobbed her head, agreeing, and Madison laughed.

"I'm glad we could have this talk. You're such a good listener. Ever consider a career as a counselor?"

Ginger nickered.

"Gid'yup." Madison shifted forward to urge Ginger into a gallop. Now that she had a game plan—a rather weak one, but it was a plan—she was eager to execute it and start her forever with Adam. If he wanted a ring on her finger, she'd wear it. If he wanted them to live together, she'd pack her bags. If he wanted her to walk down the aisle—well, she wasn't quite ready for that step yet, but an extended engagement sounded like a piece of perfect.

Without warning Ginger stopped short, rearing on her hind legs, forelegs flailing as she screamed in terror. Madison tried to grab for the startled horse's neck, but she was already flying backwards. A sickening crunch was followed by excruciating pain up her back and into her left shoulder. Her arm crumpled as she instinctively tried to catch her fall. Then her teeth clanked together as the back of her head hit the ground. All the wind left her lungs on impact, and she lay stunned, unable to move or even cry out. She gasped for air, her lungs stinging in protest. She tried to draw a hand to the back of her head, but

her arm wouldn't move. Fuck, she'd fallen off her horse dozens of times training for rodeo. She knew better than to land like that. Ouch. She winced and turned her head, but could see nothing but tall grass through the narrow tunnel of her vision.

Don't pass out, she thought as the sound of Ginger's hoof beats retreated into the distance. *They'll never find you out here. You cannot pass out.*

The sinister rattle of an angry snake alerted her to what had spooked her faithful horse.

"Adam," she whispered just before her world went dark.

CHAPTER FIFTEEN

SITTING ON A PICNIC TABLE behind the tour bus, Adam stared into the mouth of his brown bottle and let everything but the chaos in his mind fade into the background. He'd honestly thought Madison gave a shit about him. All she'd really wanted from him was some hard cock and a good time. Just like all the other girls. Why did he even bother?

Yes, he was still thinking about her. One night completely lacking sleep had not cleared his mind of her. He doubted years of sleepless nights would banish her from his thoughts. But that was what he needed to do—stop thinking about her.

He took a swig of his beer, wishing he had something stronger—much stronger—to deaden the pain. To make him forget. To make him not care. Caring about someone sucked. He wouldn't make the mistake of doing it again. He was done with women. And relationships. And all the garbage that went with them. He'd always been a loner and now he was more than ready to return to his norm. Well, most of his norm. He still planned to stay clean and mostly sober.

The wooden tabletop beside him shifted slightly and a warm, slender arm brushed his. Heart thudding with expectation, he jerked his head up, but it wasn't her. Madison hadn't come back. It was that chick Jacob had banged a few nights before, the one who was friends with Gabe's girl. The one whose room he'd been in the night before. Hell if he could remember her name. He remembered her face, though. She was quite the looker. Not that he cared. He no longer cared about anything, least of all attractive women.

"Why you out here by yourself?" she asked.

He shrugged and took another draw of his beer, hoping she'd go away and leave him to wallow in his misery.

She took the bottle from his hand, took a swig, and

returned it to the loose nook between his palms.

Okay, he was sharing whether he wanted to or not. Why had she come here to bother him? It wasn't like they had anything in common.

"What do you want?" he asked.

"Just lonely," she said. "Mel went after Gabe. I should have figured she would."

And he cared why?

"I thought," she said, staring absently at the space between the table and the white gleam of the bus's side. "I thought maybe she . . . maybe she could love me. But no, not even her. Why doesn't anyone love me?"

Maybe they did have something in common. But he had no idea why the girl thought he would be a good sounding board. Didn't she realize he was too wrapped up in his own problems to give a fuck about anyone else's? If he couldn't easily talk to the woman he loved, why would he even consider talking to this walking train wreck?

"I'm sure someone loves you," he said. "What about your parents?"

She shook her head. "My father loved to rape me and mother loved to neglect me. Does that count?"

He shook his head slightly. "Parents suck."

"Did your father rape you too?"

He lifted an eyebrow and looked at her. She smiled weakly, and he realized the question was her very inappropriate attempt at a joke. "No. He just turned me into a junkie."

Adam tossed back the rest of his beer—finishing it in three long swallows—and hurled the bottle against the bus, satisfied when the brown glass shattered. He wished the rest of what was building inside him could be destroyed so easily.

"And your mom?" she asked.

"She left me with him." And why did this woman care anyway? He hadn't even been able to help her the night before. He'd been too wrapped up in his own misery to care about hers. Too self-absorbed to remember her name. Fuck, he really was an asshole. No wonder Madison had left him. "I'm sorry, I forgot your name."

"Nikki."

"That's right. Are you doing better now?" He still wasn't sure exactly what had gone down with her, just knew that Gabe and his chick had been worried enough to fly back to New Orleans from Austin in the middle of their romantic weekend. He was pretty sure they'd taken Nikki to the hospital. She was banged up. He saw traces of bruises on her arms. Her throat. Her face.

She stared down at her knotted hands and shook her head. "I try to be fine, but I'm not. Not really. I don't know if I'll ever be fine. Melanie just makes it easier for me to pretend."

He wasn't sure what she meant by that, so he said nothing.

She sighed. "Do you ever think everyone would be much better off if you never existed?"

"Don't think that way." He rested a comforting hand against her lower back, and she jerked as if he'd punched her in the face.

"Sorry," she said. "I'm a little jumpy today. After last night I don't think I'm up for sex, but I can blow you if you want."

He'd had hundreds of women come on to him in his life, but her suggestion shocked him to his core. "I don't want to have sex with you, Nikki."

Her gaze returned to her hands. "Oh. I guess you have a girlfriend or something."

"Actually, no. She dumped me." And seeing as she had yet to text him, much less call, he was certain it was over with Madison. He just hadn't let the truth sink in yet. He was still planning to go after her in a couple days, but was convinced it would be a fruitless endeavor and he was just setting himself up for more heartache. "But that's not why I don't want to."

"Oh," she said, her brow knotted. "Am I too ugly?"

Adam rubbed a hand over his face. He was too annoyed to offer this damaged young woman the level of care she needed. "Do you really think that your only value lies between your legs?"

She didn't answer, just wrapped her arms around herself and tipped her head forward so that her silky brown hair concealed her face. A drop struck her jeans and blossomed into a dark spot on the fabric.

Shit, he hadn't meant to make her cry. He didn't need any

further complications at the moment, yet he couldn't very well walk away from a woman in so much pain.

"You're beautiful, Nik. And not just on the outside. Don't you believe that?"

Another teardrop landed beside the first. Her sniff was scarcely audible, as if she'd learned long ago how to cry in silence.

He reached to tuck her hair behind her ear so he could see her face, and her tears didn't bother him half as much as the bruise on her cheek did. His fingertips hovered over the mark, but he didn't touch her. He had no business touching her. He dropped his hand and clenched it into a fist on his knee. How could he reach this woman? He knew what it was like to be a bullet train on a collision course with a reinforced brick wall. And yes, he'd often thought that everyone would be better off if they let him run headlong into it. Jacob had tried to stop the inevitable crash, but he hadn't been able to reach Adam. Only Madison had gotten through to him. What had she done that was so different from what Jacob had done? He thought back to their early sessions, when he'd been too angry with the world to even answer her questions, and then to the session when he'd finally opened up. What had she done differently?

She'd been patient. She'd found common ground. And most importantly, she'd listened without judgment. Adam could do that for Nikki if she was willing to open up. He knew it wasn't the guy who'd bruised her face that had broken her spirit. Her wounds were deep and emotional. They'd been scored into her soul long ago.

"Sometimes I think I hate my mother more than I hate my father," Adam said. He rested his hands against the dry wood of the table on either side of his hips and leaned back, just shooting the breeze.

Nikki wiped her face on the hem of her T-shirt and angled away from him. "Why's that?" she said after a long moment.

"Maybe he's a twisted son of a bitch, but at least he was there. She knew what my father was like, knew he was an addict and abusive. She ran, and I'm glad she got away from him, but she didn't take me with her. She just left me there with him, knowing he'd hurt me. I always hoped she'd get her

shit together and come back for me and make it all better, but she never did."

It had been Madison who'd made him face the hatred toward his mother that he hadn't even recognized and move forward. What was he going to do without Madison in his life? Go back to being bitter and angry and high out of his fucking mind because it was the only way he could function through the pain? But that wasn't functioning at all. That wasn't even living.

Without Madison's direction, he didn't know where he'd end up or where was headed. He didn't want to be that guy anymore, but that guy was who he was used to being. That guy was the person he knew how to be. He knew how to avoid reality. He knew how to be a junkie. He still didn't know how to be clean. He *was* clean, but he had no idea how to feel normal in this new skin. It seemed too small for him, like he needed to climb out of it.

He glanced at Nikki, wondering if sex was how she dealt with her pain, if sex was her narcotic. "Did anyone know what your father was doing to you?"

Her head jerked slightly in his direction, and she peered at him out of the corner of her eye.

"You don't have to tell me," he said and lay back on the tabletop, his feet still resting on the bench. He threaded his fingers together, put them behind his head, and stared up at the sky. Puffs of white floated lazily across a field of azure. He searched the heavens for familiar shapes in the clouds. "That one looks like a turtle."

"What?"

"That cloud," he said. "It looks like a turtle."

Nikki turned her face upward, her eyes scanning the sky. "Where?"

"Right there." He nodded toward the turtle-shaped cloud above.

"I don't see it."

"Come down here."

She offered him a look of uncertainty, her brows drawn together, split lip puckered out slightly. He supposed she thought he was trying to make a move on her, but really, he

just wanted her to let her guard down. He had no idea why he wanted her to confide in him. Maybe he was full of himself, thinking that he might be able to offer her some comfort by showing her that he was as fucked up as she was and hey, that was okay, everyone was fucked up in one way or another. The two of them just happened to have an extra pound or two of baggage to deal with.

He turned his attention back to the sky. "Rabbit."

She lay back on the table beside him, mimicking his position, her bent elbow inches from his. "All I see is a cupcake," she said after a moment.

"Where?"

She pulled one arm out from under her head to point at a cloud. "Right there."

"Are you blind?" he said. "That's a turtle."

"It doesn't look anything like a turtle."

"It does if you squint at it like this." He squeezed his eyes completely shut, and she laughed. Music to his ears.

"There's a carrot!"

He opened his eyes and followed her pointing finger to a cloud obviously shaped like a bunny.

"That's a rabbit," he said.

"No, it's not. It's a carrot."

He took her wrist and traced the outline of a rabbit around the cloud.

"Rabbit," he insisted.

She retraced the shape of a carrot in what he'd seen as the rabbit's ears. "Carrot."

They lay there for a long while, disagreeing on cloud shapes. He always saw animals. She always saw food. After a while, she took his hand and held it gently. He let her hold it. Her touch wasn't sexual—he knew the difference—it was a hand in need of something to hold on to. A hand in search of something solid and real. He knew that feeling well. He remembered the first time Madison had held his hand during a session. It had been innocent on her part, but it had completely changed his mindset. For the first time, he'd craved someone's touch to remind him that he wasn't alone in his struggles. She was there for him. Eventually that craving had turned sexual,

but it hadn't started that way. He had to tread lightly here, with Nikki. He didn't want her to get the wrong idea. He didn't want her to think he could be interested in her. Not because she was unworthy, but because someone else already owned his heart, even if she didn't want it. He turned his head to look at Nikki and found her staring at him intently.

"My mother knew," she said.

She didn't need to explain further. He knew she was answering his question from earlier. And he'd figured that would be her answer.

One wounded beast recognized the wounds in another.

Something clicked in his mind, and he could see the two of them lying side by side in the sweltering desert sand watching things far more sinister than clouds above them. And then words echoed through his brain as if someone was whispering in his ear.

One wounded beast recognizes another
Together we watch the buzzards circle
Who will be the first torn to shreds?
I can't watch
Close my eyes
Behind blistered eyelids I see nothing but red
I still feel the pain though I must be dead
Eaten alive
I'll take the coward's way and beg it ends
I'll go first; say goodbye, my friends
Devoured from the inside
Never to finish life's ride
Better dead than outliving your screams
Better dead than forgetting your dreams
Better dead than lying in wait
Kissing the devil might change my fate
I've touched brimstone; why hesitate?
She'll wait for me at the pearly gates
But will only be disappointed
When she realizes she'll spend her eternity alone
As I rot in Hell

Adam sucked in a breath and held it, waiting for more words to come. He needed to write them down before he

forgot them. The lyrics were rough, but he could use them in a song. Part of him—that part that wrote the songs that made Sole Regret what it was—had missed this darkness, the morbid place where his creativity dwelled. But most of him missed the light in his life. Madison had been gone only hours, and already he was in full mourning. Full darkness. How dark would it get before he fractured completely? He could already feel the cracks forming in his soul. It was only a matter of time before it shattered.

Adam sat up and gently pulled his hand from Nikki's. She blinked up at him.

"Will you wait here for a minute?" he asked. He needed something to write on and had nothing with him.

"I guess."

"You want a beer while I'm up?"

"Are you going to throw the bottle against the side of the bus after I finish it?"

He lifted an eyebrow at her. "If I feel like it."

She grinned. "Yeah, I'd like a beer. Unless you have something stronger."

Adam shook his head. Something stronger always led him to trouble. And he would avoid that trouble for as long as he was able.

"A beer is fine." Nikki tilted her face to the sky. Sunlight kissed her smooth cheek and danced in the blue of her sad eyes. Watching her, Adam was struck by another spark of creative inspiration. He really needed a pencil and paper. Maybe he should start carrying a notebook around in his pocket again. He hadn't done so for a long while. Hadn't needed to. Because when his life had gotten light, his creativity had fallen silent.

On the bus he grabbed a couple of beers from the fridge before he dug one of his sketchbooks and several charcoal pencils out from under his bunk mattress. He tucked the pad under his arm and headed back to the picnic table behind the bus, replaying the lyrics in his head and searching for more.

Nikki hadn't moved from the spot he'd left her, but she wasn't staring up at the clouds. Her eyes were squeezed tightly shut, her lips pursed together, brow knotted as if she were in

pain.

"Are you okay?" he asked as he settled on the surface of the picnic table beside her.

Her hand shot out and scrambled to find his. Only when she had it clutched firmly in her own did her body relax and her breathing begin to slow.

"I don't like to be alone," she said in a whisper. "When I'm alone, bad things happen."

"Is that why you're so clingy with Melanie?"

Her eyes snapped open, and she glared at him. "I'm not clingy."

He huffed in amused disbelief. "If you say so."

Her hold loosened slowly until she released his hand. He flipped open his sketch pad and wrote *when I'm alone, bad things happen* on one page. Something about that sentence struck a chord with him. He then flipped to a clean sheet and, along the left margin, he wrote the words that had come to him earlier.

"What are you doing?" Nikki asked.

"Writing something."

"Yeah, I sort of figured that out. What are you writing?"

"Song lyrics."

She lifted her head off the table and craned her neck to try to see what he was hurriedly scrawling across the page. He pulled the notebook up against his chest and lifted an eyebrow at her.

"Do I need to ask you to leave? This is top secret."

She released a heavy sigh and flopped back on the table. "You know I'm a huge Sole Regret fan, right? You can't really expect me to not sneak a peek."

A shadow crossed one of her eyes. Reminded him of a skull. Lyrics abandoned, he began to sketch her face, half in its realistic, lovely perfection, the other half exposed to the bone, and her flesh picked clean by the two buzzards he drew flapping their wings on the stark ground beside her as they fought over the heart they'd torn free from the now empty hole in her chest.

"Are you drawing something?" Nikki asked after several long moments of silence.

"Yeah."

Before he could stop her, she grabbed the edge of the sketch pad and tipped it toward her. Her breath caught.

"It's me," she said.

He wasn't sure how upset she'd be to see herself drawn that way, half her flesh gone. Her chest an empty chasm.

"It's beautiful," she said.

Beautiful? Not exactly the reaction he'd expected.

"Where did you learn to draw like that?" She pulled herself up to sit beside him, her fingers tracing the penciled lines of her face and then the bones of her skull. Her touch was light enough that she didn't smudge the charcoal. He wasn't sure why her interest in the drawing made his heart thud against his ribs. Her fingertips hesitated over the pair of birds wrenching her heart in two directions.

"My parents . . ." she whispered and then looked up at him for validation.

He nodded and stroked a hand over the back of her head. Her brown hair was like silk beneath his fingertips. "It isn't bad enough that they rip your heart out, but it's as if they're fighting over who gets to hurt you more."

"Yes, exactly like that." Nikki considered him for a moment, her gaze searching his face and then meeting his eyes. "You're different when you're with someone one on one."

He lifted a brow at her.

"Good different," she said hurriedly. "I always thought you were so cool and pretty much an asshole, but you're really kind. And deep." She furrowed her brow at him. "And . . ."

"Scary."

She laughed. "No, not scary. Dark, but not scary. The realism of that chest wound you drew . . . Pretty gory. And those lyrics?" She grinned. "They are a little scary."

Adam hugged the sketch pad to his chest again. He'd forgotten that he'd written them along the margin.

"You weren't supposed to see those."

"Sorry. I told you I was a fan. I couldn't help it. They're truly amazing. Have you written any other lyrics?"

He snorted. "Just every song Sole Regret has ever released."

"No shit? Maybe you *are* scary," she said. "In a good way, of course."

"Lie back so I can finish my drawing," he said.

She leaned back and settled on the surface of the table again.

"I always assumed that as the singer, Shade wrote your lyrics," she said. "You have no idea how many times I've lied awake listening to him sing those words to me. Screaming them in my ear. Imagining he'd written them for me because they touched me so deeply and kept my hope alive. I was so infatuated with him and the songs he sang just for me. And all along it was you who wrote the songs." She glanced at him and grinned. "So I should have been trying to get into your pants all this time instead of Shade's."

He shook his head at her. "I already said I'm not interested in sex."

"But we can be friends?" she said, and the innocent lilt to her voice made his heart clench.

"Yeah, we can be friends."

She reached for his knee and gave it a squeeze.

"Just friends," he added, eyeing her hand pointedly.

The offending hand slid from his knee, and she moved it to rest on the top of her head as she continued to gaze up at the sky. Apparently, being *just friends* meant that she should talk his ear off while he continued to add details to his sketch. As he drew the lines of her slender arm, she told him about how she met Melanie when they were children. And as he added the details of her fingernails and the creases and texture of her delicate hands, she told him how she'd gone to college with Melanie, skipping over the horrors of her adolescent family life because it had been devoid of Melanie. And as he tried imagining her bare breasts—yeah, it was a tough job—so he could do a decent job of drawing them around the gaping wound in her chest, she told him how Melanie always saved her from herself. Nikki had a thing for Gabe's new flame. Even though it wasn't any of Adam's business, he should probably clue the guy in or someone was bound to get hurt. And in his experience, it tended to be the guy half of the relationship that was left with his heart shredded and who ended up drowning his sorrows in a bottle of beer or drawing Madison's perfect tits on another woman's body.

I have issues, he thought as he drew an elaborate butterfly resting on the side of Nikki's head—the beautiful side of her, not the skeletal side. The butterfly's wings were poised in mid-downstroke, giving the illusion of movement. The only things he like drawing as much as tits were animals. He hadn't skimped on the details of the buzzards' talons, feathers, and eyes or on the elaborate wing pattern, spindly legs, and slim abdomen of the butterfly. He also didn't skimp on the details of Nikki's breasts, because breasts deserved attention. Breasts always deserved his attention.

He was almost sad to move his work down to a slender belly and the flair of hips, with a leg bent to angle conveniently over feminine folds. It was invasive enough for him to imagine what her breasts looked like—and end up drawing them like Madison's. Adam had no business or interest in imagining what the woman's pussy looked like. He felt she had to be naked in the drawing, though. Clothes would have taken away from the feeling of exposure. But all of her secrets didn't need to be completely revealed. He was still futzing over the exact shape of her big toe when he realized she'd fallen silent.

He glanced up to her face, expecting to find her asleep, but she was simply watching him. Perhaps she was tired of talking about Melanie.

"Almost done?" she asked.

"Almost."

"I can't wait to see it. I had my portrait drawn by a caricaturist once," she said, "but I didn't care much for the results. It only managed to make me very self-conscious about my horse teeth and my chipmunk-fat cheeks and my wide-spaced eyes that are practically on the sides of my head."

Adam shook his head. He had hated the drawing that hack down by Jackson Square had done of Madison. "There should be a law about taking something beautiful and making a mockery of it."

"Can I see the drawing now?" She was like a child who couldn't wait to open a gift.

"Not yet."

She scowled at him. "You gave me horse teeth, didn't you?"

He laughed. "No, your teeth are very lifelike. Especially

where half your face is missing."

"I can't sit still anymore," she whined.

"You can move. I never said you couldn't move. Besides, you didn't have any problem jacking your jaws earlier. Plenty of movement going on there."

She slapped his leg. "Shut up."

He laughed, adding a shadow here and there to the nearly finished drawing.

She sat up beside him and opened her beer, which was sweating a huge puddle onto the wooden table near her hip. Her fingers toyed with the water as she took a swallow from the brown bottle.

"It's hot out here," she said.

It was rather warm. Adam had been so wrapped up in his work, he hadn't noticed until she'd mentioned it.

"We should go inside," he said.

"Not until I see the drawing."

Poker face in place, he said, "I think I'm going to shred this one and start over."

Her jaw dropped, and she wrenched the sketch pad from his loose grip. He'd been done for several minutes, but was a bit nervous for her to see the completed drawing. With the exception of the tattoos he'd designed for his bandmates and the sexy image he'd crafted of Madison, he usually kept his artwork to himself. His music was for the world, but his drawings were for him alone.

"I'm naked!" she squeaked, her gaze shifting as she examined every detail of the sketch. "Oh, Adam, it's beautiful. *I'm* beautiful."

"I told you that you are."

Her eyes widened, and she lifted a hand to hover over the living butterfly he'd drawn in her hair.

"Why did you draw this?" she asked, her tone accusatory. "I never told you about Melanie putting butterflies in my hair. Were you eavesdropping on us earlier? When I told her that I love her?"

Adam shrugged. "I wasn't eavesdropping. There was just a lot of white space there, and I thought a butterfly would look better than a scorpion, but if you want me to change it . . ."

He reached for the sketch pad, and she clutched it to her chest. "No, don't change it," she said. "It's perfect. Better than perfect."

"How can it be better than perfect?"

"It just *is*!" she said, her eyes a bit watery. She watched him warily and when she seemed convinced that he wasn't going to take the drawing away from her, she tilted it away from her chest to take another look. "Okay, so it isn't perfect."

He leaned closer so he could examine his work more critically. "Should have made the teeth bigger."

She smacked him half-heartedly. "It isn't that. My boobs don't look like that."

"Yeah, well, that's how I imagined them. So that's how I drew them."

"Mine are bigger than that, and this part isn't that wide," she said, matter-of-factly, pointing at the areolas. "And my nipples are larger."

She shoved the pad into his hands and reached for the hem of her tank top. "I'll show you."

Adam probably shouldn't have been shocked that Nikki was taking off her clothes outside in broad daylight—plenty of women had shown him their racks in public arenas—but they'd been bonding on a friendly level, so when her pink tank top went flying in one direction and her lacy bra in another, he could do nothing but gawk.

Apparently, he wasn't the only one gawking. Several low wolf whistles came from the area of the semi-truck parked near the bus. The road crew was taking a break from setting up the stage. Adam hadn't even noticed them until they'd directed their appreciative attention to the suddenly half-naked woman at his side.

"See," Nikki said, cupping her breasts in both hands and offering them up for his artistic examination. "My boobs look way different than those."

Well, he wouldn't say they were way different. The general structure of breasts was similar in all cases. But the devil was in the details. And she was right. He hadn't drawn hers properly.

He erased the nipples and the under curves of her breasts and took up his pencil to do a more realistic job.

"Take it all off, baby!" one of the road crew yelled.

Nikki gave them the finger. "Get lost, *baby*."

The crowd of men staring at them had gotten uncomfortably large.

"Let's take this inside," Adam suggested. "I can't concentrate with all the noise they're making."

"Okay." Nikki hopped down from the table and retrieved her tank top. She held it over her breasts with one hand, located her bra, and tossed it over one shoulder before picking up her beer and heading for the bus.

"Go get her, Adam," one of the road crew shouted. "Plow her good and hard for me."

Adam rolled his eyes and shook his head. Just because he was following a gorgeous, topless woman up the tour bus steps did not mean he was going to *plow* her. He was just going to draw her breasts properly. He had no interest in sex with anyone except Madison. And maybe once the love of his life figured out what she really wanted, he'd go back to plowing *her*, but it wasn't happening with Nikki. Nope.

"Where do you want me?" Nikki asked as she glanced around the interior of the bus.

"The bed."

Nikki laughed. "So you *are* trying to seduce me."

"If I was trying, you wouldn't have to ask," he said.

She shivered. "Mmm, I really do think I went after the wrong member of the band last weekend."

"If you don't knock it off, I'm going to draw a fifty-year age progression of your boobs."

Her jaw dropped, and she cupped a breast in either hand, rubbing her thumbs over her nipples to make them stand erect. "You wouldn't." She pouted at him. "You said there should be a law about mocking something beautiful."

"I wouldn't be mocking them. Just giving you a glimpse of the future."

He started when her tank top and bra slapped him in the face.

"You are so mean," she said.

He brushed the clothes away, and they landed at his feet. "If you're trying to insult me, you're going to have to try harder

than that."

"I wasn't trying to insult you. I just want you to make me look beautiful in your drawing." She fluttered her eyelashes at him.

"Then go lie on the bed and stop playing coy. You know damned well I'm not trying to seduce you."

"Jeez, I was just joking around," she said and stomped into the bedroom.

She stretched out on the bed and tucked one arm under her head, shoving the pillows up against the headboard. Adam kicked off his boots and climbed up on the bed beside her to sit cross-legged. He examined her breasts closely. She trailed the fingers of her free hand over one pink tip.

"Do you want them hard for the drawing?" she asked, her voice low and seductive. "I think they look better hard, don't you?"

If she didn't knock it off, his dick was going to change his mind about not having interest in sex.

"Just lie still," he said.

"They'd get really hard if you licked them." The tip of her tongue traced her lip and then disappeared into her mouth.

"Do you even know *how* to have a nonsexual relationship?" he asked.

"I know how," she said defensively.

"Then prove it."

"It's kind of hard not to get turned on when you're staring at me like that," she said.

"Like what?" He took the pencil to paper and restructured the under curves of her breasts so they no longer looked like Madison's.

"Like I'm worth looking at."

"We already established that you are. Now stop talking so I can concentrate."

She smiled and went still, watching him draw and no longer doing her best to put his dick in charge.

He turned his attention to her nipples, careful to draw every detail in perfect likeness. The soft pink buds really would look better hard, he decided, but he was not going to lick them even for the sake of art. He was tempted to draw a second image of

her with her chest intact and not marred by the gaping hole of her heart ripped out by the battling crows.

Maybe she'd allow him to draw her again sometime.

Adam yawned unexpectedly.

"I'm sorry you find my boobs so boring," Nikki said, her lips twisted into a wry grin.

"Your boobs are perfectly tantalizing," he assured her. "I just didn't get much sleep last night." And his brain had recognized that there was a bed handy for napping.

He returned to his drawing, moving faster now, because he suddenly wanted to finish as quickly as possible so he could catch a few Zs before the show.

"Once Melanie took me to bed with her last night, I slept great," Nikki said.

Adam paused and glanced at her face. She was smiling dreamily and her nipples grew hard without her even touching them. Yep, Gabe definitely needed to be warned about the puzzling relationship between the two women.

"I thought she didn't want you that way."

Nikki sighed. "She doesn't. And now that she knows I *do* want her that way, she probably won't let me cuddle up with her when I sleep. I can't sleep alone unless I take a couple of these."

She shoved her hand in the pocket of her jeans and tugged out a small baggie full of bar-shaped white pills. Adam's belly tightened. Yeah, he could use a few of those himself.

"What are those?" he asked, but he already knew.

"Bars. You want some?"

God, yes, he wanted some. He wanted the entire baggie full.

"I'm drawing," he said. His hands were shaking as he pulled the tip of his pencil over the seductive texture of the sketch paper.

She popped several Xanax into her mouth and swallowed them with a chug from her beer. She set the bottle on the night stand and then returned to resting on her back. "Adam?"

He looked over the drawing, checking for anything he missed, and added a small mole to the under curve of one full breast. Hell, he might as well make the drawing as realistic as

possible since he had a living model at his disposal.

"Hmm?"

"Will you hold me? Just until I fall asleep. And then I'll be okay. I won't dream on this stuff, so I'll be okay."

His first instinct was to refuse, but she was staring at him so hopefully that his resolve crumbled. "Yeah, okay. But just until you fall asleep."

He set the completed drawing aside, and she smiled at it. "Now those are my boobs," she said.

He chuckled and lay down beside her. "Glad you approve."

Nikki shifted, resting her head on his shoulder, and snuggled into his side.

"Thank you," she whispered.

He didn't mind. He kind of liked feeling that someone needed him. Even if it was as a pillow.

"For you," she said and pressed one of her pills into his hand. "It will help you forget her."

He stroked her silky hair with his free hand, and she relaxed against him. Soon her breathing became deep and regular. Even though he was exhausted, Adam didn't have such an easy time falling asleep. He held the pill she'd given him pinched between his thumb and forefinger and stared at it. What could it hurt? It was just one pill. It wasn't as if it would even make him all that high. It would just take the edge off, let him relax. Allow his mind to clear. Maybe even make sleep possible. A lot of power to do good in this little pill, he thought.

What could possibly be so bad about swallowing one little pill?

He should call Madison and talk to her about his thoughts, these undeniable urges to self-medicate. But she'd left him, and he had no one to turn to.

The drugs had always been there for him; they had never failed him. Fucked him up and fucked him over, oh yeah, but they had always given him exactly what he'd needed. Or so he'd thought. Through all the rehab and treatment, had anything really changed inside him?

He still wanted to live outside of reality. Reality hurt. It sucked.

So what harm could it do?

Just one little pill.
What harm?

CHAPTER SIXTEEN

SOMETHING HIT ADAM hard in the belly. He sucked a startled breath into his lungs and blinked open his eyes, trying to focus on whatever was hovering above him. Turned out to be Gabe's chick glaring down at him looking entirely pissed off. Weird.

"How could you?" Melanie bellowed at Adam and slugged him in the stomach again. "How could you take advantage of her after everything she's been through this weekend, you fricking asshole?"

Adam managed to catch her fist before she pummeled him again.

"What the hell?" he growled, not close enough to awake to put up with this sort of bullshit.

"Do you even have a conscience?"

Well, that was debatable, but in this case he didn't have a clue what had the woman so riled up.

The warm body resting against his side groaned in protest as Melanie shifted her attention elsewhere.

"Nikki," Melanie said, shaking Nikki's shoulder vigorously. "Nikki, can you hear me?"

Nikki was out cold and considering the number of Xanax she'd swallowed, Adam wasn't the least bit surprised.

"What did you give her?" Melanie said, her voice taking on an edge of desperation.

"Give *her*?" Adam said, his confusion quickly turning to annoyance. "I didn't give her shit. Why don't you ask her what she gave *me*?"

"Nikki, what did you take? Wake up. Talk to me!"

"Let her sleep, for fuck's sake," Adam grumbled. "She's emotionally exhausted."

Adam rolled out of bed and into Gabe's fist. If Adam had had solid footing, the blow to the shoulder might have

snapped his collarbone, but it merely knocked him back onto the bed. He wasn't sure why he was being attacked. He hadn't done a goddamned thing wrong.

"What the fuck is wrong with you?" Adam yelled and jumped to his feet, both hands fisted.

"Did you drug her so you could screw her?" Gabe said, his voice low and those bright green eyes of his narrowed to slits.

"What?" Adam glanced at the half-naked, unconscious woman on the bed and finally realized what it must look like to a couple of nosy jerks. "I didn't screw her."

"Then why is she naked?" Melanie screamed at him before turning her attention back to her friend. "Nikki? Nikki, open your eyes."

"She isn't naked," Adam pointed out. "Just topless."

"Melanie?" Nikki said in a slurred voice.

"Yes, it's me. What did you take?"

"She took Xanax," Adam said. "She said it helped her relax. And sleep."

"How many did she take?" Melanie asked.

"I don't know. I'm not her keeper."

"You sure you didn't take advantage of her?" Gabe asked.

"I was just drawing her." He flung a hand out toward the sketch pad propped against the lamp on the night stand. "And we were both tired, so we fell asleep."

"And how many Xanax did *you* take?" Gabe asked, a look of disappointment on his lean face.

"Not that it's any of your fucking business, but I didn't take any."

Gabe scratched his eyebrow, drawing attention to the pair of dark bruises around his eyes. Bruises Adam knew he'd earned the night before when he'd provoked the guy who'd hurt Nikki. Gabe's need to defend and protect the woman was a bit odd, but Melanie was the one truly freaking out. She had Nikki sitting on the edge of the bed, her naked torso swaddled in the covers.

"Did he do anything to you?" Melanie asked as she stroked the hair from Nikki's ashen face. "If he did, I will fucking kill him, I swear."

Nikki's lower lip trembled, and her eyes filled with tears.

She ducked her head to avoid Melanie's imploring gaze.

If she lied and told Melanie that Adam had molested her just to gain sympathy and attention from the woman she was so obsessed with, he was going to lose it. He was barely holding it together as it was. He didn't need more drama in his life.

"You can tell me," Melanie said gently, wrapping an arm around Nikki's shoulders and tugging her against her side.

"Fuck this shit," Adam said. "I didn't do anything to her."

He grabbed his sketch pad from the nightstand and headed for the open door.

Gabe stepped between him and freedom, crossing his arms over his chest. "You aren't leaving until Nikki gives us her side of the story."

"Did you see what he drew?" Nikki said. Her voice was still slurred, but there was an emotional lilt to it as well.

Gabe took the sketch pad out of his hand and examined the drawing. "Kind of gory, but remarkable, as usual." He angled the drawing toward Melanie.

"She's naked," Melanie pointed out, her nostrils flaring.

"N-not that," Nikki said and touched the side of her head. "The butterfly. He drew a butterfly in my hair."

Adam and Gabe exchanged startled looks when Nikki burst into body-racking sobs. While Melanie attempted to comfort her, the two guys rushed out of the room and closed the door to offer them privacy. Or avoid a scene. Whatever.

"That woman needs professional help," Gabe said.

"Then why are you dating her?"

Gabe's jaw dropped, but then he chuckled when he realized Adam was teasing him. "I meant Nikki. Give me that," he said, jerking the sketch pad out of Adam's hands. "Are these lyrics?"

Adam nodded. "The first I've written since we've been on tour."

"Fuck yes," Gabe said as he read the words. "Jacob was really starting to worry about you."

"I was starting to worry about me," Adam admitted.

"And this!" Gabe said, tapping the sketch of Nikki that filled in the rest of the enormous page. "This needs to be the album cover."

Adam's face went uncharacteristically hot. "What? No, I don't think—"

"Dude, it's brilliant."

Adam gnawed on his lip and scrunched his brows together as he appraised the drawing. It definitely wasn't good enough to be an album cover. But it wasn't terrible.

Gabe pulled his phone out of his pocket and started thumbing in a text. "Jacob needs to hear these lyrics," he said. "They'll blow his mind."

"They're not finished," Adam said.

"You have no idea how freaked out he's been about your dry spell, do you?" Gabe said, still typing away on his phone. "And then when you asked Dawn for advice backstage, you had us all freaked out. The rest of us could try to write lyrics, but we all know they'd never be as creative as what you come up with in volume. Jacob even asked me if he thought we could get our hands on some of the stuff we tossed aside from the last three albums that you claimed wasn't good enough."

"It isn't good enough," Adam said. But he did have the notebooks in a box in his closet if they got desperate enough to use them. Not that he had to worry about his writer's block anymore. He was so bone-deep miserable over Madison leaving that he'd have his new sketch pad full of ideas within the next twenty-four hours.

He pulled his phone from his pocket in case he'd somehow missed a call or text from her while he'd been asleep.

Nothing.

Was she just being stubborn, or was she really over him that quickly?

Maybe he should swallow his pride and call her right then.

But he wouldn't. Not yet. He didn't want to seem desperate, even though he felt that way. In two days, he wouldn't hold back, but he needed to give her the time she claimed she required.

While they waited for Jacob to make his way to the bus, Adam took his sketch pad from Gabe and sat at the table. He had another idea eating at him already.

Last Goodbye, he wrote.

How could I have known it would be our last goodbye?

The hundreds before never counted for much
A word, a glance, a simple touch
He took you
Before I could let you go
Ashes to ashes
How could I know
That you would say our last goodbye?
Dust to dust
You were gone in the blink of an eye
Now I'm alone
Never to see you
Never to touch you
Never to hear you
Again
How could I have known it would be our last goodbye?
The hundreds before now mean so much.
Any word, every glance, each touch
You gave me
I won't ever let you go
Ashes to ashes
Because now I know
A way to never say goodbye
Dust to dust
I'll be gone in the blink of an eye
Just to see you
Just to know you
Just to love you
Again

Adam caught movement in his peripheral vision and lifted his head, his eyes taking a moment to focus on Jacob's grinning face across the table from him.

"It's back?" Jacob asked, nodding eagerly.

"Yeah, I guess it is," Adam said. But at what cost? Did an artist really have to suffer for his work? Or did Adam just have to suffer for his?

"Any guitar music yet? I'm ready to harmonize," Jacob said, reaching for the sketch pad.

"And I'm ready to bang out a new tempo," Gabe said.

"And I'm ready to bang," Owen said with a wide grin.

"Where's Caitlyn when I need her?"

Adam shook his head, but was grinning a mile wide on the inside at their enthusiasm. He'd forgotten how much fun it was to create. "No guitar pieces yet. I just started on lyrics."

Jacob flipped the page to the previous verses and dropped the sketch pad. "What in the hell did you do to Nikki?"

"Isn't that awesome?" Gabe said. "That's the sketch I was talking about. It would make a fantastic album cover."

"It's sick," Jacob said. "How could you draw a living person all torn apart like that?"

"She is all torn apart like that," Adam said, pulling the sketch pad toward himself. "You're just too blind to see it."

Adam flipped to a new page and wrote *Torn Apart*
They don't see what I see when I look at you
A perfect outer shell that hides so many secrets
Scars so deep and

"What do you *mean* she's all torn apart like that?" Jacob yelled, startling Adam into looking up from his work.

Gabe rested a placating hand on Jacob's shoulder. "He doesn't mean literally. She's fine. Well, not any worse than she was the last time you saw her."

"Don't freak me out like that," Jacob said. "I don't need the nightmares. My life is enough of one already."

Adam flipped the page and wrote *My Life, I don't need the nightmares. My life is enough of one already.*

"Are you turning my comments into lyrics?" Jacob asked.

"No one is safe," Owen said and laughed.

Adam flipped the page and wrote *No One Is Safe, dark things reside deep in my thoughts. My greatest concern is if I'll get caught*

Owen fisted a hand in Adam's T-shirt.

"Hey, stop that," Owen demanded.

Adam turned to another blank page.

Hey, stop that, he wrote, just to tease Owen.

Gabe chuckled. "I think we've created a monster."

The monster I created ended up scrawled on the next page. That idea had a bit more merit.

"Pencil dick the love machine," Owen said.

Adam glanced up at him, an eyebrow lifted in question.

Owen laughed and patted Adam's shoulder a bit too

forcefully. "Just seeing if you're paying attention or just writing down everything we say."

Pay Attention Adam wrote on another blank page.

I know a guy named Owen

A civilian who wears dog tags

And they call him pencil dick the love machine

"Pencil dick the looooove machine," Jacob sang in his best impression of Barry White on a porn movie soundtrack. He even gyrated his hips for effect.

"That will be the first single off the new album for sure," Gabe said.

Adam laughed when Owen launched himself on Gabe's back and locked him in a choke hold.

"I wouldn't mess with him," Jacob said. "He's used to getting his ass kicked by professional MMA fighters."

"Semiprofessional . . . UFC . . . fighter," Gabe said breathlessly, landing a fierce blow to Owen's ribs with his elbow.

"Oh, my bad," Owen said, wincing, but not releasing his hold. "I thought he got his ass kicked by the Pillsbury Doughboy."

"You mean that was you?" Gabe taunted.

Owen squeezed harder. "Some of us have to work at perfection, chicken legs."

Jacob laughed. "You two really need to work on your insults."

"Gabe?" a soft voice said from the open bedroom door.

Adam's smile faded when he saw the look on Melanie's face. He knew that look. That was how he'd felt when Madison had closed the hotel door behind her as she'd left him.

Owen released his choke hold and slid down Gabe's back.

"What's wrong?" Gabe asked, moving to stand before her. He took her upper arms in his hands and stared down into her tear-streaked face.

"I have to leave," she said.

"What? I thought you were going to go on the road with us."

"She is?" Jacob said, but he was ignored.

"I want to, but Nikki, she . . ."

"Melanie, you can't let her rule your life."

"If I leave her alone, I'm afraid she'll try to kill herself again."

"Again?" Gabe questioned.

Nodding, Melanie tucked her hair behind her ears. Her hands were shaking so bad, Adam could see the movement from ten feet away.

"She's in a fragile state right now."

"Which is why she should be admitted," Gabe said. "You aren't a psychiatrist, Mel. She needs professional help."

"Don't you think I know that!" Melanie snapped.

Gabe jerked as if she'd slapped him.

"I'm sorry," she said and caressed his cheek. "I didn't mean to yell. And I'm not leaving forever, just until she's stable. She needs me."

"*I* need you too," Gabe said.

Adam turned his attention to his sketch pad, drawing a lionfish on the corner of the page.

"So," Owen said loudly, "how about them Cowboys? Think they have a shot at the Super Bowl this year?"

"How should I know?" Jacob said, apparently oblivious to the reason Owen was trying to change the subject. "The season hasn't even started yet."

"I'm not breaking up with you," Melanie said clearly, as if she and Gabe did not have a small yet uncomfortable audience. "I just need to do this. Okay? Please don't make it harder than it already is."

"I feel like Nikki will always come first," Gabe said.

"Lucky girl," Owen chided.

"Shut. Up. Owen," Gabe said, giving the quipster a glacial look over his shoulder.

Owen covered his lips with one finger and pressed them into his teeth.

"She doesn't always come first, Gabe. She's going through a really rough time right now. What kind of friend would I be if I turned my back on her? I'm sorry, but I just can't do it."

"You should stay," Nikki said as she ventured out of the bedroom wearing one of the band's discarded T-shirts. Melanie's face was streaked with tears, but Nikki's was

downright flooded. "I can go home by myself."

Adam offered Nikki an encouraging smile, but she was too focused on Melanie to see it.

Gabe looked Nikki over from head to foot, his gaze pausing at her throat and cheek where colorful bruises marred her flesh. He sighed and turned his attention back to Melanie.

"When will I see you again?" Gabe asked her.

"Soon," she said. "I promise."

"If I wasn't on tour, I'd follow you home and help you with this."

"I know that," she said, kissing his lips softly. "It's one of the thousands of things about you that makes it so hard for me to leave."

But she did leave. Packed up herself and her friend and headed back to Kansas.

Adam continued to toy with his new lyrics at the dining table until Gabe sank into the bench across from him after sending the two women off in a cab.

Gabe linked his hands on the table in front of him. "Why is it that we have willing women coming out of our ears, yet it's so hard to convince the ones we *actually* want to stick around?"

Adam stiffened. Did he know that Madison had left him? Adam hadn't mentioned it to anyone. It sure seemed as if Gabe were trying to commiserate, which meant he knew they had something to commiserate about. And maybe that was okay. Despite having people around him all day, he'd never felt more alone.

Adam shook his head. "No idea, but if you figure it out, be sure to let me know."

Gabe's eyes lifted and he met his gaze. "You too?"

Adam nodded curtly.

"What happened?"

He didn't really want to talk about it, so he left out all the details. "She said she needs time to think things over. So she left."

"Well, at least she doesn't have a ball and chain for a best friend."

"Don't be too hard on Nikki," Adam said. "She's been through a lot. And not just this weekend. Her entire life."

Gabe scrubbed his face with both hands and dropped forward to bang his forehead on the table. "I know. That's why I feel like such an incredible ass for even thinking she should just. Go. Away."

"She's gone now," Adam pointed out.

Gabe chuckled and lifted his head from the table. "That's true, but unfortunately she took Mel with her."

"She'll be back," Adam said, reaching across the table to slap Gabe in the upper arm. He wasn't used to comforting people. It felt kind of weird, but he had to admit there was something appealing about it too. It made him feel good about himself, which was even weirder.

"I'm sure Madison will be back too," Gabe said.

Adam wasn't—wouldn't she have at least *texted* him if she had any desire to ever see him again—but he nodded. "I hope you're right."

Adam went through the motions of preparing for the show, but his heart wasn't in it. The stupid, aching organ was fixated on someone over 500 miles away in Dallas. His muse got off on his misery, however. He'd filled several more pages with lyrics between sound check and the call for places. And as soon as his guitar was in his hands backstage, he began fiddling with new riffs.

"Nice," Owen said, mimicking Adam's string of notes on his bass.

"Yeah, I like that," Kellen said. He had completely missed sound check, but had arrived backstage moments ago.

"I assume your writer's block is gone," Kellen said with a bemused smile.

"Yep," Adam said and left it at that. He wasn't prepared to share the reasons why. He was trying very fucking hard to keep his mind *off* the cause of his sudden bout of inspiration. Or maybe it was his focused attempts to keep his thoughts from wandering that made him concentrate on writing lyrics and now, guitar riffs.

"Well, keep it up," Kellen said, giving Adam's back a hard smack. "Sounds great."

The cellphone in Adam's front pocket vibrated against his thigh. His heart skipped a beat. *Please be Madison*, he thought as

he fished the phone from his jeans. His heart thudded faster as he recognized her name displayed across the screen. He accepted the call with a trembling finger and drew the phone to his ear.

"Madison?" he said breathlessly. "I'm so glad you called. I thought—"

"This isn't Madison," said someone who sounded a hell of a lot like Madison.

"What?"

"This is her sister, Kennedy. Look, Adam, I don't like you. Well, I don't really know you, but I don't like who my sister has become since she started dating you. She's changed and not for the better."

"Why are you calling me?" He could only think that Madison had been too chicken to tear him to shreds and had asked her sister to do it. And could she have picked a worse time? He had to be on the stage in a few minutes. Madison knew that.

"There's been an accident."

Something kicked him in the gut and knocked the wind from him. "What?"

"Madison was thrown from her horse. She hit her head and is completely incoherent, except she keeps calling your name. I decided to leave my personal feelings concerning your unhealthy relationship aside and ask you to come to the hospital. Maybe you can reach her. She doesn't want anything to do with me."

A strange feeling of calm settled over him. He could be there for Madison. He *would* be there for her. As far as he was concerned, nothing could stop him. Not even her. He lifted his guitar strap over his head, set the instrument on a stand, and headed for the exit. "Where is she?" he asked her sister.

"Baylor Medical Center."

"I'm on my way," he said.

CHAPTER SEVENTEEN

"ADAM?" MADISON WHISPERED for the thousandth time that night, but this time he actually answered.

"I'm here." A strong hand squeezed her fingers.

She pried her eyes open, her thoughts hazy from all the pain medication they were pumping into her vein through an IV. Or maybe it was the concussion. At least she knew what a concussion was now. She'd never been more terrified than when they'd been trying to explain her injuries to her and none of the words made any sense. Nothing had made any sense. Nothing except for Adam. Her feelings for him had been the only thing she'd been sure of since Ginger had tossed her. Maybe even before that rather painful moment.

"Is it really you?" she asked. Maybe she was hallucinating again. She was sure she'd seen her grandmother earlier, standing by her bed, but that was ridiculous. Nana had been dead for years.

"It's me," Adam said, leaning over her and stroking her hair from her face so he could drop a tender kiss on her forehead. "I got here as fast as I could."

"What time is it?" Through the window, she could see it was dark outside, but she had no idea how many hours had passed since she'd been brought out of surgery. She tried to pull her body upright to search for a clock, but due to the weight of the huge cast on her arm and the traction device holding the pins in her shoulder in place, she couldn't manage more than the tightening of her abs.

"Around five, I think," he said.

"In the morning?" She searched his face, noting the lines of fatigue around his eyes.

"Yeah."

"Did I lose an entire day?"

He shook his head. "No, I drove all night." He glanced over his shoulder at the open door. "I'm not sure how long I can stay. They didn't want me in here disturbing your rest, but after driving all night, I wasn't about to listen." He grinned crookedly and stroked her cheek. "I'm sure security is on the way to toss me out."

"You always have been a troublemaker," she said, her heart full to bursting because he'd come—driven all night—to be there for her. She never expected him to go to such lengths for her, to be so selfless. She was glad so many people were wrong about him and the she was an excellent judge of character.

"Can't help it," he said, cracking his knuckles. "It's how I roll."

She laughed and then groaned as her side protested. If not for the pain medication, she knew that simple laugh would have brought her to tears. The doctor had determined that her ribs weren't broken, merely bruised, but they sure as hell felt broken.

"So what's the damage?" Adam asked. "Your sister rushed me in here without telling me much."

The traitorous bitch, was Madison's first thought. "You talked to her?"

"Briefly. She's the one who called me and told me you needed me here."

"Oh." Well, Madison was still pissed at Kennedy, but maybe eventually they could mend their damaged relationship. Maybe.

Madison tossed her blanket aside with her uninjured arm, and he gasped.

"Broken radius and ulna, sprained elbow, dislocated shoulder," she said, pointing to her right arm. "I tried to catch my fall. That was a mistake."

"I thought you were good at riding horses."

"I am good at riding horses," she said defensively. "My horse was spooked. By a snake."

Adam shook his head as if he were angry with her. "Why'd you take your horse near a snake? Don't you remember what that fortune-teller in New Orleans said?"

She shook her head in disbelief. "I didn't *mean* to take her

near a snake. It was hiding . . ." The fortune-teller's words echoed through her mind.

"In the grass?"

She nodded. "It doesn't matter. I had to go for a ride." She smiled. "I was looking for you."

"Huh?"

"Don't worry, I found you."

He touched her temple with gentle fingertips. "Are you sure your head is okay?"

"No worse than it was before," she assured him.

"Your sister said you have a concussion."

"I do. But I'm feeling much better. Especially now that you're here."

He smiled, holding her gaze for a long moment. When his eyes became shiny with tears, he diverted his attention to the bandage on her shoulder. "What's under here?" he asked, running a finger along the tape.

"That's for my fractured collarbone. They had to screw the pieces to a metal plate."

"Ouch." He took in her body from head to toe and then met her eyes. "You're in an awfully good mood for someone so broken," he observed.

"I feel less broken now than I did when I left you."

He let out a shaky breath. "You do?"

She nodded, reaching out to him with her good arm. "You came."

"Of course I came. Jesus, Madison, you could have died. Why do you have to be so fucking reckless?"

Despite her damaged ribs, she laughed until her belly ached. "Me? You're the reckless one."

"Then I'm a bad influence on you. I'm going to end up getting you killed."

She didn't care about anything but him being there. "Are you going to kiss me, or what?" she asked.

"May I?"

She lifted an eyebrow at him. "You've never felt inclined to ask before."

"Yeah, well, I'm trying not to be an asshole here. I'm doing my best to change for you."

Now she was really confused. Even more than she'd been when her brains had been scrambled.

"Change?" she blurted. "Why would you change for me?"

"Because . . ." He lowered his gaze and rubbed a finger along the solid length of her cast. "You're so good and I'm, I'm not."

"I don't want you to change, Adam," she said. "I happen to love everything about you."

"Then why did you leave?"

"Because it's scary to love someone as much as I love you. And I couldn't figure out why you encouraging the insanity between us was activating my fight or flight response. So I chose flight. But I should have chosen fight. I'm choosing fight now, Adam. I'll fight for you. I won't run again."

His gray eyes lifted, and he met her gaze. "She never fought for me."

"Who?"

"My mother."

"I'm not your mother."

"I'm well aware of that."

"And I will fight for you, Adam. I will. I promise you that."

He stared into her eyes and then dipped his head slightly. "I believe you," he said. "But maybe you should wait to fight until you've healed a bit. Though one good whack with this cast would take out a charging bull." He touched the plaster gingerly, as if afraid touching it would hurt her.

"I love you," she said and swallowed the lump of nervousness in her throat. Was she really going to do this? What if he'd changed his mind? "Adam?"

He lifted his head, and she was surprised to see his eyes brimming with tears.

"I love you too," he said.

She nodded, her own vision swimming. "If you still want to marry me, I . . . I accept your proposal."

He again looked her over. "I don't know, Madison," he said. "I'm not sure you'll ever be able to give me a proper hand job again."

She lifted a spare pillow and hit him with it, grateful she was feeling no pain. "The doctor says I should recover

completely with rest and physical therapy. You'll get plenty of spectacular hand jobs."

"If you're sure."

She nodded and stared at his pocket expectantly.

"I'm not asking you yet," he told her.

"You're not?" The disappointment of his words crushed her chest. "It's the whole 'in sickness and in health' thing, isn't it? I promise I'll be back to normal in no time." Six to eight weeks wasn't so long when they had the rest of their lives to spend together.

"That's not it. I think I'd like to meet your family first. See what kind of crazy I'd be marrying into."

"*My* family? What about *your* family?" She'd talked to his dad on the phone and found him to be as difficult to reach as his son had been.

He laughed. "You already know my family is crazy. And your sister seems pretty cool. Maybe I could win her over if we got to know each other."

As much as she loved her family, she was still angry with Kennedy. She didn't care if she ever approved of Adam. Screw her. "She's not as cool as you think she is. I found out who ratted on us to my boss," she said.

"Not—"

"Yeah, it was Kennedy."

Adam's eyes widened. "Your sister? Why would she do that? I know she doesn't like me, but I thought you two were close."

"I thought so too."

She fumed silently for a moment, her jaw aching with tension. "You know, I was always taught to turn the other cheek and passively accept my fate. To take the path of least resistance."

"It's okay to be that way. It makes you a good person." Adam traced her eyebrow with his thumb, his callused fingers resting lightly against her jaw.

"Not always," she said. "Sometimes you have to fight for what is right."

"It's exhausting to constantly fight. I should know. I have very little compromise in me."

She laughed and then rubbed her ribs, which had started to sting. Must be time to up those pain meds. "And I tend to have too much compromise, so when I find something I want passionately—"

"Like me?" He grinned at her.

"Yes, exactly like you. I don't know how to claim what I want without feeling guilty."

His brows drew together. "Guilty? Why in the hell would taking what you want make you feel guilty? Especially when it's something offered willingly."

"It's weird, isn't it? I know it is. It's being with you that has shown me that it's okay to take what I want sometimes. I don't have to compromise. I don't have to hold back or deny myself. Not always."

She reached for his belt and tugged him closer so she could dig into the front pocket of his jeans. The side of her hand brushed the length of his cock and even in her hazy not-quite-there pain, a thrill of excitement made her breath catch and her core tighten.

"You know you can have that any time you want, baby," he said with a teasing grin. "No compromise required."

"I'm glad you see this my way." Her fingertip dipped into the ring nestled deep in his pocket, and she held onto it with her thumb so she could pull it free. "I want this," she said, holding the engagement ring up to him, "and all the scary and wonderful promises that go along with it."

"You're sure? If I put this on your finger, I won't let you walk away from me again. Not ever."

Her heart fluttered, and she nodded, surprised her eyes were filling with tears. "I've never been more sure of anything in my life."

"You don't think we should *talk* about this more?"

"Do you want to talk about it?" she asked, wondering at his sudden hesitation.

"No, but I thought that's what you wanted. I'm trying to be better at compromising. For you."

"Well, knock it off. We can compromise later; after you agree to my demands."

He grinned as he stared into her eyes and lifted her

uninjured left hand. His hands were trembling when he slid the ring onto her ring finger.

"Do you really want to marry me?" he asked, and the uncertainty in his eyes tugged at her heart strings.

"I said I did, didn't I?"

His brows drew together. "No, you said—"

She covered his mouth with her good hand. "I want to marry you, Adam Taylor. I love you more than anything in the entire universe, and I can't wait to get out of the hospital so I can follow you on tour whether you want me to or not."

"It won't matter," he said.

"What won't matter?"

"I'm pretty sure I not only stepped over the line but leaped it when I walked out before the show last night without so much as a word. The tour, the band? Over for me."

Madison's face fell. "You did *what*?"

"Kennedy called and said you needed me, so I came. And I'm not sorry I did. I might have lost my band, but you said yes."

Damn, the man was impulsive. She loved him for it, but it would definitely be a constant challenge for her. "You didn't even tell them why you were leaving?"

He shook his head. "It didn't seem important at the time. All I could think about was getting here as fast as possible."

She reached up and wrapped her good hand in his chains to tug him closer for a kiss. "That's the sweetest thing anyone has ever done for me," she said.

He grinned. "You're welcome."

"If I could move properly, I would kick your ass. I can't believe you left without explaining. You have to make this right, Adam. Call the guys. Let them know what's going on, that it was an emergency."

Adam shook his head slightly. "I'll call them later. I'm too happy that you're mine and too upset that you're hurt to listen to a bitch session from Jacob. It would probably be best to wait until I've had some sleep. I'm sure I'll just make it worse if I talk to anyone but you right now."

It was an ungodly hour to call someone. Especially a rock star.

"You do look tired," she said, patting the mattress near her left hip. There wasn't much room for him, but if he squeezed in close, he could rest beside her. "Why don't you lie down with me? We'll call the guys in the morning. I'll send them pictures of my wounds and my CAT scan so they know it's serious."

Adam glanced at the door. "I wonder why no one has come to kick me out of your room yet," he said.

"Maybe they forgot you were in here."

"I have a feeling your sister is keeping them at bay."

"Well, she *is* a stubborn know-it-all cow."

"Who looks disturbingly like you," Adam said. He kicked off his boots and removed his leather jacket, tossing it onto the empty chair at the end of the bed. He slid onto the bed beside her, moving in close to her uninjured side. He held her hand gently and traced the ring he'd just placed on her finger.

"This must have been the shittiest weekend of your life," he said.

She squeezed his fingers. "Are you kidding? I got *engaged* this weekend."

He chuckled. "And that's supposed to make up for all the shit you've endured?"

"It totally does. You couldn't make me any happier if you tried."

"Is that a challenge?"

She wished she had two working arms so she could hug him. She settled for squeezing his hand even tighter. "If you want to take it that way."

He nuzzled her neck and stroked her instep with his big toe. "Is this okay?" he asked.

"It's a start, but a little tame by your standards," she said with a giggle.

"I don't want to hurt you. Seeing you injured like this tears my heart out. Makes me want to write lyrics and guitar solos and shit."

She wasn't sure why her injuries would give him a sudden desire to create music. "I'll be okay," she said, tingles of delight coursing down her neck as he placed gentle kisses on her skin. She went completely still as something terrible occurred to her.

"This injury really is going to cut into our sex life, isn't it?"

"I'll just figure out new ways to excite you until you're fully healed."

He was already exciting her as his teeth scraped across her earlobe.

"That's eight weeks!" she protested.

"Don't blame me," he said, his breath warming her neck. "You're the one who fell off a horse."

She squeezed his hand, the new ring on her finger feeling heavy and delightfully foreign. "Excuse me? I was thrown off a horse."

"So until you're better, I'll take it easy on you. Gentle kisses, soft touches, slow licks, easy sucking, but absolutely no fucking."

"I'll never be able to handle it," she complained. "Two *days* of that just about killed me."

He kissed the corner of her mouth. "I'll teach you to love every minute of it."

"I do love every moment with you," she said before capturing his lips in a searing kiss. "So do as you must, Adam. Tease me."

ABOUT THE AUTHOR

Combining her love for romantic fiction and rock 'n roll, Olivia Cunning writes erotic romance centered around rock musicians. Raised on hard rock music from the cradle, she attended her first Styx concert at age six and fell instantly in love with live music. She's been known to travel over a thousand miles just to see a favorite band in concert. As a teen, she discovered her second love, romantic fiction—first, voraciously reading steamy romance novels and then penning her own. Growing up as the daughter of a career soldier, she's lived all over the country and overseas. She currently lives in Illinois. To learn more about Olivia and her books, please visit www.oliviacunning.com.

4279381LV00011B/79/P

LVOW04s2146220215
Printed in the USA
CPSIA information can be obtained at www.ICGtesting.com